How to Control Your College Costs

The Path to College Affordability

Claire Law, M. S. Nationally Certified Educational Planner

IECA Professional Member, Expert in College Admission and Financial Aid

ISBN-13: 978-1-7362609-2-0 (paperback), 978-1-7362609-1-3 (Kindle)

Illustrations by Ellis Fox.

The author's advice and opinions are based on her professional experience. The information is believed to be accurate and reliable at the time of publication.

The anecdotes are based on real cases she encountered in her practice. Financial aid awards posted as examples are real and recent. All names and identifiers were redacted to protect the privacy of students and parents.

This book contains information concerning federal student financial aid programs, including Title IV federal student aid. Although the author and publisher believe this information to be accurate, this information has not been reviewed or approved by the U.S. Department of Education.

PUBLIC INSTITUTION
AFFORDABILITY
COMMUNITY COLLEGE
PRIVATE
ELITE
IVY LEAGUE
UNIVERSITY
FLAGSHIP
COMMUNITY

TABLE OF CONTENTS

Dedication

I dedicate this book to parents, students, school counselors, Independent Educational Consultants (IECs) and anyone who is interested in higher education and taming college costs. I want to thank the people who supported me through writing this book: my husband, Chip Law, my IECA colleagues: Steven Roy Goodman, Dr. Steven Antonoff and Lora Block, who founded the IECA College Subcommittee on Affordability and influenced my thinking about financial aid, Mark Kantrowitz, Paula Bishop, and Gary Carpenter, Founder of NCAG Association. I am thankful for my UCI Student, Karen Hott, a talented IEC, who edited parts of this manuscript. Ellis Fox is the gifted artist from the School of the Arts in N. Charleston, who designed the illustrations. My orange tabby, Flopper, kept me company and even typed a few strange words, like ghhaaa, reminding me to laugh!

About the Author

C. Claire Law, M.S., is a Professional Member of IECA, a Certified Educational Planner (CEP) since 2001. She's a graduate of Carleton University and the University of Rhode Island, "And Proud of It," as the slogan goes. She worked in college admission and financial aid at Bryant University, The Art Institute of Atlanta and Carleton University (Canada). During the FFEL Program, she worked in education loan sales for a Sallie Mae lender. She founded Educational Avenues, Inc. in E. Greenwich, RI, in 1999, where she guided students through the college application process. She is the co-author of *Find the Perfect College for You*, examining personality type in college. She currently lives in Charleston, S.C., with her husband Chip and her cat Flopper, now forever in her heart. She teaches financial aid to Independent Educational Consultants (IECs) at UC-Irvine Continuing Education. She guides first-time undergraduate students to their best-matched colleges while minimizing parents' costs, whether they're in a high, low, or middle-income bracket.

Connect with her on LinkedIn https://www.linkedin.com/in/cclairelaw/

Download pdfs, family budget excel spreadsheet, and other articles from www.eduave.com or email claire@eduave.com.

Praise for How to Control Your College Costs

In this book, Claire Law introduces the concept of an Affordable Family Contribution, or AFC. The AFC is a measure of how much the family feels it can afford to pay for college. If a college's net price is higher than the AFC, she encourages the family to choose a less expensive college."
– **Mark Kantrowitz**, Financial Aid Expert

If I were hiring an expert in the area of college financial aid, it would be Claire Law. She is widely respected for her knowledge of college affordability and for her ability to make it understandable.
– **The Miller Family**

How to Control Your College Costs is a must-read for all families planning to send their children to college. Financial aid is complicated. This book breaks it down into understandable parts. Read this book, get the facts before you start the college process. It will save you time and money.
– **Gary Carpenter, CPA, Founder, NCAGonline.org**

This book demystifies and unmasks the financial aid process! Claire Law is a national leader in explaining financial aid and affordability issues. Heed her advice and find a college that's a great fit — and that's affordable!
– **Dr. Steven R. Antonoff**, Author, Certified Educational Planner

How to Use this Book

Welcome to the world of College Financial Aid, a term that may in and of itself define the college selection process, the outcome of a student's life, and the future well being of a family's fiscal health. Before we begin to explore this mysterious and complex subject, let me give you a real-world example of why you need this book.

Not that long ago, a previous client referred a family to me that had an immediate need to understand college costs for their son. The son had applied to a number of highly-selective private schools and was accepted to many of them. In the spring these schools sent the family awards letters that spelled out what the actual costs each institution would be. The family was in "sticker shock" when they learned that the annual cost for one year for their son at his preferred college would be over $80,000 per year or over $320,000 for his undergraduate degree. The family could not come close to affording this price for their son AND they also had two other children to educate!

This family was in dire straits and I was able to help them out by getting them to rethink their college list. These incidents are only too common and unnerve me each time. As a result, I committed to create a knowledge base that families can access all in one place.

This book is similar to a reference workbook, an encyclopedia with a large glossary of all the terms and processes related to college financial aid.

I then went further to show how a family and their student are assessed, so they can find a great college that the family can afford.

Finally, I created a "How To" process that will enable families, educational consultants and students to understand the intricacies of financial aid.

This book will allow the reader to take charge of the college selection process by using a common theme: the Affordable Family Contribution or AFC.

My book provides its reader with everything they need to know to find the "right" college for their child, matched with a price tag that the family can afford. That said, this book is not intended to be consumed in one sitting, rather, it is multifaceted, and can be used as a reference guide, a college section tool, a process for family budgeting, and a road map to get to the best outcome for a student when combined with family affordability.

You will now have the means to CONTROL your college costs!

Enjoy the journey...Claire.

Dear Reader

Thank you for buying my book! I've felt compelled to write it after discovering that college affordability is possible, even though the costs of higher education continue to increase at the speed of a Ferrari.

I am writing this book to benefit three audiences: 1) parents and students, 2) school counselors and 3) my colleagues, who are Independent Education Consultants (IECs.) When I refer to "you" in my writing, I'm speaking to either students, parents, college advisors, or all of you!

The examples in this book come from my experience working with students and parents, and I removed all identifying information. Any resemblance to a person you may know is entirely coincidental. However, I hope that by reading the stories you will see how you can position yourself to your best advantage.

I've worked in private practice as an Independent Educational Consultant for the last 21 years, and helped families feel less stressed over college costs for their children.

Parents will spend generously and even overspend for the benefit of their children. Yet everyone wants to spend their hard-earned money well, and not squander it.

It's even more important that the right educational fit for our students be affordable for at least the four or more years of study.

That's where I want to help families and college advisors go a step further in helping families identify fit and affordability.

Prior to working as an Independent Educational Consultant, I worked in college admission, financial aid and for a Sallie Mae lender. In the late 1990's, when the Family Federal Education Loan Program still existed, I called on Financial Aid Administrators to persuade them to use my company's FFEL Stafford, PLUS and alternative loans. I discovered that loans are the lifeline of colleges and the bane of consumers.

Consumers are students, parents, aunts, and uncles who borrow or co-sign loans. I shuddered to see financially needy students borrow amounts they would never pay back. Getting students and parents to sign promissory notes was the easiest thing to do. In fact, I presented the "entrance counseling" in an auditorium filled with parents and students who then lined up to sign the master promissory notes. Nowadays, this step is on the federal student aid website and I think the loan fees, interest rates, and financial side of the transaction are better explained.

If I learned anything, I learned that Sallie Mae, Wells Fargo and Nellie Mae are not friends. They are businesses. I'm not picking on them, on Sallie or Wells Fargo or Nellie alone, because there were over 300 lenders under the FFEL Program.

The CARES Act provided federal loan borrowers with a payment pause, but these old FFELP loans were not included. Molly Webster wrote in the New York Times, "Millions of Americans were forgotten when Congress extended protection for student loan holders."

My point is that it's too easy to sign a promissory note when the anticipation of getting a college degree and a good-paying job looks rosy at the end of the road. It's even more painless now to sign a promissory note online than when students and parents were required to sit in front of a financial aid administrator each time they took loans out.

The U.S. Department of Education provides some controls by limiting the loan amounts that dependent undergraduate students can borrow. Parents, however, can borrow up to the full cost of education minus any other aid already awarded.

It's not uncommon to find parents who are nearing retirement and are still having to make payments on student loans.

Graduate students borrow the largest amounts. Medical and veterinary schools cost over $100,000 per year. Law school graduates end up with huge debt if they don't select the right school with the right funding.

When parents don't qualify for federal loans, many resort to private loans which are more difficult to assess. Although this book isn't all about loans, I offer several chapters on federal and private loans for the reader to examine.

Even though you may think that it won't happen to you, the national student loan debt of $1.7 Trillion tells us that *someone* incurred excessive loan debt. I hope my book will prevent the reader from becoming a statistic.

The choice of college matters a great deal, but so do the net costs, especially for families who will need to borrow. The financial aid application process can feel like it is being run by the man behind the curtain and I hope to shed light on how to maximize the educational benefit and minimize the costs.

I've met many families at all levels of income and wealth, who wanted to allocate their resources according to their needs and values, not the constraints of the federal financial aid regulations or the colleges' policies.

The formulas don't take into consideration that a family may not be able to spend every last cent on the first child because perhaps the second or third child has special needs and more resources need to be saved for that child.

Parents may not realize that colleges have significant agendas and goals that are apart from providing education and training to students. It's not all about kids.

Colleges are tasked with meeting their budget each year. By necessity, they sort through their many inquiries, then parcel out scholarships and financial aid to incentivize those students who help the college meet its goals.

These goals are separate from the consideration families hope to receive when their student applies for admission and financial aid.

Many families depended on the advice of IECs to provide a balanced and affordable college list. This is a step in the right direction because IECs visit many colleges and special needs programs. They meet in person with learning specialists at colleges and have expertise, knowledge and contacts beyond what parents could develop when the college application process comes around.

By becoming informed consumers of higher education, parents will be better prepared to pay for college. Educational Consultants and College Advisors will select those colleges that will likely treat students preferentially in the admission and financial aid process.

When students enter colleges where they fit in well academically, socially, and financially, they will persist longer, and the colleges will enjoy higher retention and graduation rates.

If you'll take 20 minutes each day to complete the surveys in this book, and read the following pages, a little at a time, you will gain a clear view of how you can take control of your college costs.

Yours for college success,

Claire Law, M.S. IECA Professional Member
Certified Educational Planner

Introduction

I love working with students and parents to help them navigate the college admission and financial aid process. Every student is different. Some are super-achievers and heavy hitters, others work hard and get average grades, still others have diagnosed or undiagnosed learning disabilities, or are on the spectrum. Yet each student has their superpower.

I enjoy working with parents, aunts, uncles and grandparents who call me because they want to help their children, nephews and grandchildren. They too are different. They bring their views, values and expectations to their children's college selection and application process.

I take many variables into consideration before assigning a college list. I assess the academic profile of the student and the financial situation of the parents. Then, I identify the colleges that would treat this family preferentially through both the admission and financial aid process.

Some students have the wrong college list.

My process starts with identifying the natural gifts that each student possesses. As a Certified MBTI® professional, I administer this and other assessments to help students better understand themselves and others. According to Catherine Briggs and her daughter, Isabel Briggs Myers, each person has innate tendencies and characteristics that define their personality preferences and learning style. My students realize they will find more satisfaction in fields of study that support and honor their innate abilities.

Nowadays, so many teenagers suffer from anxiety and depression, and doing well in school adds another layer of pressure. However, the struggle is a part of living, and we must talk about it. Nobody is born with encyclopedic knowledge and critical thinking skills. The growth comes from working through the challenges and wrenching within an area that is outside of one's comfort zone.

It's essential for each student to understand and believe in their individual strengths. These are their superpowers. If you're interested in how I use personality preferences and learning style to match students with colleges, fields of study and careers, you will find many examples in the book I co-authored, *Find the Perfect College For You*.

This is all I'll say about personality type in college and my college process. If you can afford the help of Independent Educational Consultants, you will be on the right path. Consultants will take the time to get to know your family and your student's needs. They will steer you toward well-suited colleges.

Consultants also work pro-bono with students who are on free or reduced lunch programs or families that receive federal means-tested benefit programs.

In this book, I focus on giving you the training needed to navigate the world of college financial aid. Fasten your seat belt because, together, we will evaluate the financial resources that are available from the government and private colleges. I will never try to advise you on how to invest your money. I will give you the tools to evaluate your personal finances, show you how they will be evaluated by colleges, and then you can establish your criteria for paying for college.

Why did I write this book? College fit and affordability are essential for students to develop and reach their potential. Once they start college they need to have the funds to remain there until they graduate. Earning a degree or even just a certificate will open doors in the workplace.

I work with parents willing to do anything and everything possible for their children. Too often they believe that their student must get accepted to the most selective college they can get into. Often, this turns out to be the most expensive college.

I am writing this book to help families navigate the admission and financial aid process so that students and parents can choose the right school, which balances academic fit, social fit and financial fit.

If you like facts, figures, and formulas you will enjoy the detailed explanations of how public and private colleges award financial aid. If the alphabet soup gets confusing you can always refer to the glossary.

If it gets too technical, read the student's stories because they illustrate the formulas with real life examples.

It's why I write about students' experiences, and I hope that by reading their stories you fill find nuggets of wisdom that will guide your college selection.

I've never found college financial aid boring, because the rules and regulations affect real people's lives. You will find that the rationale behind the aid policies aligns with this nation's history, national sentiment and political initiatives.

More than ever, college affordability is critical for everyone in this 21st century. The workforce needs to be trained for the jobs that exist today. I will show you how to shop wisely for elite private, public flagship and smaller liberal arts colleges. I will remind you that community colleges are the closest to providing quick training that results in immediate employment.

Higher education tends to be more abstract, and a degree in Sociology or History will not yield as good a salary as an Associate's degree in Nursing from a community college. However, Bachelor's degrees in business, engineering computer science and the medical professions are always in demand, with research and development continuing to advance the body of knowledge.

I will discuss how you can evaluate your college options relative to the cost of attendance. Your return on investment is important. Don't forget that higher education is an industry, a sector like agriculture, manufacturing, and hospitality.

Colleges and universities continue to charge more because they receive less and less funding from state government, and have to rely on tuition dollars to make budget. I provide strategies for families to make their best informed, student-appropriate and family-affordable choices. IECs reading this book will learn the back of the house rules that affect what families will pay. IECs can and will save money for their clients.

This book starts with an explanation of the Cost of Attendance (COA). This is determined by law (Section 472 of the Higher Education Act of 1965) and is not currently subject to regulation by the U.S. Department of Education (DoE). The law specifies the types of costs that are included in the COA, but each school must determine the appropriate and reasonable amounts to include for each eligible COA category for its students.

(There are many abbreviations in this field. If you forget what they are, refer to the glossary at the end of the book.)

It's essential for the reader to understand how the COA works for the college and for the consumer. My focus is on college affordability and the financial aid available for families in different financial situations and marital status.

You will find exercises to test your awareness of college costs. The questionnaires always infuse reality into the process. Elite colleges from Brown University to UCLA have broken the $80,000 mark per academic year. Sadly, the academic year that is supposed to last nine months has so many breaks that the number of teaching hours are shorter and remote learning is here to stay.

In the chapter "**Know Thyself**," you will find questionnaires to start you thinking about what is important to you in the college process. You will sort your values and select variables that will drive your college search. Parents can take these surveys with their children, and Independent Educational Consultants can use them for their clients.

The family budget sheet is critically important because it leads to the family's formulation of their **Affordable Family Contribution**, (AFC). You may have heard of the "EFC" or Expected Family Contribution, an acronym that will be renamed to Student Aid Index (SAI) in 2023. Regardless of name changes, it remains essential for families to discuss and determine for themselves an amount that they are able and willing to pay. I call this amount your "Affordable Family Contribution" or AFC.

IECs and readers will learn all about the Federal Methodology (FM) which regulates the federal student financial aid that families are eligible to receive. You'll find a few quiz questions here too, which will help you to deepen your knowledge. I teach an entire course on college affordability at the University of California-Irvine Continuing Education, and I couldn't resist checking up on you with a quiz or two. You can't take the teacher out of me!

Your next assignment will be to use several Net Price Calculators (NPCs) for the colleges that may interest your students and parents. Although they may not be 100% accurate, they give a ball-park range estimate of net costs.

In addition to learning how to file the FAFSA, you will learn how to file the **CSS Profile** form. Some colleges require parents to file an additional financial form, the CSS Profile. You will learn the **Institutional Methodology** (IM) that regulates the CSS Profile. If you're applying to private colleges and certain public universities, you will need to know how you will be assessed under the private school's lens, which could add or subtract from your expected family contribution, depending on your financial positioning and the college's own financial aid policies.

FAFSA changes in 2023-24: I include a review of the changes to the FAFSA financial aid formulas that were enacted by the Consolidated Appropriations Act, 2021. These changes will take effect on July 1, 2023, for academic year 2023-24. The changes affect families with high school students graduating in 2023. They will be filing this "new" FAFSA on or after October 1, 2022 and the income considered will be from the year 2021.

The **"Meet the Students"** chapter contains stories with real examples of students, their college lists, the rationale for selecting them, and the financial aid awards they received. All names and identifiable information were changed, redacted or deleted.

Strategic Enrollment Management (SEM) and You reveals the man behind the curtain: colleges have agendas of their own. It's not all about kids. With federal and state funding dwindling, colleges are increasingly more reliant on tuition revenue. Families and students need to be aware of these enrollment tactics, play the game when it's to their advantage, and don't fall for the marketing.

Why is college so expensive? Beth Akers, *A New Approach for Curbing College Tuition Inflation*, Manhattan Institute, August 2020, writes: "The Bennet Hypothesis is that a consumer's willingness to pay increases by the amount of the subsidy, which allows sellers to ask for a higher price. When sellers of a product or service are aware of this change in consumers' willingness to pay for a product, they can strategically raise the cost to capture some of that subsidy for themselves. This is particularly true in markets, such higher education, with high entry barriers that prevent new suppliers from entering the market in response to higher prices.

Award letters are often confusing to families and I wrote a chapter explaining how to evaluate award offers. Most financial aid consists of loans, so the following chapters explain the terms and conditions of federal loans. Read my section on private and alternative loans, and other sources of funding, such as 529 plans. I also include information on an unusual way to pay for college, but only if you have a pension under ERISA.

Appeals will become more common, since the new Consolidated Appropriations Act, 2021, prohibits Financial Aid Administrators (FAAs) from having a policy of dismissing all financial aid appeals filed by students or parents. When award offers are unclear to you, when you have questions about an award, I'll tell you when you can call the financial aid office and appeal it.

State aid: Don't forget that each state provides some funding for first-year students. Funding may be need or merit based. Toward the end of this book, you will find an explanation of the state aid offered at many of the 50 U.S. States.

Glossary: Refer to the Glossary when you don't understand a term or abbreviation. The concepts are well explained there.

Resources and links are listed after each sentence where appropriate, or at the end of each chapter. A complete list of "Resources" is at the back of the book.

Downloads: You can download excel spreadsheets, like the family budget, the award comparison sheet, and additional articles from my website: www.eduave.com

Happy reading and learning! May this book enable you to choose fit and affordable colleges.

Advice to IECs, School Counselors and College Advisors

Dear IEC, School Counselor, and College Advisors, I am sure you will find this book especially useful to you in your work because most families need financial aid to pay for college. Whether you work with wealthy, middle-class or low-income families, it helps to know which colleges have financial aid policies that favor your clients.

It's no longer enough to calculate grade point averages and estimate whether standardized scores are on the line or a shoo-in. Along with identifying where our students can be successful, we need to identify the colleges' financial aid awarding policies which affect different families in different ways.

For example, some colleges will be generous for students with a high financial need while others will only award federal aid and loans.

The students' academic performance, extra-curricular activities and special abilities or "hook" remain the essential variables that lower college costs. IECs are already adept at matching the student with the colleges. Those who would like to know more may want to check out Dr. Steven Antonoff's book *IECs: Students of Colleges*. It's an incredible resource!

Parents who hire IECs for their children will receive many hours of one-on-one, expert guidance. As IECs, we have the privilege and pleasure of getting to know our families well. This is time that guidance counselors typically don't have, since they have administrative duties and serve hundreds of students.

IECs are in continuous education to keep up with the most recent changes in higher education. They collect reliable, first-hand information through in-person college visits, conversations with students, faculty members, and directors of admission and financial aid.

They know how to find the right colleges for the super-achiever, the student with average scores and the learning-disabled student. IECs are professionally trained in placing students where they can grow their potential. IECs reduce the guessing game and the risks, and thus lessen the anxiety while empowering students to become responsible for driving their application process.

Families at large may not know that IECs are committed to the highest level of ethical standards and professional practice. Many of us abide by the Principles of Good Practices established by IECA, NACAC and HECA.

I realize that some families prefer to go through the college admission and financial aid applications on their own, just like not everyone uses an accountant to file their taxes. However, while we file taxes each year, most families don't go through the college admission and financial aid process each year of their adult lives. College admissions and financial aid has changed a lot since we went to college ourselves, so parents who rely on personal experience might be using old information.

Parents and students may not realize how the financial aid formulas work, or why the net cost is different for each family. Colleges are very adept at processing applications for financial aid while families are not.

I believe that IECs, College Advisors, and School Counselors can provide more of 'wrap-around' services if they become aware of the college' individual financial aid processed and policies.

This book isn't about gaming the system or advising families financially. It's about explaining a process that is not transparent. It's about giving parents and students the facts, so they can make decisions based on reality and not wishful thinking.

Some families consult with their financial planners or accountants but few know how financial aid works. Often, tax deductions increase the expected family contribution on the FAFSA.

Accountants don't meet with students one-on-one, and don't know which colleges match the student's educational and social needs. IECs are uniquely suited to creating college lists that are fit and affordable.

Many IECs work with high-net-worth clients who have plenty of funds, and affordability isn't a major concern for them. However, even wealthy families like to save money and spend it well. As my colleague Betsy says: "There are lots of Range Rovers parked outside the Dollar store. Rich people, too, like to save money!" I'd add that all people want to spend their money well.

At a time when a college degree no longer guarantees a lifetime of employment, families like to examine the return on investment. The worth of a college education comes into question when graduates are unable to find work that pays more than the minimum wage. Families don't want to invest in a college that over-charges for what it delivers.

I've come across parents who ask me how they can be exempted from paying for their children's higher education. The federal and institutional methodologies assess parents' ability to pay, not their willingness to pay.

College costs can negatively affect a family and their planning to save for retirement. Parents may borrow large PLUS loans and defer all payments until the student graduates, thinking the student will repay the loan. By then, the payments may come as a shock. It's well worth it for these families to work with IECs who are likely to find less expensive schools that still meet the student's needs.

In this book I explain how IECs can open viable options for parents and students. They will see how families' expected family contribution sets them up financially, under the federal methodology and institutional methodology.

As IECs, we know how the student's academics and extracurricular activities will play out at colleges that are safety, match or reach. If we explain how certain colleges award aid, our students and parents will have more choices that will be affordable.

I'm confident that as you go through this book, you will tweak those college lists to include choices the family can pay for all four years.

I've included questionnaires to help IECs start the conversation with parents about financial costs and financial fit. Use "beginning questions" during your initial meetings to assess whether your clients are concerned about costs.

You'll gauge how to talk about finances once you get to know the family. Do involve the student in the conversation of college costs, to the extent that is possible. They bear responsibilities relative to the repayment of undergraduate federal loans.

Only occasionally, I felt that a student might not be ready for this discussion. Some teens are painfully aware of their family's financial situation and worry about not being able to attend their "dream college." One girl burst into tears when I showed her the cost of her super-expensive art school.

It's very difficult for teens to comprehend how long it would take to earn $73,000 as an artist, which was the cost per year. In such cases, check with the parents before discussing costs.

Other students could care less, especially if they've been indulged and always got what they wanted. One such student asked me: "Which college is the most expensive? That's the one I want to go to." I kid you not.

Our job as college advisors is to dispel the myth that high costs equate with a better quality education.

Then there are parents who are terribly afraid of loans. Some need the reassurance to know that even if it entails paying with loans, college is worth it.

The key is not to borrow excessively. Some of the borrowers from prior decades did just that and are still stuck in income-driven repayment plans that are not all that advantageous.

Others went to graduate school and took on additional amounts of loans. We don't want to quash these sensitive students' enthusiasm for college by going into too many financial details. However, the reality needs to be explained and exposed.

We must remember that our students are 17 to 18 years old when they start college. Some naïve, gullible and even reckless. I have a conversation with them about the fact that while parents are paying the larger share of college costs, they have an obligation to contribute and take ownership. The loans for undergraduates are theirs and will need to be paid back with interest and fees.

We can educate each student about school choices that will affect the quality of their life after college.

This book may give you more of a deep dive than you want. I teach an entire course at UC- Irvine about navigating college financial aid, and I spend seven weeks training other professionals.

You may not absorb all the information at once, so be patient with yourself and review one chapter at a time. You may incorporate as much or as little of this content as you feel comfortable and competent to use in your practice.

As an IEC myself, I encourage you to embrace affordability because it's a factor that affects most families. As students and parents grow in their ability to evaluate their choices, they become more realistic about how much they can afford to pay for one year and for the four years.

We're opening their eyes by making the process more transparent. You can do this! And don't forget to seek out some clients who can't pay for services. You will find it very rewarding. I want to thank my colleagues, who work pro-bono with under-resourced students. These IECs make up for the inequity in access to higher education. Thank you for all you do!

Advice to Parents

Dear Parents, if you're reading this, you might have a student (or two) headed for college, and you may be wondering how to give your children an appropriate college education that fits their needs and fits your wallet. Congratulations! You're on the right path. I wrote this book for parents just like you!

College costs are not easy to figure out because many variables focus on the "academic and social fit" and if we include the "financial fit" it's even more complicated.

Who gets funding, and why? Does it make sense to file all those forms even if you don't qualify for any "free" aid? As I shed light on the current financial aid process in this book, the answers will become clear.

You already know the choice of college matters a great deal. As parents, we make many sacrifices to take care of our children, raise them well, and make them feel safe and happy.

Paying for college is often the last push we give them to help them become independent. Leave the nest, little bird! Fly away and see the world! That's our bitter-sweet job as parents.

Paying for the best-fit college for our kids is a choice that takes some thinking and calculation. Whether you would classify yourself as "poor" or "middle-class" or "rich," paying for college involves giving up resources and involves some compromising.

Unless your child is a wiz or athlete who can obtain a "free ride," which are very rare, parents end up footing the bill. IECs can help with finding schools that will treat your student "preferentially," which means you will borrow less.

Mark Kantrowitz, an expert in financial aid and a wiz at statistics, presents facts and figures about student loan debt in an article on the Savingforcollege.com web site, *Average Student Loan Debt at Graduation*. I encourage you to read the article because few families think of researching the usual amount of debt of graduating students and parents.

The statistics don't cover the non-education loans parents may have taken out through commercial banks, such as home-equity, business loans, cash-outs from investments and other sources.

As the coronavirus pandemic caused colleges to pivot and re-invent themselves, the costs of attending college continued to rise. The pandemic simply accelerated the online teaching trend.

Colleges continually face cuts in federal and state funding, thus relying more heavily on tuition revenues. It's unclear to me how much costs have risen. Yahoo finance says today's average college tuition is 31 times more costly than it was in 1969 (Average Cost of College Has Jumped an Incredible 3,009% in 50 Years). "From 1969 to 2019, the average annual cost of a four-year public university has soared 3,009 percent." Those increases are greater than increases in any other sector of the economy, including medical costs. Bloomberg studies report that college costs increased 1,332% from 1979 to 2019, while wages have been slow and unequal in their growth over the last 40 years.

Public institutions have also increased costs following the trend of private colleges. However, whereas private colleges can inflate their total costs of attendance and then offer huge discounts in the way of scholarships, public universities are limited in how much they can discount because the costs are set by the state. Once approved, they award very small scholarships. It's worrisome when even public universities have become too expensive for the average family.

Despite the high costs of a four-year education, students still need to pursue it to further grow and develop intellectually and socially.

Parents of students with special needs may end up paying more for college, and in many cases, it's well worth it. For example, the social fit is essential for students on the autism spectrum. College is a social experience, and these students often need more support in order to learn and grow socially, emotionally and academically.

Students with language-based learning disabilities, ADHD, executive function, and processing issues also need to find colleges that will provide the supports they need to succeed. All these variables are significant but not sustainable if the starting college costs are out of the parents' financial range.

Going to college is synonymous with taking out loans. We can't expect our students to assess the financial viability when, after all, they are still teenagers. Psychologists tell us the teen brain isn't fully grown until the mid-twenties.

The prefrontal cortex, the seat for executive function and decision making, is still maturing. Parents can't leave college choices entirely to their student if the costs affect the family's financial well-being. Again, if the student needs extra-support, parents may have to borrow much more, and it will be worth it.

The key is to not borrow excessively. What is excessive borrowing? I think it happens when all repayments are put off until after graduation, and interest has accumulated upon interest on top of the principal.

Anecdotally, I just met a successful media professional who told me he's still paying for his daughter and his wife's education loans, and he's about to be retired. He borrowed PLUS loans and he knows that the balance will be forgiven if he dies, and he plans to string out the payments as long as possible. What a way to pay for college!

Then there are parents who don't plan but for one year of college. I'll never forget this student, Robert, referred to me by my client who wanted me to help him pro-bono. He loved, loved, loved his small, liberal arts college in Pennsylvania. The student was upset because his mother, who took out a large PLUS loan to get him started, wouldn't sign for another one to pay for his sophomore year. Since Robert was a "dependent" student, he couldn't borrow more than the $5,500 undergraduate loan in first year and $6,500 in second year.

I explained that even if he were classified "independent" the maximum allowed loan wouldn't begin to cover the costs. I told him he could go to the local community college and transfer to the local four-year college. He wasn't happy. He ended up working as a waiter for one semester, at the restaurant where my client was a regular.

When he came back to my office, he was ready to consider other options. I helped him to find suitable classes at the local community college that were transferable to the in-state public universities. I hoped that he would be more forgiving of his mom who wouldn't take out more PLUS loans. I should have told him to try to make the payments…

Who carries the largest student loan debt? It turns out that graduate students end up with the largest debt burdens. According to www.tcf.org, postgraduate students end up with $66,000 worth of loans on average. These don't include loans accumulated in undergraduate school. Medical, veterinary and law school graduates can end up with nearly half-a million dollars in loans.

While medical school graduates will likely earn the money to pay back their loans, many Master's degree graduates end up with sizeable debt and meager wages upon graduation.

I just met a young mom who graduated from the University of Phoenix online with a Master's degree in psychology or counseling. She owes nearly $150,000. I'm losing sleep just thinking of her!

I hope this book will give you ways to plan ahead, select colleges that fit financially, and will save money. Uninformed parents take on more debt than anticipated. One reason is lack of exposure to colleges in general and lack of preparedness for the costs.

Colleges themselves will tell parents that it's unrealistic to expect they can pay for four years of college without taking out loans. The Federal Parent PLUS loan has supplanted the need-based aid that colleges would otherwise have to offer.

It seems that the more federal aid becomes available, the more colleges raise costs and families perceive the higher-cost colleges more worthy. These higher priced colleges can offer larger tuition discounts along with more federal aid, because the more expensive the college, the more likely that the family demonstrates financial need.

These bigger scholarships and more federal aid are effective ways to attract students. Their parents are willing to pay because they think: "Hey, the college costs $76,000 dollars, my student received a Presidential scholarship for $26,000, and the subsidized Direct loan for undergraduate students." The bigger discounts look like a better bargain than a college that cost $50,000 and doesn't discount. Is the student really getting more value?

These expensive colleges also prevent the competition from entering or staying in the marketplace. Post-Covid we may find that some of the smaller, non-profit private colleges will end up closing.

An institution's enrollment strategies can lead students to the wrong colleges. Every decision involves some degree of compromise, and attending a college that still fits and will result in less debt for students and parents isn't a bad compromise.

Besides, it's not what the college can do for the student that matters, rather, it's what a student puts in. I will borrow JKF's quote here: "Ask not what college can do for you. Ask what you can do for the college!"

Advice to Students

Dear Student, how do you shop for a pair of shoes? Yes, shoes! There are many types, styles, and sizes of shoes, boots, and sneakers. How will you wear the shoes? What do you want the shoes to do for you? These are the same questions students need to ask about colleges.

Do you want running shoes so that you can run faster? Do you play tennis and want shoes that will give you more lateral support? Do you intend to hike parts of the Appalachian trail next summer? Maybe you're shopping for shoes to wear at your graduation or comfortable sandals because June graduation will be outdoors, and it will be hot!

Even before you've entered the store or ordered online, you've already considered the purpose of your shoes. Have you thought about colleges in the same way? How will you use a college education? What do you want it to do for you?

Some students seek intellectual development because they love the life of the mind. Theoretical and abstract topics are right up their alley. Others prefer to learn practical matters. Which college will help you get where you want to go?

Just as you try on shoes to see how they fit you, you can do the same with colleges! Check their size. Are they too large? Too small? Just right? How does the location and distance from home feel? Too far, too near, or just right?

Remember that Goldilocks tried papa's porridge, and it was too hot. She tried mama's porridge, and it was too cold. Then she tried little bear's porridge, and it was just right! Who knows, maybe the little bear's shoes would have fit her too.

If at all possible, try to visit the campuses in person. It's even better if you can visit while the classes are in session. You'll be able to observe the students and experience a college campus in action. It's an excellent way to test drive it!

Colleges work very hard to explain who they are, what they believe in, and how they are different from one another. Each college has something different to offer. It's up you to try them on, just like a new pair of shoes.

Different Shoes. Different Colleges

You're not like one of Cinderella's sisters, trying to fit into the glass slipper! You don't want to feel uncomfortable in college.

There are many types of colleges that you may never have heard of that provide excellent, personalized education. When you graduate, the major income differentiator is the field of study.

Let's consider the college location: Millennials tend to prefer large cities to the countryside. They may never have heard of the "city drain" effect, which city colleges that want to remain "residential campuses" spend much money to combat.

The "city drain" means that the on-campus, residential experience is diluted by the goings-on in the city. Student move off campus into local housing, find employment off campus, and form relationships with people who are not students.

Take Boston University, and I don't mean to single out BU because I don't mean to discredit any college here, only to point out that the campus of many urban colleges is the city. I noticed that students either love or hate the city. Nothing in between. What is your preference?

Rural campuses provide a different social life, such as Hamilton College or Colgate University in upstate New York. To get there, you'd drive through miles of countryside, by farms with horses, pigs and llamas. You'll pass the national baseball hall of fame and museum in Cooperstown, NY.

The students at BU, or NYU, or UCLA, love the pulse of large cities. The drawback is the cost of living .

On rural campuses, student spend more time socializing with each other and in their dorms, maybe planning hiking, canoeing or skiing trips together.

It's amazing when I ask graduates of small colleges "did you know my student who attended there ten years ago?" they would say "yes," with a certainty that indicated a high level of connectedness with that peer.

How can students evaluate the differences among colleges?

One quick way to do so is to read the colleges' mission statement. For example, the mission of the former college where I worked, Bryant College (now Bryant University) is to train students "to become innovative leaders around the world."

This college recruited many international students from Europe, Turkey, Korea, Hong Kong, the Philippines, and Latin America. A U.S. student could make good friends with international students and even visit them in their home country. Bryant University is a small, private school. Its mission is to give students a business education that will serve them well at home and internationally.

Nearby Providence College (RI), on the other hand, has a different mission: "Providence College is a Catholic, Dominican, liberal arts institution of higher education and a community committed to academic excellence in pursuit of the truth, growth in virtue, and service of God and neighbor."

As you can see, you'd be walking in two very different types of shoes if you enrolled in one of these two colleges!

How well does the shoe fit?

Does the shoe have enough toe space? Arch support? Or, are you more interested in the shoes look on your feet?

I've bought shoes for many occasions, weddings, offices, working out, and so on. I purchased shoes because they looked nice. It's like when I went to college and chose to attend a more popular university. It was higher ranked than others at the time. I was walking in high heels in the first year, just to keep up with all the assignments!

It's easy to forget that once you're accepted, there's lots of work ahead. If you wear the right shoe, it will be easier to travel that road.

How can students judge the level of the academic rigor of different colleges? Ask the three Goldilocks questions: Does the college provide the right amount of intellectual challenge? It is too rigorous, not rigorous enough, or just right?

The most selective institutions will make that determination for you. They want to make sure that you will be successful at their school.

I appreciate those smaller colleges that take a personalized approach to teach students and pick them up from where they are.

The elite and highly-ranked schools admit students who have practically already done college-level work and research. Harvard's Dean of Admissions and Financial

Aid, William R. Fitzsimmons, is known have said that it's not the school that makes the student. It's what they bring to Harvard.

The highly selective universities look for more than grades and scores. They look for students who are resourceful, confident, and able to solve their problems efficiently. Students gauge how many hours of study are needed to earn an A or B in a course, so they have time to enjoy other out-of-classroom activities. College is not only about studying but also socializing, debating, and growing. Your perspectives of people and the world will likely change.

Occasionally, some students apply to colleges that are way above their academic performance. They don't question, however, whether they could sustain a high level of academic rigor.

Granted, some students will blossom at the right college. But those who are unprepared will struggle.

Grades and test scores are the litmus tests that prevent students from gaining acceptance to colleges out of their range. On the off chance that a student does get in, he/she may find the level of challenge will become stressful.

Don't let that happen to you! Choose a college where you can kick off your shoes, step onto a campus that offers you a comfortable walk through your four years of education.

How to Control Your College Costs

Not that long ago, a previous client referred a family to me that had an immediate need to understand college costs for their son.

The son, Parker, had applied to several highly selective private schools and was accepted to many of them. In the spring, these schools sent the family awards letters that spelled out what the actual costs for each institution would be.

The family was in "sticker shock" when they received the financial aid award letters, and each college cost over $80,000 per year or over $320,000 for his undergraduate degree.

Both parents were working professionals, with an adjusted gross income of roughly $300,000. The colleges were: UC Berkeley, UCLA, University of Southern California (USC). He was deferred from the University of Miami (FL) and Brown University.

The student, to his credit, called all the schools and one of them offered a $3,000 scholarship, bringing the cost down to $79,000.

Parker was going to graduate from a predominantly white, suburban high school. He hadn't visited any of the California schools. I told him the University of California system enrolls ethnically diverse students and Parker shrugged his shoulders. At such large and far-away universities, how would he fit in? On the other hand, by getting ready to step outside his safety zone, he could be entering a space of personal growth.

How to control your college costs

Academic and social fit need affordability for balance.

Academic Fit

It's essential that students enroll where they can be academically successful. When they apply for admission, if they are at the top of a college's applicant pool, they likely receive more merit aid to reward their school performance. Colleges can decide how much to offer their more desirable applicants. Students who get in but are at the bottom of the applicant pool typically pay more, like the full cost of attendance.

Social Fit

Students who know who they are and the kinds of friends they like to socialize with, can more easily find "their herd" in college. According to social scientists, people tend to affiliate with others like themselves. If you're interested in personality type in college, you will find lots of information in my book, *Find the Perfect College For You*.

Affordability

This book focuses on affordability more than social fit and academic fit. These three variables overlap one another. The student needs to find all three in a college, to be able to have a stress-free, beneficial college experience.

Parent end up paying the larger portion of college costs. This book shows families how they are assessed under the federal and institutional methodologies. The family's financial position and the college's aid policies will interact to yield more or less favorable financial aid packages.

Students can contribute to lowering their college costs by doing their best academic work. The highest levels of merit scholarships are awarded to first-time undergraduate students. Provided the student maintains a reasonable Grade Point Average, the scholarships are renewed each year.

However, if a student is swimming against the current, and can't keep up with the demands of college, they may become more than stressed out. Anxiety and depression are only too common in schools and colleges.

The college experience should build up your sense of confidence, resilience and efficacy. Take the following survey and reflect on your strengths and blind spots.

The General Self-Efficacy Scale

The general self-efficacy scale is designed to assess a general sense of how you perceive yourself and your ability to handle problems. Self-efficacy is the belief that you can accomplish important tasks and achieve your goals. The scale can be helpful in predicting how you cope with daily problems at home and in college, and how you will adapt to more serious stressful life events.

Directions: Rate each statement as honestly as you can using the following scale:

1 = not at all true 2 = hardly true 3 = moderately true
4 = definitely true

	Self-Efficacy Scale Assessment Descriptions	Score
1	I can always manage to solve difficult problems if I try hard enough.	
2	If someone opposes me, I can find the means and ways to get what I want.	
3	It is easy for me to stick to my aims and accomplish my goals.	
4	I am confident that I could deal efficiently with unexpected events.	
5	Thanks to my resourcefulness, I know how to handle unforeseen situations.	
6	I can solve most problems if I invest the necessary effort.	
7	I can remain calm when facing difficulties because I can rely on my coping abilities.	
8	When I am confronted with a problem, I can usually find several solutions.	
9	If I am in trouble, I can usually think of a solution.	
10	I can usually handle whatever comes my way.	
	Total Score	

Source: General Self-efficacy Scale (GES): Ralf Schwarzer & Matthias Jerusalem

Interpretive results: the higher your score, the more self-assured and "efficacious" you are. Then examine the answers where your scored low and examine what you can do to gain more grit and resilience.

The mark of a student who has self-efficacy is that they know the amount of work and challenge they can handle. College is a time for intellectual growth along with an enjoyment of social life.

I remember a student who was accepted to all his colleges and then, at the eleventh hour, decided to throw in a last-minute application to a highly selective university.

I was surprised when he was accepted and congratulated him. When I met him the following year, he confessed that he didn't realize the school would be so stressful. His roommate would sit at his desk with a "Don't disturb me, I have to write a report" sign and would not talk for hours. My student said he would not wish this kind of intense experience on his younger siblings.

Let me assure you that these "wild-card" applications to highly selective colleges or universities at the last minute seldom pan out.

On the off chance they do, who knows if the more selective college will be as enjoyable as those you carefully examined? Will the last-minute application that you send fit your personality, values, academic pursuits, and your family budget?

Some students end up over their heads at a college where metaphorically, they have to wear a pair of shoes two sizes too large or two sizes too small!

How do you know if a college or university will be a good fit for you? Unfortunately, you don't get to try colleges on for size before you enroll, as you would a pair of shoes!

It's a good idea to spend time reading the admission and financial aid website pages, connecting with your regional representative, and visiting the campus in person, with your parents, preferably.

Take the guided tour, ask your questions, and attend the presentations offered in the admission office. Bring a list of questions that are important to you to ask the admission representative. Ask for their business card so you can send them a thank you card.

The college visit will open your eyes to the physical campus and students living there. Try to visit while the classes are in session so that you'll be able to see the students who live on campus.

An in-person college visit will give you a concrete sense of what's right for you. The drive or flight to and from the school will put concreteness into the logistics. Would your comings and goings involve a plane ride each time?

Many students return home for Columbus Day weekend, Thanksgiving week, Christmas, MLK and President's Day, winter and spring breaks. Think about it in terms of four years.

Online classes are here to stay. If you learn better in person than virtually, you may want to ask how first-year courses are taught, so that you will enter an institution that will meet your learning needs.

What Are the Major Differences Between Colleges?

In order to compare apples with apples, let me explain the classifications that colleges fall into. It will help you assess their value rather than comparing apples with oranges.

Public vs Private universities, large vs. small liberal arts colleges, and for-profit vs. non-profit institutions.

You may have heard of the Carnegie classification, which categorizes colleges by their mission, type of education they offer, and students they serve best. For example, Doctoral Research One institutions typically conduct very high levels of research. You may have heard of the refrain: "Publish or perish." Well, if professors don't continue to conduct research, the funding will go away.

Colleges that fall into the Master's Degree classification may offer as many as 50 research programs but fewer Ph.D. programs than Research One Universities.

Baccalaureate colleges offer more Bachelor's degrees than graduate programs and expend their resources in teaching undergraduate students.

Community colleges offer two-year Associate degrees in trade and technical professions, provide foundational preparation for transferring into 4-year programs, and meet the needs of traditional and non-traditional students.

Single-gender colleges, Historically Black Colleges and Universities (HBCUs), and Tribal Colleges tailor their education to the needs of these specific groups of students. The focus is on developing and meeting their educational needs. The colleges' financial resources are invested for the specific benefit of these groups.

I have visited many single-gender colleges and it's clear to me that the women gain self-confidence, respect for the intellect and capabilities of other women, and break out of the limiting societal roles attached to gender. Women's colleges build women's self-esteem and send them out with an empowering perspective on life.

Many high school students don't want to hear me mention women's colleges, but I always put one on their list, and guess what. Some end up attending and never regret it.

Women's Colleges: When I look at where successful women went to college, I find that Erin Burnett, CNN Anchor of "Out Front" graduated with a Bachelor's degree from Hollins University (VA.) She went quite far with her Bachelor's Degree. Hillary Clinton (Wellesley College.) You may not know Meredith College in NC, but Silda Wall Spitzer, founder of Children for Children, went there.

Historically Black Colleges and Universities (HBCUs) fulfill the educational, emotional, social and developmental needs of these minority students, who are often underserved in a "regular" college environment. Studies show that when low-income, Black students graduate from college, they lift their entire family out of poverty. American novelist, poet and social activist Alice Malsenior Walker who wrote *The Color Purple* went to Spellman College, as did Marian Wright Eleman, an activist for children's rights.

Men's Colleges: Wabash College (IN) forms an enclave of intellectually-oriented young men, who gain depth in the liberal arts mode of thought. Hampden-Sydney

College (VA) educates guys in a southern gentleman tradition. Students are hunting, fishing, and engaged in sports activities. HSC supports their highest-level of academic and social development.

Associate's Degrees at Community Colleges: If you missed any foundations, say in Math or Spanish, you can re-start here. Consider that the computer languages Java, C++, or Python are the same whether you learn them at an expensive college or community college. Here students will get the best hands-on, technical training that will lead to immediate, gainful employment, or transfer to a four-year college.

Flagship: Every U.S. State has a major public university that is the "flagship." Typically, it's the oldest university in the state with the strongest reputation. The admission requirements are higher at the flagship than at its satellite campuses. Whereas small public colleges may accept a student with borderline standardized scores, public flagships cannot bend the rules.

Public universities were established as land-grant or sea-grant institutions. Their mission is to provide education and training to the population of their state and nearby county residents. After all, it's the residents' taxes that support their public flagship and the corollary branches.

If residents of other states enroll at your local public university, the tuition costs will be close to three times as much as what they would pay in their state. For example, the College of Charleston tuition is roughly $12,939 a year for SC residents, but $33,270 for out-of-state residents.

I am sorry to report that I met a young girl, Jenna, (not her name) from New Jersey who loves Charleston, SC. She is Pell eligible and her single parent is paying the entire cost via a PLUS loan. If you consider that she can only borrow $5,500 in first year and her Pell Grant gives her approximately another $6,345, her mother is borrowing around $30,000 and over four years she will owe $120,000. Jenna mentioned that she has three other younger sisters. Had Jenna attended any public college in New Jersey she would have paid next to nothing. Upon graduation, she could have moved to Charleston, SC, with a lot less debt for her mother and herself.

If her grades and test scores were not enough to get into Rutgers in New Brunswick, the flagship institution, New Jersey has numerous public colleges that offer excellent art programs, from Stockton to Rowan to Ramapo College.

Regional campuses may also be a good fit. For example, the University of California campuses are the largest and hardest to get into, whereas the Cal State regional campuses have lower admission requirements and are less expensive.

Regional campuses may offer as many as 80 to 100 programs, and within these, there are unique programs. For example, in SC, Coastal Carolina has the "Coastal Education Leadership" and marine-biology programs that are unrivaled in the South East among public universities. Its location near Myrtle Beach provides the ideal environment for hands-on, real lab-training and experience in the marine sciences.

Another example, the University of Massachusetts at Amherst, is the land-grant flagship its State, and typically is the most selective campus. However, UMass

Lowell (also public) is very selective for its nursing, pre-med, and engineering programs. A department within a college may be stronger and more selective than one at the flagship institution.

In South Carolina, the flagship is the University of South Carolina, in Columbia, and there are seven regional colleges made up of three senior campuses and four regional campuses.

However, I'd say that Clemson University is even more selective than USC for mechanical engineering, STEM programs and nursing. Generally, Clemson's degrees lead to realistic, concrete, and practical outcomes. On the other hand, the USC-Columbia campus offers an honors program, the best public policy major in the South East, and enough "ologies" to satisfy the creative, forward-looking students interested in improving the world. The location in Columbia, the state capital, makes it possible for students to attend political events and become interested in journalism, public policy, and state issues.

To make sure the shoe fits, evaluate not just the college itself but also the strength of the individual department you're interested in. Pour over the college catalog, read the mission statements, and read those course descriptions.

Private Colleges: Many private colleges were religiously affiliated and received the seed money from a specific religious branch. They offer a decidedly different academic and social environments than secular, public universities.

You will find religious similarities among Catholic Colleges, from Holy Cross, Boston College, Providence College, Notre Dame, Villanova, Catholic University, Benedictine University, Walsh University. If they follow Cardinal Newman Society's precepts, they will have weekly and daily mass and a catholic thread in the social life and the curriculum, no matter where the college is located in the U.S.

When I visited Gonzaga University in Spokane, WA, I enjoyed the well-tended trees, buildings that grew around the cathedral. There was a wedding going on, and both bride and groom had graduated from Gonzaga. Nowadays, I don't hear many students finding their soul mate in college. It may happen more often on Catholic or religious campuses.

Speaking of dating, I have noticed that there's more dating going on at all-women colleges than in co-ed colleges. I remember my multiple visits at Mount Holyoke College (MA) and noticing how the boys would lean over toward the girls. It was strange in a way to see young boys hang on every word the girls were saying. My student who was enrolled there confirmed my suspicion that the boys from Hampshire, Amherst and William Colleges were finding ways to meet the Mount Holyoke women. It's as if on a co-ed campus it's not cool to become "an item" with someone, as if an exclusive relationship is a denial of group friendship, or, one denies oneself inclusion with others.

Differences between private, secular colleges are many. Some are small in size, and the religious thread runs through the fabric of the curriculum and social life. Others are just like a secular school. Many elite secular universities started out as religious institutions.

Forget for-profit schools. These typically offer short programs in flashy majors, from music-entertainment-management to fashion-design, to culinary arts. These for-profit schools prepare you for entry-level, minimum wage jobs, so they are quite expensive for what they deliver. Even well-known universities can be for profit. I see them advertised on CNN and MSNBC. It's important to ask whether the school is non-profit or for-profit.

How to Find the Right College for You

Do take the surveys in this book. These will help with identifying the variables that will drive your college search. Discuss the results and your thoughts with your parents, school counselor, or Independent Educational Consultants.

Do write down your "must-haves." Once you have written down a list of important values to you, your strengths, interests, and academic needs, read each college's mission carefully. Explore the catalogs. How does the college align with your personality preferences, values, and educational goals?

Do the colleges have the fields of study that interest you? Do the course descriptions sound right up your alley?

Check the difference between the title of a class and the description of the content. Does the teaching approach to the subjects sound abstract or concrete? For example, students may love the sound of "Astronomy," but after reading the course description, they may realize that it's a Physics class.

Are you a concrete or abstract learner? Some students are good at learning practical matters, while others are excited by discovering meanings and relationships beyond the written page.

The course catalog is key to understanding the depth of content of each class. After each visit, write down your impressions. All these factors can reveal to you if the college you just visited will provide a learning environment that will contribute to your academic and social growth.

Personality Type in College: If you want to know more about personality type in college, please refer to my previous book, *Find The Perfect College For YOU!*, which I co-authored with another MBTI professional, Rosalind P. Marie. If you're confused by the way I described Clemson and USC, you may want to refer to this book where we explain how each of the 16 MBTI types fit in college and why. In this book I also describe the physical environment and activities it enables students to engage in. For example, a college in the city of Boston offers a different experience than one located near ski resorts. The latter is conducive to skiing, and, therefore, attracts students who like cold weather, like the outdoors and like to ski. The section on the social environment explains what students care about, the important issues on campus, and the various activities that enable students to express themselves. This is good reading for prospective students who want to gain a deeper understanding of a college physical and social environment, and how their MBTI personality preferences fit with the college.

There's a perfect college for you! Juniors in high school are the most stressed-out students I know. It's the year when, if anything can go wrong, it will. A student struggles in an AP class. Another drops out of the baseball team because it takes too much time out of their study or work schedule. But, there's light at the end of the tunnel.

As the high school senior year approaches, students get ready to complete their applications, essays, personal statements, and become intensely focused on the admission side of the process. I challenge students to consider the cost of their future education. "Along with the academic and social fit, consider the costs," I tell them, as we develop a balanced college list with safe, possible and reach schools. I dispel myths about lower ranked colleges because we know that out of 6,000 colleges not every college can rank #1.

Lesser-known colleges may offer more of what you want, and more money. There are many lesser-known colleges that can provide great experiences, education and training. Less selective colleges will likely grant you larger scholarships, which means less debt for you and your parents. These colleges have a relatively high admit rate, especially starting in 2025, when the demographic cliff impacts college enrollments, due to the decline of college-age students.

Many colleges didn't fill their classes in 2019 and 2020. This means good news for students who will receive more incentives to enroll. Top performing students could get significant scholarships here, if not full-tuition.

Clearly, the highest scholarships still go to students who rank at the top of their class, and as we noticed, not everyone can be "number one." For example, at Muhlenberg College students would need to have something around 1500 SATs, 3.99 GPA (out of 4.0) and several 4s or 5s in AP exams, or a complete IB Diploma.

Note that **public universities** award fewer and smaller merit scholarships, but, for in-state students, the starting price is much lower. Public colleges focus on meeting the financial needs of the residents in their state and nearby area. The admission requirements are not as flexible as those at private colleges.

However, at the height of the Covid-19 pandemic, even public universities changed their admission criteria, pivoted to a holistic review of students, and accepted them without standardized test scores!

It remains to be seen if colleges will do away with requiring standardized test scores. The College Board cancelled the SAT tests and ETS did the same for the ACTs. Colleges understood the medical risks of sitting in the same room for hours to take these tests. They were able to admit students nevertheless. I would hope to see this trend continue!

The strategy for students is that if they don't test well, (and how many students are used to being quizzed in such a manner?) then going test optional is easier. However, most merit scholarships and even state aid is tied to these standardized scores. Students with high grades and test scores regularly obtain larger academic scholarships.

After the smaller private colleges apply all discounts, the cost may not be much more than the in-state public flagship and certainly, an out-of-state university.

I invite my students to cast a wide net and consider different public and private colleges. If they are considering an out-of-state university is want to know why and how it compares with the local university.

Some of my students need more foundational knowledge, and these classes are best at community colleges, where teachers don't assume a pre-established level of knowledge and start from the beginning. For example, a student may think they have a math disability. However, my student started from scratch at a community college, learning fractions, then linear equation, then quadratic ones. He was able to "get it!" Repetition helped him to learn math, which was his Achilles' heel. He went on to major in business and is now considering an MBA.

There are many ways to gain a fine education besides going to the more expensive private or out-of-state universities! It just takes one professor to light a spark and motivate a student to put forth their best! In a small college environment, teachers and students get to know one another and become family. Some students produce their best work when they can lean into these relationships. It's easier to find a mentor on a small campus and become a rock star, a big fish in a small pond!

One last reminder I give my students is to consider that every opportunity has a cost. Students will be unable to be employed full-time while they are in college. The cost of going to college is equivalent to losing about four or more years of wages. Students do so in the hope that they will earn more over their lifetime if they obtain a college degree and will recoup their expenses. Make sure you invest your energy and efforts wisely, and make the most of the next four years! Choose a college that fits you academically, socially, and financially!

What Is the Cost of Attendance?

The Cost of Attendance, or COA, is the sticker price of a college before any discounts are applied. The COA is a term that financial aid administrators use to refer to the costs of tuition, fees, room and meals, books and supplies, transportation and personal expenses.

The COA is the cornerstone of establishing a student's demonstrated need for financial assistance, as it sets a limit on the total aid that a student may receive.

Since the 1980s, the Cost of Attendance at private and public universities across the U.S. has increased each year by three to six percent. Despite these increases, colleges are chronically fearful of not meeting budget. While the pandemic forced colleges to pivot to online classes and thereby shaving some costs, they continue to reach for enrollments to pay the bills.

The most deeply affected are the small private colleges with fewer than 2,500 students. Colleges need this critical mass of students who can pay the larger portion of costs to function properly. Small colleges are more likely to go close out majors that have few students or even go out of business. Public flagships have the most staying power because they can raise funds from alumni, tap into endowments, and utilize aid from the state and federal government.

However, even elite flagships will behave more like private colleges by recruiting out-of-state students who pay two or three times as much as in-state residents. The more expensive colleges may turn out to be the more affordable. For example, Brown University crossed the $80,000 a year sticker price, but they meet the full demonstrated financial need of families. This could result in students paying less at a college that meets 100% of demonstrated need than at a public flagship. During the 2020 pandemic, some colleges froze tuition increases as a gesture of good will during tough times, when students learned online and couldn't have the "full experience." Many students saved on the cost of room and board by staying home and learning remotely. The pandemic set online education as a trend that is sure to stay. With online learning well established, my hope is that the overall costs will decrease.

What Makes Up the Cost of Attendance?

DIRECT COSTS	INDIRECT COSTS
Tuition Fees (library, fitness center) Room and Board (on campus)	Books and Supplies Equipment (e.g., computer/tablet) Transportation Personal expenses

What's the Difference between Direct and Indirect Costs?

Direct Costs such as tuition and fees, room and meals are fixed and predictable and the college bills them directly to the student's account each semester or term.

Indirect Costs are less predictable because they depend on the student's cost of transportation to and from school, books and supplies, and an allowance for living expenses if they are not living on campus. Students can often save money by economizing on indirect costs.

The COA listed on college websites are estimates based on averages, and financial aid administrators adjust the final costs after students accept the financial aid offer and complete the selection of a room and board. A few colleges, like Ithaca College in NY, require students to live on campus housing all four years, which makes the COA more predictable but leaves less choice of housing for the student.

The net cost for each family will be different depending on their ability to pay and how much gift aid (grants and scholarships) the college offered.

Students cannot get more aid than the allowances established in the COA each year or it would result in an "over-award." If this happens, the student needs to return the amount of over-award.

If the funding came from the federal government, the college would return the amount there. If the student fails to make "Satisfactory Academic Progress" (SAP) the funds may also need to be returned.

I came across a young girl, Bella, at a retail store who was trying to repay $700 of her Pell Grant to the community college. I inquired further and it turned out that she didn't attend school nor drop the classes before the add/drop date because she was tending to her dying mother in hospital. I told her to appeal and she said she had, but the school didn't budge. Finally, Bella's uncle paid the $700 and she was able to return to school. I'm happy to report that she's attending a four-year college and getting excellent grades.

Most students don't end up having to return funds. If a college over-awards federal aid they know how to fix it. It's called COD or "Common Origination and Disbursement" which gives me a headache just thinking of it, and I'm glad that as an Independent Educational Consultant I don't have to deal with collecting the funds from an over-awarded student and then returning them to the U.S. Department of Education (DoE).

When students are spending more than the sums established in the COA, they can ask the financial aid administrator for more funding. If the school covers 100% of demonstrated need, students could end up with additional free assistance from the institution. Otherwise, it could result in a larger loan.

The point of indirect costs is that these depend on the student's lifestyle and spending habits. These are under the student's control. "Indirect" costs vary depending on whether the student shops judiciously and stays on budget. For example, to save on transportation, it's best to not bring a car to campus. Carpool with friends who live near your town, buy airline or train tickets well ahead of travel time and minimize the number of trips home from school. You can also save on the cost of the room by checking them out before enrolling. Usually, the newer, larger, suite-style dorms are more expensive.

However, because the pandemic has resulted in many students attending classes remotely, I suspect that colleges have had trouble filling the residence halls. It remains to be seen if they will be able to continue to raise room prices.

Many first-year students tend to sign up for complete meal plans, which explains the typical "freshmen 15" weight gain! By sophomore year, students figure out more accurately how many meals they will really use and select the plans more carefully. On a flight out of Providence, RI, a Brown University student sat next to me, and we started to chat. I had brought a sandwich and fruit aboard, and I offered her some. I was surprised that she was so glad to accept them. She said she hadn't eaten since the previous night because she had no more meals on her plan. I thought, "Here's a student who is trying to make do so she doesn't run up more indirect charges!" I was impressed that she was living within the school's budget. She lived on the left coast and couldn't wait to get home and enjoy a momma meal.

On the other hand, it made me consider that by trying to economize some students may not get enough to eat throughout the academic year. This may be the reason why the U.S. Department of Education will be requiring colleges to change the "room and board" name to "room and meals," and colleges will need to include the price of three meals a day in the published COA.

One of the most common complaints I hear from students is that college food gets tiresome. It's the reason why students don't stay on budget and end up eating out or purchasing food off campus. Parents are surprised because they are already paying for a full meal plan.

I learned long ago that the quality of college food varies by the quality level the college purchases. Aramark sells several tiers of food. This affects the "board" cost. Students may complain about Aramark, Sodexo, or Compass Group's vitals, but the issue may rest with the tier of food the college purchases.

The more costly plans feature more fresh fruit and vegetables, and the menu of options don't repeat as often. Nevertheless, I have eaten meals in many dining halls, and I have always found lots of foods and enough selections to provide something for everyone.

I ate the most memorable meals at Muhlenberg College, PA, UCLA-Los Angeles, and Bowdoin College, ME. Muhlenberg College had the freshest farm-to-fork vegetables and attractive buffets. UCLA's cuisine had the widest selection of oriental foods, including sushi. Bowdoin College featured buffets with lobsters, little-neck clams, assorted mussels, lobster chowder, fresh blueberries, and blueberry pies. I thought I'd died and gone to heaven!

Textbooks: Another way to save money on those "indirect" costs is to buy used books. Some courses and majors require more expensive textbooks. Liberal arts classes typically require less costly books that can be more easily found second-hand, whereas one biochemistry textbook can cost upwards of $300. (See Dan Kopf, *Which Major Has the Most Expensive Textbooks*.) Some students are able to rent textbooks online on Amazon. College libraries keep on reference one or two textbooks per course which students can borrow and use, thereby establishing a habit of studying in the library, with other like-minded students.

I noticed that Brown University gives a standard allowance of $1,642 for books, and if students spend more, they can bring their receipts to the financial aid administrator and ask for a larger book allowance. Being able to buy the textbooks for a course can be essential in helping students pass that course. In 2020-21, Brown University enacted an agreement with their bookstore so that high-need students can get textbooks even if they maxed their allowance. This isn't a regular practice at most colleges.

Supplies: If students are in a fine arts program, the cost of art supplies can quickly deplete any budget. In 2019-20 my student who was not on financial aid started at the School of Visual Design at Kent State University. He needed to purchase a MacBook Pro for about $2,250 and a graphics software suite costing additional funds. It's important for families to calculate these additional fees.

Another student at Cornell University in architecture spent about $2,000 on drafting supplies. Sometimes the indirect costs are unavoidable. Students must compare what they expect to pay with the amount that the college allocated for indirect costs. This exercise helps figure out if the college's allowance for indirect costs is realistic and manageable. The student can either decide to live within the "indirect costs" budget or have parents provide additional resources.

Computers, laptops and tablets are increasingly considered essential for a college student. Some colleges include the costs into indirect costs as a personal expense, but more and more, colleges provide computers to first year students and include the price into the COA.

This means that in some cases, it may be cheaper to wait until the student starts college to buy a new computer rather than to get one while in high school. For example, in Winchester, Virginia, Shenandoah University gives each incoming student a MacBook Pro and an iPad with an Apple pencil. If the laptop or tablet goes on the fritz, it can be repaired on campus, and the student can take out a loaner while waiting for the repair. This way, professors know they can expect students to submit assignments on time. The college technology department becomes more efficient in fixing computer problems since they are all the same. Also, students can't one-up each other on who has the niftier computer! Of course, unless a school has a substantial grant to cover these purchases, the laptop increases the cost of attendance.

Rutgers University in New Brunswick NJ explains their computer policy: "Students may appeal to include the cost of a one-time purchase of a computer for school use. However, including the cost of a computer does not guarantee that you will have enough funding to pay for the purchase of a computer after your other charges are paid. Only if you have aid in excess of tuition, fees, room and board (if you contract with the school) will you receive a refund to assist with the purchase of a computer."

I think that it's foolish to put up road barriers toward students who need a computer because many textbooks are now available online, can be purchased cheaply, thereby saving hundreds of dollars for each student.

Next, let's think about **transportation costs**. The COA must allow for transportation costs to and from school. If a student lives far from home or returns home more often, transportation costs may vary significantly. When budgeting for transportation, students need to figure on gas and maintenance costs if driving, or bus, train, or plane tickets, which are more expensive during holidays, along with the ride to and from the station or airport without a car. Then estimate how often you will travel to and from home during the year.

Keeping a car on campus is most expensive, because parking is always scarce, and students will most likely have to pay for parking. I'm sorry to reveal that one of my students at Hobart and William Smith Colleges ran up 18 parking tickets with no way to pay them. Colleges have leverage and can keep students from officially graduating if all fees, including parking tickets, are not paid. I remember that Jilly, who attended Northeastern University in Boston, used to set the clock for four AM because if it snowed, his car that was legally parked on the street would be booted and removed to make room for the snowplows. Parking is in short supply at most colleges, and there are more parking hazards in big cities like Boston, New York and Los Angeles.

You're getting the gist that "Indirect Costs" are personal expenses, which ultimately depend upon the student's lifestyle. Parents also run into hidden costs when they move their children into college.

This celebrated rite of passage is so exciting for parents and students that it's easy to forget the costs, which are never part of the COA. When parents move their student into the dorm, there may be items to buy, such as reading lamps, extra-long twin sheets, pillows, curtains, wastebaskets, the hanging shoe bag, the plastic space makers under the bed, the Brita filter, the shower caddy, and so on. You get the idea. You need to make a run for Bed Bath and Beyond. When you took that college tour and peeked into a model dorm room, it was outfitted with the cutest linens, curtains, and towels. That's the image the students are left with, and now the items become must-have necessities. What parent dropping off their child to college is going to skimp on those? But wait! There's more. There are additional charges in renting a small refrigerator and a microwave oven. You will have to rent from the college because they won't allow you to bring your appliances from home for fear of electrical overload. By then, parents need a place to stay overnight.

Soon after dropping off the kids comes "parents' weekend." It's the first time you'll see your child since you dropped them off. I remember talking with this parent, who was a banker, and had created a beautiful balance sheet of all the college costs and savings.

He'd listed the COA on the debits column and the savings on the credits column. He was convinced he would be saving money with his son in college. He said the costs of heavy water usage, heat, electricity, not to mention food, would go away. He planned to drop him off at college, without a car, to avoid any parking costs. He pointed out that personal items, such as shampoo, conditioner, hair products, deodorant, body wash and such would be the same if he lived at home. I agreed with him. Personal toiletries are not included in "indirect" costs anyway. "What if he wants to go out to a restaurant?" I asked. "Well, he's not going to school to learn to dine out," he said in a gruff. The next time I met him, I asked him how his visit went during parents' weekend. He let it slip that he'd invited his son's suitemates to eat out at a restaurant, one of the fanciest ones in town. I figured that set him back a few hundreds. But, he didn't seem displeased. He said he met other parents and even played golf with them. The plan was to meet these other couples again for a longer weekend. I could tell he was a father who not only was enjoying his son's college years, but also was enjoying meeting other parents and, like his son, was making friends with new people. He never mentioned the water and electricity savings again.

Luckily, this father was well to do and, as a banker, was trying to teach his son some financial accountability. If the family is low or middle income, they must pay attention at the out-of-pocket costs not just for one year, but for all four years. When an undergraduate first-time student starts at a university that is too expensive for the family, parents will feel a financial stress that likely felt by the student also.

Let's Take a Look at the Cost of Colleges

The Cost of Attendance (COA) of Well-Known Colleges

Take a look at the Cost of Attendance (COA) of these well-known colleges.

University of Virginia College of Arts & Sciences (public)

College of Arts and Sciences	Virginian	Non-Virginian
Tuition	$14,188	$48,036
Fees	$3,116	$3,798
Subtotal	$17,304	$51,834
Additional Categories (Room and Board)	$16,776	$16,776 to $18,016
Sticker Price / COA	$34,080	$68,610 to $69,850

The University of Southern California (private)

Fee	Cost
Tuition	$55,320
Books and Supplies	$1,200
Other Fees	$905
Room and Board	$15,400
Other Expenses Budget	$2,000
Sticker Price / COA	$74,825

Northeastern University (private)

The cost is the same for in-state, out-of-state residents and international students.

Fee	Cost
Tuition	$54,360
Fees	$1,092
Room and Board	$17,480
Sticker Price / COA	$72,932

The University of Michigan - Ann Arbor (public)

	Michigan Resident	Non-Michigan Resident
Tuition	$15,948	$55,292
Direct Loan Fees	$72	$72
Room and Board	$12,034	$12,034
Books	$1,048	$1,048
Personal	$2,454	$2,454
Sticker Price / COA	31,556	$70,900

Brown University (Private)

Direct/Billed Charges	Cost
Tuition	$59,254
Fees (includes $100 Academic record fee for first- time students)	$1,442
Room (Housing)	$9,774
Board (Meals)	$6,134
Subtotal - Direct charges	$76,604
Indirect Estimated Expenses	Cost
Books	$1,642
Personal	$2,202
Travel	****
Total Direct and Indirect Charges	$80,448

From the website: "Not included in your Brown University Cost of Attendance are individual expenses that may be specific only to you. For example, you are required to have health insurance while attending Brown. If you do not waive the University's health insurance plan, your Cost of Attendance will include an additional component for this charge, which for the academic year 2020-21 is $4,077. Additional individual expenses not included may include clothing for the New England climate, computer expense, additional trips home during the academic year, etc."

Community College Costs (Public)

Listed below are the 2020-2021 cost of attendance amounts for a full-time student at Trident Technical College (SC) based on 12 credit hours per semester for the fall and spring semesters. Note that very few community colleges provide on-campus housing.

	TriCounty		In-State		Out of State	
Budget Components	With Family	Off Campus	With Family	Off Campus	With Family	Off campus
Tuition (@ 12 credit hrs. / semester)	$4,608	$4,608	$5,112	$5,112	$8,736	$8,736
Registration Fee	$36	$36	$36	$36	$36	$36
Room and Board	$4,072	$7,768	$4,072	$7,768	$4,072	$7,768
Books/Supplies	$1,460	$1,460	$1,460	$1,460	$1,460	$1,460
Transportation	$2,016	$2,016	$2,144	$2,144	$2,144	$2,144
Personal	$680	$680	$680	$680	$680	$680
Total	$12,872	$16,568	$13,504	$17,200	$17,128	$20,824

What did you notice about in-state and out-of-state costs? I will draw some generalizations about in-state and out-of-state costs of **tuition**, bearing in mind that private colleges charge the same for in-state, out-of-state students, and international students.

The out-of-pocket price is the price that families pay after financial aid awards. The results depend on the family's ability to pay and the college's aid awarding policies.

Ohio State University is $11,518 (Tuition & Fees) for in-state, and **$33,502 (Tuition & Fees)** for out-of-state students, so with room and board, the total COA is In-State $28,074 and **Out-of-State COA $50,648.**

University of Virginia Arts and Science total cost for in-state residents $34,080; Out-of-State COA $68,610 to 69,850 depending on the major.

University of Southern California COA: $78,054. (private colleges charge the same whether students are in or out of state)

Note that **Out-of-State Tuition** is typically three times more expensive than in-state.

UC Berkeley for in-state Californians is $37,468 which is reasonable, given that the school is highly regarded. Note that the Cal States are less expensive than the

UCs. Also, many Californians start at community colleges and then transfer to four-year institutions.

Arizona Out-of-State COA: $47,410 is well priced compared to colleges in California which is why it attracts CA students.

Public flagship universities (e.g., Michigan, Virginia, UNH) provide more aid to their in-state residents while non-resident tuition is nearly three times higher. During the Covid-19 pandemic, many students were learning remotely from home while paying out-of-state tuition. It's difficult to justify the out-of-state expense when the student can't have the full experience of joining a campus community in person.

Smaller liberal arts, private colleges: Tuition costs are the same for in-state and out-of-state students, and COA vary. For example, the College of Wooster (OH) $68,250 to $68,750; Chapman University (CA) $80,710; Furman (SC) $68,952; Colorado College $78,080.

Room and board costs vary across the board anywhere from $11,000 to $19,000. I predict that by 2025 some colleges will charge over $20,000 per year, due to increasing food costs and the amenities that colleges provide to remain competitive.

Community colleges offer "in-state" and "in-district" residents the lowest priced tuition, from $2,000 to $4,500. They are the least expensive way to get two years of college for students who live at home. The drawback is that few community colleges have dorms, so it's harder for first-time non-residents to enroll there. However, I found Valencia College and Central Wyoming College in Riverton do offer dorms. Wikipedia publishes a list of community colleges with dorms.

More observations:

1. Private colleges tend to have a COA between $62,000 and $82,000 (2021-22).
2. Public universities costs range between $20,000 and $30,000 for in-state residents; from $30,000 to $60,000 for out-of-state residents.
3. As public universities increase costs especially for out-of-state students, and private universities discounted their sticker price, the net costs of these two options may be very similar.
4. Public universities don't have as much merit aid to give out as private colleges do. Why? Costs are set by the state's legislature, whereas private colleges have more flexibility in raising tuition and then offer larger scholarships to discount it.
5. Public universities may freeze tuition but increase fees to make up for the shortfall. Some public universities have higher fees than private colleges.
6. Students who consider an out-of-state public university (e.g., University of New Hampshire, University of Vermont, University of Delaware, Rutgers) with a COA upward of the $50,000, may find that the cost ends up nearly similar to private colleges. For example, in the case of Sonia in the Meet the

Students section, you will see that the private college ends up costing slightly less than her in-state flagship university, which would be too high a reach for her.

7. When the price of a public university and a private college are similar, families need to zero in on the better fit for the student. This is the area where students can find their "hidden gem."
8. Out-of-state COA at public universities runs between $40,000 and $60,000, (International students pay the out-of-state COA)
9. Public universities have increased costs so much that they can be as expensive as some private colleges, after subtracting the larger discounts provided by the private colleges.
10. Student health insurance is another charge that can range from $1,800 to $5,000. Some parents pay it without realizing they don't have to, if their child is covered under their family insurance. Dependent students can stay on their parents' medical insurance policy until they reach 26 years of age.
11. International students often are required to purchase the college's health insurance. (Room and board charges are the same, whether you're in or out of state.)
12. As you know, colleges that are more selective are more sought after. They are perceived as a better calling card when students graduate and look for jobs. We know that anyone graduating in engineering or computer science from MIT, Stanford, Caltech and Harvey Mudd will find well-paying jobs. However, there are many students who graduate from Podunk University and end up being successful and happy in many fields. It's all about what students do when they are on campus that matters, more than the name school.
13. High grades, test scores, rank-in-class and other "hooks" strengthen students' chances for scholarships, and these students raise the school's academic profile and ranking. I tell my students they're like money in the bank.
14. Excellent grades don't guarantee that the student will gain admission to the highly selective and competitive colleges. The admission decisions are often arbitrary in that a student may be over-qualified for a college and yet be denied because the college has a different agenda and goals. It may be looking for students who want to major in history instead of pre-med. It's an arbitrary, unpredictable, unfair selection process and it's not necessarily a reflection on the student.
15. Costs of books and digital supplies are dropping, according to the College Board's Trends in College Pricing and Student Aid publications.

How Costs Add Up and How You Can Save!

Indirect Costs: Colleges can set their indirect costs based on several variables, from living expenses by region or metropolitan areas, or based on increases in the consumer price index, as calculated by the U.S. Bureau of Labor Statistics (BLS).

While financial aid administrators can tweak the allowances budgeted if there are extenuating circumstances, they expect students to stay on budget. I remember my own children being unaware of their "indirect costs." This is a conversation that I should have had with them before they left for college. It might have mitigated the many calls I received for "pizza money!"

How can students save on the costs of living on campus? What if they decide to live off campus? I don't profess to know all the ways, but some of these tips may help.

On campus, students can select a less-expensive dorm room that still allows them to succeed. Some students can study in the library or an empty classroom. During the pandemic, many students remained at home, and it was common for the few students who decided to reside on campus to have an entire room to themselves. Some ended up paying for the room and board that they had previously signed for.

Once the Covid-19 vaccine makes it into the arms of those young people 17 years of age and older, the residence halls should return to being full, like old times, and I dare say that students will be glad. Their preferred residences remain the suite-style dorms, where tenants have their own room and a large living area where they can socialize or watch TV. We will continue to hear roommate complaints when the rooms are small and the occupants are incompatible! Getting along with someone different than oneself is also a valuable educational lesson.

In a few foreign countries, like the U.K., a single room per student is a standard. When I traveled with the British Council to visit colleges in London, I noticed that students lived in single rooms. It caused me to reflect upon the American approach to higher education and the reasons why first-year students in the U.S. traditionally have a roommate. The benefit is that the first-year student can have an immediate friend as they adjust to a new place. They have a built-in companion to walk to the dining hall and enter it together. U.K. students seemed older to me, probably because they spend at least one extra year of high school preparing for the A level exams and, then, many take time out to work and experience life before enrolling in university. The typical American experience is designed for entering college immediately upon high school graduation.

Many American students have their own room when they live at home. When they start college, they share space for the first time. Studies show that having a roommate teaches students how to get along with others and enhances social, emotional and intellectual development. Going to college isn't all about hitting the books. The full college experience involves meeting people with different perspectives, debating newly learned concepts and forming solid principles to live by.

Living on campus confers more benefits than living alone or at home. The intellectual and social benefits of living with peers are tangible and long-lasting. However, few students reside on campus all four years. Many will rent an apartment near the college and set up house with other students. This budget involves different types of "indirect costs," from paying rent to buying groceries to learning how to cook.

Resident Advisors (RA): Students can cut costs by applying for RA positions. If you're the type of student who likes to help others and is comfortable with resolving conflicts, you may make an ideal RA. This is a leadership position and a resume builder for students in the upper years, who are mature and able to mitigate the conflicts that arise among floor mates. Resident advisers keep an eye on the goings-on, report unruly behaviors on their floor and keep everything copasetic. Typically, this position grants the student free room and board.

Transfer Credits: Another way to reduce costs is to take the liberal arts courses at a community college. Many students take dual enrollment courses that count toward both high school graduation and college credit. Students with Advanced Placement (AP) classes can get credit if they score at least a three in the AP exam, though many colleges require a score of four or five. Credits through CLEP (College Level Examination Program) can also reduce the number of introductory classes students would take in the first year. These advanced credits can result in savings for up to a semester or more. Even if the college requires students to attend all four years, bringing in AP credits can mean taking fewer introductory courses, giving students more time to dive into courses of their interest. You could go further and graduate with a double major or even a dual degree, such as a B.A. in Political Science and Economics or a dual degree in English Literature and Psychology. The combinations are endless!

Don't overdo it! A word of caution: don't take more credits than the standard amount unless you have the time to dedicate to each class and are fairly sure that you can handle the extra workload. There's a reason why a college is on a semester or quarter calendar with a specific number of credits. It's because students learn best within those parameters.

Some students are so excited and motivated by all the classes available in college that they take more than the required credits, usually15 per semester or 30 per year. A typical four-year degree requires the completion of 120 credits. If you take 30 credits each year, you will have enough to graduate in four years. However, some students take one or more additional courses per semester and stretch themselves too thin. The mark of a good student is one who can be realistic about their abilities and do well in the required courses.

Advanced credits and community college credits: Students can shorten their college years by bringing in advanced AP credits. However, they should be careful not to enroll in too many classes before starting college. With too many dual-enrollment classes students risk becoming classified as "transfer students," if they have more than several semesters of classes. Transfer students don't receive the same level of scholarships, state aid and merit scholarships as "first-year" or "first-time" college students.

Check out your state aid: Make sure you know how your state aid works. Some students don't realize they will get additional aid from the state where they reside. If you apply to an out-of-state university, chances are your state aid won't follow you.

State Aid: Please refer to the section at the back of this book on "State Aid Sampler" and the information supplied. Also, note the state aid deadlines posted for each state on the front of the FAFSA form. In many states, students get state aid automatically when they file the FAFSA. You may need to list an in-state public college first on the FAFSA to be considered for state aid.

In states such as SC, FL, GA, the state scholarships are funded by the lottery and are given out based on grades, class rank and standardized test scores. In this case, the office of admission calculates your GPA and sends your scores to the state higher education office.

I've come across cases where the student's GPA was under-reported to the state. By knowing the criteria for receiving aid, my student called the financial aid office and clarified her GPA. The officer rectified the error and my student received the next level up of scholarship.

One-year masters: If you plan to obtain a graduate degree, another way to save on college costs is to shop at colleges that offer a free fifth-year master's degree. This is becoming more available; for example, at Clark University in Worcester, Massachusetts, students can earn a one-year master's degree at no additional charge. Oglethorpe University in Atlanta has the "Petrel Promise," guaranteeing that students will graduate in four years and will find employment within six months, otherwise, Oglethorpe will give them a one-year Masters' degree for free.

The only catch here is that students must take advantage of this fifth-year plan. Otherwise, it's no benefit. I remember meeting this student in his last year of a Bachelor's degree program and although he enrolled because of the fifth-year, free-Master's degree offer, he was tired of the college and didn't want to remain there for yet another year. He realized that the free tuition was a bonus, but by remaining in school he'd be missing out on one year of salary in the workforce. This type of incentive can work if students stick with their original plan and bring it to conclusion!

Accelerated Programs, Anyone? If students are fairly certain they will go to graduate school, the "combined" and "accelerated" programs can shave some of the costs. For example, Brown University's Liberal Medical Education or PLME consists of an eight-year plan that combines a Bachelor's degree with a medical degree. Naturally, this is a very selective program. The University of Richmond

(VA) offers a 3+3 program that allows students to study for three years, rather than four, in an undergraduate program and then start law school in what would be their fourth year of a Bachelor's degree.

Many **accelerated programs** are unique to the institution and therefore, not well-known or understood. These can save time and money. For example, the Biomedical Engineering program at Johns Hopkins University allows students to utilize their AP or IB credits to advance to the next level. According to Shannon Miller, Office of Undergraduate Admissions, students with such advanced credits can complete a Master's degree in their fourth year. They graduate with a Bachelor's degree in three years and are automatically admitted to a master's program. They are even exempted from taking the GRE exams.

Dual Degrees: A dual degree program lets the student work on two degrees at the same institution or in parallel with another institution. For example, a student may graduate with a Bachelor's degree in two majors, or complete a degree from one school in Linguistics, for example and one in Russian from another college.

These dual degrees may also be called "**Combined Degrees.**" For example, it is possible at John's Hopkins University to complete the Master's in Biomedical Engineering (BME) in four years.

Speaking of Baltimore, I remember that one of my artsy students enrolled at Goucher College in Towson, MD, and took classes at the Maryland College Institute of Art. Another took advanced courses in Russian at Johns Hopkins. My students enjoyed being able to take classes at two different campuses and meet different students.

These degrees work well for students who like to plan and work their plan. They like to follow a roadmap, and stay the course. In my practice, I use the Myers Briggs Type® Indicator and STRONG® Interest Inventory to help students assess their personality preferences and likelihood that they will be satisfied with following a plan. I posted a "mock" personality-preferences questionnaire on my website (www.eduave.com) that you can take.

One by one, my student assesses their level of interest, dedication and abilities. Students who know themselves well will feel more confident in the choice of accelerated or dual degrees. To help with this assessment, I shared some "Starting Questions and Self-Assessment" and "The Value Sort" exercises. These can help students bring into focus what's important to them. They can use those questions to engage their parents in a heart-to-heart discussion.

Did I mention the 3+2 professional programs? These are available at colleges that have strong articulation agreements with other institutions. I say "strong" agreements meaning that it's a true and tried articulation and many students have successfully done it. This plan of study involves spending three undergraduate years at a rigorous liberal arts college and then transferring to another college, perhaps a totally different one, such as a technical institute. For example, in New York State, Siena and Union colleges have agreements with Rensselaer Polytechnic Institute (RPI), the Medical College in Albany, and the Albany College of Pharmacy. For example, a student who enrolls at Union College will gain a Bachelor's degree in liberal arts and a Bachelor's degree in engineering from RPI in five years.

A student who applies and is admitted to both Union College and the Albany College of Pharmacy will earn a Bachelor's Degree from Union College and a terminal degree in Pharmacy for the Albany College of Pharmacy. They also have an articulation agreement with the Albany Medical College, which is highly accelerated compared to the usual trajectory. Students apply to both Union College and the Medical College in Albany. They must be accepted by both schools to follow through with the plan.

Be Steadfast! This means that students must be relatively mature, determined, and sure of what they want. Typically, first-generation immigrant students with parents in the medical field are more successful in completing these programs. Perhaps it's because they don't question what they could do in other areas of study. They take for granted that their career must follow in their parents' footsteps. It's worth looking into these lesser-known articulation agreements because they can offer a varied-type training and real value for the determined student who knows what they want. Many students are not sure of what they want to be or what they want to study in college. These programs are not so productive then. These students will thrive at liberal arts colleges where they can explore their interests from anthropology to sociology and the rest of the "ologies." Once they discover their passions, they will be ready to consider the combined programs.

Opportunity Cost: Earning a college degree opens many opportunities, although staying in college also means that some other opportunities are lost. While in college, students are not working and earning a salary. If colleges made it easier to graduate in three years, students would be able to enter the workforce and start earning a salary one year earlier. This would result in fewer loans and more earnings over one's lifetime.

In conclusion, students may want to know that there are colleges that offer dual, combined and accelerated degrees. Many colleges accept AP tests, CLEP and dual enrollment classes for advanced credit, thereby reducing the number of semesters needed to graduate. Sometimes, colleges have articulation agreements with graduate schools, that may reduce the years to a Master's degree. These may be ways to reduce costs for students who know what path they want and will stay the course.

More Ways to Save Money on College Costs

- Ask for advanced credit for your dual-enrollment classes, AP test scores and CLEP tests. If you are in the International Baccalaureate (IBprogram, plan to complete the full higher-level diploma to gain more advanced credits in college. Some colleges will award as much as the entire first year.
- Save on textbooks by buying them used or online (betterworldbooks.com, chegg.com, amazon.com, etc.) You can use the ISBN from the class syllabus to find the books. Once the class is over, sell them back. The library will have a couple of textbooks on reserve for each course offered at the college.
- Use and re-use items that you already own. For example, bring towels, sheets, pillows, curtains from home.
- Share laundry chores with your roommate so that you have enough clothes to launder whites and darks separately.
- Use the meals you're paying for, and limit outside food vendors. If you have money left over on your swipe card, make sure the funds can be transferred to the next semester or year.
- If your college costs are significantly higher than the allowances in the cost of attendance, you can ask for more aid. Keep your receipts and submit them to the financial aid administrator. If you need additional funds to sit for a test or certification, ask the administrator to help you. If the college meets 100% of demonstrated need you may get more free aid. However, if the college doesn't meet financial need, the financial aid administrator will offer more loans.
- Don't bring a car to campus, so you will avoid parking costs, parking tickets, wear-and-tear on the car, and car repairs.
- Use public transportation. Carpool if you have a friend who is a reliably safe driver. Some colleges provide students with a bus pass.
- If you need to fly to get to college, buy flights well ahead of time. Remember, flights are more expensive during the holidays, especially Thanksgiving and Christmas.
- Examine the choice of dorms and select a room that will be less expensive. For example, older buildings tend to cost less than brand new residence halls.
- Internet costs, microwave and refrigerator rental costs add up. Avoid them or share the costs with your roommate.
- Avoid purchasing a new computer in your senior year in high school if you can. Your college may offer a better buy along with tech support.
- Establish a budget. This will be even more critical if you move off-campus and pay rent, utilities, food, and transportation.
- Parents who plan to attend "parents' weekend" can cut costs by booking hotels early. Some residence halls have guest rooms that can be rented out for minimal costs.

The Benefits of a College Education

You'll earn more money over your lifetime if you have a college degree.

Go for the highest degree you can get.

Do it while you're young, like, when you're in your late teens and early twenties. It's harder to go back to school as an adult, although online learning makes college more accessible to working parents.

Did you know that people with higher levels of college education stay married longer? Apparently, they live healthier lives, enjoy more benefits, and over their lifetime, they earn more than high school graduates.

A liberal arts education can free students to explore many subjects. If you constantly read, approach new ideas and information with curiosity, stay in school. If you seek true understanding, if you like to discuss concepts ad infinitum, talk with many people about why a solution is what it is, and examine it from many different perspectives, then the life of the mind is for you.

If academics, possibilities, and broad approaches to theoretical concepts aren't your thing, go for a fouryear program in a practical field, from manufacturing to business. If you're detail-oriented, look for administrative positions where your organizational skills can be put to use. Get an Associate's degree at a community college.

If you're good with hands-on tasks and enjoy seeing the results of your work, look for programs that offer tangible and practical outcomes: aircraft or auto mechanic, electrician, heating-ventilation technician, welder, pipefitter, nursing, computer hardware tech.

Once you learn a trade well, and know how to get clients, you could become an independent contractor, or, open your business. You could employ other people.

Choose training and a field of study you like and are good at.

How much time do you have? If you don't have two-years for an Associate's degree at a community college, at least complete a community college Certificate. They take less than a year! The key is to graduate with a Certification.

You may find that once you earn a Certificate, you can continue to take more classes toward your Associate Degree. Once you complete your Associate's degree, you'll be able to transfer your credits to a 4-year college. Rome wasn't built in one day! In Aesop's tale, the slow and steady turtle, not the hare, won the race.

Visit https://www.onetonline.org/ to explore your interests, careers, and "sunrise" occupations (jobs that are in demand.)

If you like computer networking, routing-switching, you could earn an excellent salary with a CISCO certification.

Avoid for-profit, expensive, short-term programs.

Get the most education you can for the least cost.

Stay true to who you are. It will enhance your lifelong growth.

Control Your Costs

Choose the right door! Does it sound like the old TV show "Let's make a deal?" The old Monty Hall problem was one of probability. You stood a better chance of winning is you switched doors.

You improve your chances of choosing the right door when you research your options, debunk myths, and plan ahead.

Families who understand how the financial aid system works stand a better chance of getting more aid.

High-income families typically have high expected family contributions. Even they may balk at having to pay $82,000 to send their student to Northeastern University, Wake Forest or NYU. If their estimated contribution is higher than the cost of attendance, they will pay the list price.

Where can high net-worth families find the best buys? Their in-state, public institutions will be very affordable. Private colleges that offer sizeable scholarships will be their best bet. If the student applies to colleges that offer aid based on financial need, such as Amherst or Swarthmore Colleges, they will pay the full sticker price.

Where can middle-income families find the best buys? At colleges where the student ranks in top 10% of the applicant pool. They will need both merit and need-based aid.

Where can low-income families find the best buys? At colleges like Amherst, Williams, Swarthmore among others, low-income students will have 100% of their financial need met.

Those who try to game the system need to consider that federal grants are meant for families that live near the poverty line. There may be some loopholes that may be even legal, but I'm not one who could help millionaire get need-based grants.

If you hear of these successes, be skeptical! As the federal FAFSA form aligns more closely with the IRS 1040 tax return, there's a fine line between tax avoidance and tax evasion. Cheating on the FAFSA can result in a $20,000 penalty and time in prison. Private colleges that use their internal forms or the Profile comb through every possible source of funding.

Students can choose to open the right door by applying to schools where they rank high in the applicant pool.

If they are what I call "emerging learners," the less selective, public, regional campuses, and community colleges are ideal places for reviewing and rebuilding the skill that were not learned in high school.

Smaller, less-selective, liberal arts colleges often offer a supportive learning environment for these “emerging learners” who wouldn’t be admissible to state schools. If the student is athletic or has a special skill needed by the school, the price will likely be lower.

Choose the door that opens to an education that fits your current academic, social and developmental needs. The odds will be in your favor that you will pay less and enjoy it more.

Please read the chapter “Meet the Students” and you will see examples of college financial aid awards, merit scholarships, needbased aid, and more examples of how to compare costs and value.

The Family Budget

Complete the "Family Budget" form, and calculate your "Affordable Family Contribution." Your budget is a record of your expenses, compared with your monthly income. These are items you can control and spend them in a way that maximizes your resources. Keep pay stubs, expense receipts, any documents that can prove your financial situation. The budget can give you potential financial information to present to financial aid administrators. Your budget shows you what you can afford to pay for college. You can make a plan to borrow only a certain amount, for example.

However, colleges don't expect you to pay just from your current income and savings. They expect families to pay through borrowing. You need to decide how much debt is doable for you and how much debt would be excessive for you. We will review the federal financial aid formulas in later chapters, but suffice to say that a certain percentage is expected from your current income and assets.

You need to decide for yourself how much you are willing to pay from your savings, from your current income, and from future borrowing. It's up to you to control those parameters, not financial aid administrators. Every family's debt-tolerance is different. It's like investing: every person's risk tolerance for loan debt is different.

The "Affordable Family Contribution" or AFC, is an amount you decide you can pay from savings, income, and borrowing. Once you have defined your AFC, you have an amount of funding in mind which fits your risk tolerance. Your AFC is an amount you can and are willing to pay, regardless of what colleges say you should pay.

Your family budget gives you ammunition to explain and prove where your income goes each month and why your expected family contribution is not representative of what you can pay. Note that as far as colleges are concerned, willingness to pay is not a reason to refuse to pay. Such an argument won't fly with a financial aid administrator. However, financial aid administrators will respond to your appeal and the documentation that supports your financial position.

One way to check on what individual colleges would charge is to use the "Net Price Calculators" or NPCs found on each college website. NPCs are mandated by the federal government and colleges must publish them in the financial aid section.

The net cost, or net price, is the difference between the cost of attendance and the grants and scholarships (money that does not need to be repaid) awarded by the government and the colleges. This is the amount you will have to pay to cover one year of college costs. Note that the net price does not subject loans from college costs. Loans must be repaid, usually with interest.

NPCs give you an approximate net cost, and some are more accurate than others. Make sure the data you enter is as accurate as possible. This can give you a starting point for how much this college would cost you, and you can use this information for judging if it's worth it for your student to apply. Consider calling the financial aid office if you need clarification, if you don't understand the NPC questions or if the cost of attendance for the upcoming year are not posted. You can also check to find your EFC by entering your financial information on the EFC calculator on the College Board website. Compare your EFC to your Affordable Family Contribution and see how similar it is to each college's Net Price Calculator.

Reference: Laura Perna, Jeremy Wright-Kim and Nathan Jiang, *Are Colleges Complying With Federal And Ethical Mandates For Providing Students With Estimated Costs?*

In future chapters, you will learn how to file the FAFSA and CSS Profile. Read the case studies. Some will resonate with your individual family situation. Pay careful attention to your SAR, "Student Aid Report." You will receive it after you file the FAFSA. Your federal EFC will be on the first page. Also, it will say if your file was selected for verification. It recaps the financial information you entered on FAFSA or downloaded through the Data Retrieval Tool. If you are eligible, this first page indicates the amount of Pell Grant.

Pell and FSEOG grants are federal entitlement programs that you can use or "spend" at any college of your choosing. "Award Letters" can be confusing and I post one for my student, Sonia, in the chapter "Meet the Students."

The completed credential from any college will launch people onto more lucrative employment. It's the key that enables families to control this process, lower stress, and purchase an education that fits the student academically and is fiscally fit for parents.

You will save money by applying to the colleges where your student ranks near the top of the applicant pool, because those colleges that will treat your student "preferentially."

A student's academic record may be average or below average for college A but at college B it may be above average. Depending on your student's academic abilities, your financial situation, and the college's aid policies, your net price will vary.

Many do well to work with IECs because the know colleges and get to know students. You will pay less if you knock on the door of colleges where the student ranks near the top of the applicant pool. Cast a wide net to different colleges until you find a couple that fit your AFC.

Please note: **I will never try to advise you about your investments for the scope of managing your finances**. Although high college costs can affect parents' retirement, you will not need to shift assets or change your current investment strategies with me.

Please refer to the Glossary at the end of the book to review what each term or acronym means.

PS: When I use the word "You," I'm referring to students, parents, school counselors, IECs, and anyone reading this book.

Beginning Questions and Self-Assessments

Beginning Questions for Parents and Students

Directions: Both student and parent(s) need to answer the questionnaires below separately. Then, they need to compare the answers together.

IECs and School Counselors: use this survey with your families to ascertain whether college costs are a consideration and to what extent the student is on board with the parents.

The answers on this questionnaire will support the family's need to identify their Affordable Family Contribution or "AFC."

Questions for Parents	YES	NO
Have you discussed with your student the cost of going to college?		
Will the cost of college influence the decision of which school the student will attend?		
Have you discussed how much you, the parents, are able to contribute?		
Have you discussed how much you expect your student to contribute through savings, money earned from a job, obtaining scholarships, and/or loans?		
Do you think your student appreciates the need to have affordable options on a college list?		
Do you feel that your family can easily cover the cost of four years or more of college?		
Do you feel there will be a financial need that is larger than what you can cover?		

Is it desirable to attend a slightly lesser-ranked school in exchange for more merit aid?		
Would it be acceptable for you as the parent to encourage your student to go to community college for a semester or a year to save money?		
Is graduate or professional school a consideration?		
If so, have you discussed who will pay for graduate school after the bachelor's degree?		
Do you have other children who are in college or who will be going to college? Will you have more than one child in college at the same time?		
If so, have you thought of how you will pay for more than one child going to college?		

Based on this questionnaire, how concerned are you about college costs?

____

Could you pay for any college your student got into?

____

How much have you saved already for college? (for each child)

____

How are you planning to pay for college?

____

Parents can use the answers to create a parental framework for talking about college costs with their student.

IECs and School Counselors can give this survey to their families, discuss the implications, and the need for identifying "Affordable Colleges."

Questions for Students	YES	NO
Have you discussed with your parents the cost of going to college?		
Will the cost of college influence the decision of which school you will attend?		
Have you discussed how much you will contribute to your own education through your savings, money earned from a job, or scholarships? Are you aware that the federal government allows every student to borrow a certain amount of loans?		
Do you believe that you should have affordable options on your college list?		
Do you feel that your family can easily cover the cost of four years or more of college?		
Do you expect your parents to pay for college?		
Are you aware of the different ways that are possible to pay for college? Self-help aid, such as loans, work-study, and other student work? Grants and scholarships? Did you know that when you file the FAFSA you will receive some amounts of federal loans that are your responsibility to pay back with interest? Do you know the difference between simple interest and compound interest?		

Do you feel you should go to the "best," most selective college you get into, no matter the cost?		
Would you attend a slightly lesser-ranked school in exchange for more merit aid?		
Would you accept going to community college for a semester or more to save money?		
Is graduate or professional school a consideration?		
If so, have you discussed who will pay for graduate school after the bachelor's degree?		

Discuss the results of this questionnaire with your parents, IEC, or school counselor:

What concerns do you have with the potential costs of college?

____

How do you plan to pay for college?

____

Call to action: Students and parents make the best decisions when they can talk about their feelings relative to college costs. Families working with IECs (Independent Educational Consultants) will receive lots of support and guidance if they know your concerns. Families need to have a college (or two) on the list that fit the student academically, socially, AND are affordable for two or four years. The price can be driven down by simply applying to colleges that fit the student well.

Students can help pay less by doing their best work in high school. When you start college, you can help by continuing to perform your best academically and graduating in four years or less. (Consider that that graduation rates are quoted based on six years!) This means students are spending money on college tuition, fees, living expenses, when they could be earning a salary in their industry, or gaining a graduate degree.) Plan ahead so you will enjoy your college years and graduate without a lot of debt!)

Test Your Knowledge of Your Local Colleges

Do this exercise to test your knowledge of colleges in your local area and within your state. Guess the tuition costs without looking online! Both the student and the parents need to answer each section separately. Have fun with this quiz!

Once you've completed it, then verify the costs on the colleges' websites. You may be surprised! If you hit the bull's eye, then you're close to a genius in my books!

(IECs, School Counselors: use this survey with your families to ascertain their knowledge of college costs.)

What is this year's total Cost-of-Attendance (COA) at your in-state public university? Note the name here:________________	$______
What is this year's total Cost-of-Attendance (COA) at an out-of-state public university, just over the border from your state? Note the name here:________________	$______
What is the total Cost-of-Attendance (COA) of a well-known elite, private College? Note the name here:________________	$______
What is the total Cost-of-Attendance (COA) of a lesser-known private College? Note the name here:________________	$______
What is the COA at your local Community College?	$______

Now check your answers by visiting the websites for the colleges you selected. Search on the financial aid web pages for "Cost of Attendance." You can also use the College Navigator tool provided by the National Center for Education Statistics (NCES) at nces.ed.gov/collegenavigator/ to check on cost increases over the last few years, as well as retention rates from first to second year and overall graduation rates.

How did you do? Were your first guesses (without checking online) close to the verified costs you found on each college's website?

Did you notice that tuition and fees are fixed costs? These are the "Direct Costs."

Room and "Board," also called Room and "Meals," are the "Indirect Costs" because they can vary.

Now break down the cost for room and meals for each college here:

What is this year's cost of room and meals at your in-state public university? (use average meal plan for first-year students)	$______
What is this year's cost of room and meals at an out-of-state public university? (use average meal plan for first-year students)	$______
What is the cost of room and meals of a well-known elite, private College? (use average meal plan for first-year students)	$______
What is the cost of room and meals of an elite, little-known private College? (use average meal plan for first-year students)	$______

What did you notice about the costs of room and meals?

____

Do you think you will live on campus all four years?

____

I hope you will have noticed that the room and meals costs vary somewhat from college to college, from $10,000 to $14,000 per academic year. The costs vary depending on the type of room students select and the size of the meal plan. First-year students typically sign up for the full-week plan of 21 meals. Some schools require this of first-year students. Eventually, students discover that they don't use all 21 meals, because they don't make it to breakfast or sometimes skip lunch due to their class schedule. After students become oriented to the pace of college, in the upper years they may select a cheaper room and a smaller meal plan. Some students spend little time in their dorms because they prefer to study in the library, or, in an empty classroom rather than in their dorm room where there may be more interruptions. Post Covid-19, some students may continue taking classes online. The first year of college is when students make many new friends and in later years, they may choose to reside campus and share apartments with friends.

Know Thyself

Families have values they hold dear. Students often embody their parents' values without knowing it. This next exercise helps students identify values pertaining to the academic experience they're looking for in a college, the physical campus, the physical location, and the plans for the future. Take the time to do this exercise. Then, you will have a yardstick by which to examine whether a college is in line with what is important to you.

Every college has a clearly spelled out mission. By reading the mission you will gain an understanding of what the college values.

- Some colleges focus on teaching undergraduate students primarily and may have a religious feel if it was founded by a religious order that is still active on campus, like Catholic University, Fairfield College, Boston College or College of the Holy Cross. Providence College (RI) provides education founded on the Catholic tradition of the Dominican friars.
- Public institutions tend to be large and were founded by federal land-grants to provide undergraduate and graduate education to the residents of their state. For example, the College of Charleston (SC) is a public institution and its mission to provide education for the residents of South Carolina and the Low Country locals.
- Smaller liberal arts colleges have a distinguishing feel, flavor, and social appeal. Because they're smaller institutions, the physical and social environment exist in a more definable context. Willamette University provides rigorous education in the liberal arts and selected professional fields.

You can learn a lot by reading the mission statement of a college. Compare then the mission with your values. Are you looking for a rigorous liberal arts education? Is your religion a significant part of your life? Are you interested in social justice? Liberal arts colleges hold an unapologetic goal to make the world a better place. For example, Swarthmore College (PA) looks for intellectually curious students who are interested in making the world a better place. At the admission level, it will help you express why you want to attend their college as you link their ethos to your values.

When it comes to paying for college, the financial aid policies often align with the mission. For example, Swarthmore College (PA) started out as a Quaker-affiliated colleges and emphases tolerance, collaborative learning and "purposeful application of knowledge." Their financial aid policies align to these principles. Swarthmore believes that access to higher education is a right that everyone, regardless of ability to pay, should be able to access. The financial aid policies at Swarthmore reflect this mission and the college meets 100% of each student's demonstrated need.

Carson's story: After several meetings with Carson, a rising high school senior, I felt that her college list wasn't exactly hitting the bull's eye. Then, my cat jumped on the table, positioned itself in front of Carson, and looked at her with owl-like, all-knowing feline eyes. We laughed. It occurred to me that both Carson and I had been analyzing colleges so closely that we were missing something. I loved seeing Carson laugh, so I asked her to think about her happiest times and describe them to me. She said she was happy when she spent time with her peers. I asked her to describe her peers. It turned out her favorite peers were the kids in her church youth group. Those were her "real" friends. She felt she could count on them and felt safe there.

This was a turning point for her, and for me, as her guidance counselor. We hadn't been looking specifically for religiously affiliated colleges. This changed the college list. Carson made several "virtual" visits and after she identified a couple of "fits", she asked her mother to take her to visit the campuses. She returned looking confident and happy, having made her choice, and feeling on top of the world. Apparently, she'd spoken not only with admissions representatives but also with a few students, whom she met in the restroom, of all places, and around campus. She felt she could make friends there and be her authentic self. Had she not discovered that she was happiest when she was with her church peers, Carson might have ended up at a different school. Granted, secular campuses also have ministries, like a Catholic group, or a Hillel or a Muslim group. However, the religiously affiliated college that Carson chose had religion as a thread woven throughout the curriculum and in the students' heart.

By identifying your values, principles you hold dear, and matching your academic abilities with the colleges' admission requirement will go a long way toward identifying colleges that may treat you preferentially. When you rank at the top of the applicant pool, you're likely to get a merit scholarship and pay less in the end.

Take the time to sort go through the Value Sort Exercise to help identify what's important to you.

Value Sort Exercise

The Value Sort Exercise should be taken by the student and parent(s) separately. Then, they can meet to compare results.

Did dad select "security" as the number one value while the student selected "socializing?" What does the student really mean by choosing "socializing?" Does this mean partying, fraternities, sorority life or simply meeting new and different people? Does the student come from a small high school in suburbia and thinks a mega college will offer more people to meet? If so, with whom does the student plan to make friends?

Use the Value Sort questionnaire to pinpoint what you value the most. Then write down the four values that are most important to you, and share them with your parents. This will help you remain faithful to your values even when you may be tempted to stray. These will be the values that you will keep in mind as you drive your college search.

Match your values to colleges that are affordable.

Use this scale to rate what's important to you.

4 = This is most important to me.

3 = This is important to me.

2 = I'm indifferent – I can take it or leave it.

1 = This is not at all important to me, or this is the opposite of what I want.

© Claire Law	Values Pertaining to Academic Experience	
Value	**Explanation**	**Rating (1 to 4)**
Tangible results	I want my classes to be practical and realistic, producing tangible, real results.	
Creativity	I want college to allow me to express my creativity and delve into anything I value.	
Independence	I want college to foster my independence, to allow me to make my own choices and to give me a high level of autonomy.	
Intellectual stimulation	I want to be challenged intellectually in my classes.	
Clear expectations	I want my teachers to set clear expectations.	
Competence	I want college to give me the skills to be competent in my career.	
Interest	I want most of my classes to be interesting to me.	
Leadership	I want to be a leader in the college I attend.	

Teachers	I want my classes taught by professors, not TA's (teacher assistants).	
Class size	I want all of my classes, including introductory ones, to be small.	
Graduation	I want to be at a school where most people graduate in four years.	
Work ethic	I want to be at a school where most of the students care deeply about their education and study intensely.	
Party ethic	I want to be with students who work hard and play hard.	
Competition	I want to be in a competitive academic atmosphere. I learn best when everyone in class is high-achieving.	
Cooperation	I want to be in a cooperative academic atmosphere. I learn best when students in the classes have differing levels of ability.	
Work-life balance	I want to enjoy my college experience and not have to constantly work hard.	
Match	I want to be in a school with students whose standardized test scores and GPA are similar to mine.	
Accommodations	I want a school that can accommodate my learning differences.	
Services	I want the school I attend to have good study resources, such as a writing center or math lab.	

© Claire Law	Values Pertaining to The On-Campus xperience	
Value	**Explanation**	**Rating (1 to 4)**
Socializing	I want to spend a lot of my time in college socializing with friends.	
Greek life	I want to be on a campus that has a strong presence of fraternities and sororities.	
Clubs	I want a college that has lots of clubs and activities, like intramural sports.	
School spirit	I want a college where the school spirit is strong. (This may be shown through support of team sports like football, soccer, and basketball.)	
Sports	I want to participate in team sports. If so, name the sport(s): ________________	
Nature	I want to go to a school where I can easily experience nature and enjoy the outdoors.	
Solitude	I want to be able to have some time by myself when I'm at college.	
Volunteer work	I want to do volunteer work in college.	
Leadership	I want to take on leadership roles in college.	
Social approval	I want the college I attend to impress others.	

Honesty	I want a college environment that allows me to be myself.	
Adventure	I want to have adventures at college, to do something new, different, or exciting.	
Living situation	I want to be on a campus where most students live on campus at least through sophomore year.	
Living quarters	I want my living quarters to be nicer than most.	
Facilities	I want the school to have great facilities (gym, library, student union, etc.)	
Fashion	I like to wear good clothes, and name brands are important to me.	
Culture	I want to be part of a school that is tolerant of people's differences. I want a school that is service-oriented.	
Opportunities	I want the college to provide plenty of opportunities for internships, service learning, and study abroad.	
Student body	I want the student body to be mostly made up of people who are like me. If this is important to you, indicate what "like me" means: ________________________	

© Claire Law	Values Pertaining To Location	
Value	**Explanation**	**Rating (1 to 4)**
Location	Where the campus is located is important to me. If this is important, indicate whether you prefer a large city, small city/town, suburban, or rural environment: ________________________________	
Climate	The climate of the school's location is important to me. If this is important, indicate the type of climate you prefer (warm most of the year, cool most of the year, clear change of seasons; humid, dry):________________	
Distance from home	It's important that I be within a ____-hour drive from home. If this is important, indicate how close to home you want to be.	
Community	I want the surrounding area of the college campus to be appealing to me.	
Safety	I want the campus and the surrounding area to be safe.	

© Claire Law	Values Pertaining To School Characteristics	
Value	**Explanation**	**Rating (1 to 4)**
Size	I know what size of school would suit me best: small, medium, or large.	
Coed or single-gender	I want a coed, or single gender, or LGBTQ-friendly campus.	
Affiliation	The school's affiliation is important to me. It should be ________________ (public, private, religious, nonsectarian).	
Campus	I want my school to have an attractive campus.	
Cost	I think about college costs.	
Awareness	I will apply for financial aid.	

© Claire Law	Values Pertaining to Preparation for the Future	
Value	**Explanation**	**Rating (1 to 4)**
Affordability	I want to graduate with the minimum amount of debt for me and my parents.	
Service to others	I want my college degree to align with a career that is helpful to others.	
Advancement	I want college to help me get ahead in life.	
Status	I want my college degree to align with a career that results in high status and prestige, a career that will impress others.	
Material comfort	I want my college years to lead me to a lucrative career.	
Leadership	I want college to prepare me to be a leader.	
Duty	Doing what is right is important to me. For example, I want to serve my country.	
Power	I want my college years to lead me to a position of power.	
Security	I want my college degree to align with a career that will result in long-term employment.	

Service to others	I want my college degree to align with a career that is helpful to others.	
Career or grad school placement	I want the college I attend to have excellent resources for career and graduate school placement.	
Opportunities	I want the college to provide plenty of opportunities for internships, service learning, and study abroad.	

Assign #1 to the most important value to you. Then #2 to the second most important value. Then #3 to the third most important value, and so on., #32 will be the least important value to you.

Parent's most important values that will drive the college search are:

1. ___________ **2.** ___________ **3.** ___________ **4.** ___________

Student's most important values that will drive the college search are:

1. ___________ **2.** ___________ **3.** ___________ **4.** ___________

After the student and at least one parent complete the Value Sort exercise, take the time to compare notes. Use this survey as a launching point to open a dialogue and verify what is important to keep in mind when selecting colleges to consider.

**Students: continue to discuss your values, plans, and expected outcomes with your parents, School Counselors, and Independent Educational Consultant IEC. Be mindful of costs as your parents figure out their budget and what they can pay for college. Even though your parents will help you financially, earning a college education and paying for a small part of it is your responsibility. Students who apply for financial aid (by filing the FAFSA) will be responsible to repay their loans. Studies show that if they graduate, students can repay the nearly $30,000 over ten years. Many pay the entire balance earlier. You can lower the balance you owe after four years by paying your loan while in school. For example, even paying the yearly interest of a few hundred dollars will lower the balance you will owe at graduation. I will explain this in future chapters. The StudentAid.gov web site provides information about interest rates here and how interest is calculated.

Family Budget

Good job in identifying your values! Highlight or write down the variables that were most important to you so you can check back as you continue to explore your colleges. Going forward, I assume that students have a list of colleges they have researched. Students should focus on the fit, not the brand name. They should make sure the pair of shoes they want to buy fit well: too tight it will be uncomfortable and hurt, too loose and the foot will slip and slide resulting in blisters. Don't lose your footing!

The college list and associated costs are critical parts of taking the right next step. Often, parents talk with other parents, peruse websites and buy the thick college guides. I am an Educational Consultant and I know that IECs are experts in placing students in the right school, or college, or gap-year program. IECs know the academic and social environment of many individual colleges and can develop a realistic college list based on the student's credentials, learning style and social needs. They know if a college would be too competitive and would result in rejection letters. They know how teenagers react to rejection and can save the student from the angst that accompanies this process and they can save money for the entire family by giving appropriate college lists.

If a list contains many "selective" or "competitive" colleges, the student may set himself up for receiving many rejections and end up feeling like a failure. Students can't bank on going to colleges that admit fewer than 50% of students. If students apply to colleges that receive tens of thousands of applications for a class size of 2000, they have to accept that the odds aren't in their favor, even though these students were at the top of their high school class. Just because a college has great name recognition doesn't mean it would be a good fit for all students.

Colleges have many add-ons that students never use. I always chuckle when a tour guide tells me that there are 300 "interest and activities" groups on campus, and "if you don't find one you like, you can create a new group!" I've never replied to these assertions, but let's be real: there are only so many hours in a day, and if the student plans to study at all, there's little time left to explore 300 groups!

Now that I think about it, when I went to college, I was like a kid in a candy store and wanted to do everything, from swimming, to taking yoga and modern dance classes, art and drama classes, and several other extra-curricular activities. This now explains why I did so poorly in my first-year classes!

There are forces at work behind the college admission and financial aid processes that are not transparent. There's always a gamble involved when students reach for the "popular," "highly ranked" and "hot" colleges that typically select students with high credentials.

Stick with colleges where you rank at least above the middle of the applicant pool. Selectivity has nothing to do with whether a college can meet your academic, social and emotional needs, in addition to the financial needs of the family. IECs help students and parents grow through the personal development embedded in the college search. For these and other reasons, IECs are invaluable in helping students find the right fit, that special place the family didn't notice, where this student will grow, where the expenses will be doable for the parents for all four years.

In future chapters I will discuss how costs add up, how to look into the forms the colleges use, and how to minimize costs. For now, I'll assume that the student has a realistic college list. Just as students need to have a realistic college list, parents need to examine their finances realistically.

You can control the college costs by becoming savvy shoppers. The goal is to gain a college education that fits our student and doesn't send parents into the poor house!

Parents are more than willing to pay for their children's college education, but some colleges are simply too expensive, and families need to decide whether the costs and value are worthwhile for both the student and parents.

It starts with knowing what you can afford, and this starts with looking at your family budget. I provide the budget sheet below and you can download the active excel sheet from my website. If you have a better family budget sheet feel free to use it. I'm providing this one for you to tally your monthly costs as compared to your income. If you file for financial aid and use the budget sheet to ask for more aid, don't include lots of discretionary items like vacations and donations. The budget sheet is more appropriate for parents, although some students have money of their own that most certainly will be counted by colleges.

Your Affordable Family Contribution (AFC) will likely be different from what colleges expect you to pay. Just so you know. colleges expect families to pay a percentage from 22% to 47% from current income after the necessary deductions are subtracted. Surely you must save some money to pay federal, state and local taxes.

The expected family contribution works out to be about $3,000 to $5,000 for each $10,000 in income. The federal formula also assesses a contribution of up to 5.64% from your current assets, not including the home you live in. You are expected to be willing to borrow as much as you need to pay the balance of costs.

What should families consider? Their budget! It's how you can take control of your college costs. After expenses, what do you have left to contribute to college costs each month? What can you pay from savings? What amount can you borrow and pay back with interest and fees?

The same questions apply to the student. What can the student contribute from work earnings? From savings? From borrowing?

Students can create their own budget on the StudentAid.gov web site.

The amount of loans a dependent undergraduate student can borrow is limited each year: $5,500 in first year, $6,500 in second year, and $7,500 in each of the third and fourth years. Students can "spend" these loans at any college of their choosing.

Community colleges offer the least expensive way to get a good education for the first two years. Although they are often overlooked, they provide practical training for immediate job entry at a minimal cost.

From nursing to engineering to computer science, many community technical colleges offer programs that are selective and challenging. Studies show that students who complete an Associate's degree are successful in the last two years of a Bachelor's degree program. It's also possible to enter directly into a graduate degree bypassing the Bachelor's degree, as my nursing student did.

Some uninformed families, perhaps in low or middle-income, end up borrowing excessively for their children to earn that first degree. It's easy and painless to receive the Federal Parent PLUS loan. It's a seamless process for both parents, students, and colleges. Borrowing is a decision parents need to make carefully. The best advice is "borrow only what you absolutely need and can afford to repay" and not a penny more.

Parents can compute college affordability independently, in the privacy of their home. The federal computations assess families' ability to pay by taking a percentage from the available current income after the mandatory expenses are subtracted and assets, and also consider ability to sustain future debt.

In the FAFSA and CSS Profile chapters, I explain the percentage of income and assets that the federal and institutional formulas consider available funding for college. You can use those percentages to assess your contribution under the federal and institutional methodologies and your own Affordable Family Contribution Methodology. For example, if the institutional formula will require a minimal contribution of 3% to 5% of your home equity or business equity, how much does that increase your contribution? Is it within the amount you calculated for yourself? It's useful to have a handle on what you can contribute because then you will have a strategy and starting point of your own.

You may have other priorities to take care of besides breathing, working, and living for the sole purpose of paying for college. Surely families should be able to allocate their resources in a way that serves their financial well-being. There are many colleges out there that will be more than happy to take your student for less money and still provide a great education.

In my experience, parents are more than willing to do anything to make their children successful. They often overspend on a degree that will not yield returns. I like to refer them to the College Scorecard, a federal website where they can check the salaries after graduation from each college in specific fields of study.

The Affordable Family Contribution is not a way to skirt any parental obligation to contribute. It's an amount that families who want to make sure they can keep their student in college for all four years need to consider. Colleges give financial aid offers for one year at a time, because they balance their budget one year at a time. If a family can pay for one year but not for the remaining three, the student will likely suffer. Low- and middle-income families are most at risk if they have to borrow large Parent PLUS loans starting in the first year of college. It's different if they need a Parent PLUS loan in the fourth year as a bridge to enable their student to finish with a degree

Your Affordable Family Contribution (AFC)

CALCULATE YOUR AFFORDABLE FAMILY CONTRIBUTION (AFC)!

Your financial contribution is the amount that you and your family alone can establish. You can control college costs by setting your AFC. Would this amount be sufficient to cover a year or two at the local public colleges? Is this amount you've calculated reasonable, doable, and viable for your family? If colleges expect more, then you have the right to shop around until you find the college that fits your student and is affordable.

When you decide to buy a car, you know how much you want to spend. You have a budget in mind. Letting students apply to any college they want is like letting them walk onto a dealership and buy any car they want. Kids and colleges end up telling parents how to spend their money!

College expenses can derail families that buy more college than they can afford. This causes the parents' retirement to not get funded or uses it to pay for college.

When you buy a house, you get pre-qualified for a mortgage and can't buy more house than you can afford. But, colleges can certify parents for federal and private loans. Parents just need to put their signature on the promissory note and click "enter." It's never been easier to become a debtor.

Regardless of whether the U.S. Department of Education changes the name from "Expected Family Contribution" to "Student Aid Index," the crux of the matter remains the same. Don't let other people tell you how to spend your money!

It's up to the parents to decide how much they'll spend for each child for two, four or more years. Under the current financial aid formulas, parents may end up spending the most on the first child.

The Affordable Family Contribution enables families to decide if they need to set aside more resources for a younger sibling who may have special needs. If they know what they can pay, they can explain it to financial aid administrators.

Families are more than willing to pay for college. Parents will do anything to help their children become successful and enjoy a good future. It's an emotional process that pulls at parents' heart strings.

Parents have bought into the benefits of a college education lock, stock and barrel, and take on federal loans and even private loans, when they exhaust the federal options. Often they haven't even read the college course catalog.

Most sane people won't sign a contract without knowing the net cost after all discounts. Yet, this is what students do when they send a commitment deposit to a college before they receive an offer of financial aid.

Typically, students apply to college at the start of their senior year in high school and receive offers in the new year.

The most selective universities typically send offers of admissions by April 1, followed by financial aid award letters soon afterward. Then, students have 30 days to reply with a yes or no.

(The National Candidates Reply Day of May 1 is no longer enforced, due to a settlement between the National Association for College Admissions Counseling (NACAC) and the U.S. Department of Justice, but many colleges may still expect students to respond to the offer of admission by May 1.)

Colleges are experts at telling families how to pay for college, and since they are authorized to release federal parent loans, they provide a quick solution to parents who can't pay cash.

You notice I harp on the plight of parents. I do so because college costs come at a time when parents are closer to retirement. Undergraduate students have their whole life ahead of them to pay the limited amount of loans for undergraduate students.

I've often seen students persuade their parents to pay for colleges that are too expensive, even when students barely scraped in. Parents feel proud and happy that their kid made it into a "well-known" school but may not stop to consider that students might pay much less at a school where they rank at the top of the applicant pool.

There's a common phenomenon out there where students who got into perfectly suitable colleges continue to apply to more selective schools. If by chance they got in, they'd rank at the bottom of the applicant pool and would end up paying the full sticker price.

Independent Educational Consultants are well aware that there's no wisdom in placing reach schools on a students' college list. The momentary happiness of getting into a "reach" school quickly turns into a fight to keep up academically and financially.

Families hear from admissions representatives that you never know if you don't apply, and, no matter the costs, there's financial aid. But, financial aid consists mainly of loans! Families don't discover the net cost of these colleges until the spring of the senior year and must commit to a college by May 1. By then, there's little time to evaluate the awards, return on investment, and apply to different colleges. There are only a few days to decide on a purchase that over four years could amount to a quarter of a million dollars!

Imagine having to close on a home purchase just a few days after your offer is accepted, with no home inspection or other contingencies. Paying for college can be just as expensive as buying a home.

Assess Your Finances. Just as undergraduate students need to assess their academic strengths to choose the right college, parents need to evaluate their financial stability. Before awarding any federal or institutional aid, colleges obtain your financial information and tax returns from the IRS. Colleges are experts at researching where you might have additional sources of funds that you may not have thought of. For example, by looking at your dividends and capital gains, they can impute your non-retirement investments' value. They can gauge your ability to sustain debt. They do this day in and out. It's their job. Parents on the other hand don't know how the rules work because they may go through this process only a few times in their lives. I still hear from parents who ask if they will pay less if they enroll in college themselves. The answer is still no. In fact, even with multiple children in college at the same time there'll be no reduction of the expected family contribution, starting July 1, 2023. Financial aid rules can change on a dime.

The name Expected Family Contribution (EFC) is supposed to change to "Student Aid Index" or SAI on July 1, 2023. The reason for the name change is that families expect to pay their contribution and not much more than that. Colleges charge much more than the Expected Family Contribution because they don't meet 100% of demonstrated need. By changing the name families will be more confused about what's fair of them to pay. It will be harder to detect the gap, the amount between what the family is reasonably supposed to provide and what the college charges. Hence, it's even more important that families keep a monthly budget updated and calculate on their own an amount they can feasibly pay.

The family budget: Some of the families I work with don't have a budget. They have an idea of monthly expenses and income, though not on paper. Some don't like to do a budget. In fact, they hate it. They may never have done one. I empathize with these people because I too, am not particularly interested in accounting. For this reason, I have created this simple budget sheet on the next page. It just calls for basic adding and subtracting. I encourage you to fill it out each month, or, complete any budget form that works for you. The Budget is the most critical piece of homework you must do before your children go to college. Then you will be able to decide what is affordable for you. I call such an amount "Your Affordable Family Contribution" or AFC.

Family Budget Worksheet

Your family budget is a working document that shows exactly where your monthly income goes. It's the first step toward defining your Affordable Family Contribution, AFC. This simple family budget provides documentation to explain yourself and advocate for your student. If you meet with a Financial Aid Administrator for a short conversation, or if you plan to file an appeal, your family budget will support your statements. Keep receipts and bank statements in case you have to provide proof of expenses.

	Expenses	**Monthly**
Home	Rent/Mortgage	$0.00
	Internet/Cable/Phone	$0.00
	Home Repairs/Maintenance	$0.00
	Groceries	$0.00
	Laundry/Dry Cleaning	$0.00
	Total	**$0.00**
Bills	Loans (Student, Home Equity, Etc.)	$0.00
	Credit Cards	$0.00
	Car Payments	$0.00
	Insurance (Auto, Home, Life)	$0.00
	Total	**$0.00**
Transportation	Public Transportation/Taxis	$0.00
	Gas	$0.00
	Parking/Tolls	$0.00
	Car Repairs/Maintenance	$0.00
	Total	**$0.00**

Health	Prescriptions, Medical	$0.00
	Vision, Dental	$0.00
	Gym Membership	$0.00
	Total	**$0.00**
Personal	Gifts/Special Occasions	$0.00
	Travel	$0.00
	Dining Out	$0.00
	Entertainment	$0.00
	Clothing	$0.00
	Total	**$0.00**
Misc.	Child Support Paid	$0.00
	Alimony	$0.00
	Total	**$0.00**
	Total Monthly Expenses	**$0.00**
Hypothetical income example	**Income**	**Monthly**
	Salary (Annual)	$115,000.00
	Federal and State Income Tax, etc.	$7,800.00
	Net Income (Annual)	$107,200.00
	Child Support Received	$0.00
	Untaxed Social Security Benefits/401(k) Contributions	$0.00
	Pensions and Distributions	$0.00
	Other income (after taxes)	$0.00
	Monthly Income (Divide by 12)	**$8,933.00**
Summary	Total Monthly Income	$8,933.00
	Total Monthly Expenses	$0.00
	Monthly Available Funds	**$0.00**

After you subtract your expenses from your monthly income, how much are you able to pay each month for college? Set your rationale and parameters. Perhaps you could pay a bit more each month by cutting out other expenses. You must decide how much you can pay each year. Will you save an amount for nine months or twelve months? Then scroll down to calculate amounts you can pay from savings and borrowing.

You may also use a budget sheet from Mapping Your Future to help you figure out what you can pay monthly out of current income. Some families keep an updated budget on Quick Books or some such programs, in which case the above budget sheet will seem too simple.

However, I caution parents to stick to a simple budget that keeps discretionary expenses low. If you're applying for more financial aid, you don't have discretionary money for donations, charity and vacations.

If your children are not yet of college-age and you want to see how much you'd need to save for college, use the College Board savings calculator to know if you're on track.

Your AFC

Your Affordable Family Contribution (AFC) is an amount that you are able and willing to pay.

Start with your income from the budget exercise above, and then calculate how much you can pay from your savings. Then calculate how much you feel able to borrow each semester. It's up to you. Now you have some control over your expenditures. If you put aside an amount of income for 12 months, you may be able to borrow less.

The federal methodology (FAFSA) is heavily based on your current income: it assumes you can pay from 22% to 47% of your available income (your adjusted gross income minus allowances for taxes and basic living expenses), and considers up to 5.64% of your assets. These percentages are slightly different at schools that also require your CSS Profile form. For now, let's assume your student is applying to colleges that require the FAFSA only.

After you complete your budget sheet, and calculate what you'll contribute from current income, compute the amount you can contribute from savings and borrowing. What total amount is doable for you? Now you can shop for colleges that will approximate what you are able and willing to pay. This amount is what I call your *Affordable Family Contribution.*

YOUR AFFORDABLE FAMILY CONTRIBUTION	
Amount parents will pay from current income:	$
Amount parents will pay from savings:	$
Amount parents will pay from borrowing:	$
Amount student will pay from savings:	$

Amount student will pay from working:	$
Amount student will pay from fed loan:	$5,500
Total = AFC (Affordable Family Contribution)	$

Congratulations! You calculated your AFC, Affordable Family Contribution!

Regardless of what colleges ask you (the parents/students) to pay, you now know which amount is doable, fair and reasonable for you.

This very simple exercise gives families control over the current financial aid system. Regardless of whether the EFC changes name from Expected Family Contribution to Student Aid Index (SAI) the family needs to establish for themselves the price point they can afford. We do this with everything we buy, from houses to cars to groceries. There's a price limit beyond which we don't think it's worth it to pay more. Even families who can pay more want to make sure the investment is worth it.

The AFC reflects the same methodology that colleges have used for years to assess family's ability to pay. Colleges consider three major sources of funding:

1) the family's savings
2) the parents' current income and
3) parents' ability to absorb debt by taking out loans

When the colleges' net cost if much greater than the family's AFC, they are asking parents to take on more risk by borrowing more. The question students and parents need to ask is: How are we being assessed? How did the school arrive to such a contribution? Your AFC will show that you are more than willing to contribute your share of college costs. Your AFC will also help you avoid overspending on a college education. If a college expects you to pay more, consider other colleges that are more affordable.

It's not unusual for colleges to give more aid in the first year, called the "base year," to entice families, and less in the upper years. This is called front-loading. Students' borrowing limits increase in the upper years so they can pay more by taking out larger amounts of loans. One question to ask the colleges is which amount of grant aid or scholarship offered in the first year will continue to be available in years two, three, and four. Students can borrow $1,000 more each year from the federal government. Will college costs be more or less than $1,000?

If those college costs increase by more than $1,000 each year, parents end up borrowing more. What would be an amount beyond which parents wouldn't borrow?

Additional questions related to the family budget:

Is there any wiggle room for contributing more?

____

Does the student have a trust fund?

____

Are there relatives willing to help?

____

Is there a 529 plan? Who owns it?

____

A UTMA/UGMA account? In whose name?

____

What is the utmost amount you can contribute out of your current monthly income?

____

What is the utmost you can contribute from savings?

____

What amount of loans would be the most you could borrow?

____

Add all this up. What is the "the most" you would and could possibly pay?

____

If the amount at the bottom of the Family Budget is it, then enter the amount here

____

Will you remain steadfast and shop for colleges that meet your AFC amount?

____

Budget considerations: It's entirely possible and very easy in fact, to go over budget, and spend much more on college than you intended. Families pay much more than their EFC. It's why you need to examine your budget and establish your Affordable Family Contribution (AFC).

Otherwise, you may end up buying your seventeen-year-old the equivalent of a shiny new car. Never mind you told yourself you would not pay more than $20,000. The smell of a new car is inebriating and to you, at this very moment, it's beautiful, and your child deserves this. The entrapment is like when you buy real estate. In that case, however, the broker, mortgage company and other people will monitor the mortgage amount you pre-qualified. If you don't qualify for a mortgage, they will be the first to sell you a less expensive house.

There are many colleges, some with more beautiful campuses than others. Most students fall in love with the campus more than with the classes that are offered.

A professor once told me the groundskeepers have more to do with whether students enroll than the quality of the teaching! With so many colleges, with friends touting the merits of going to Colorado, or California, or New York, or Florida, the possibilities are endless. Everyone has an opinion about this college being better than another. It's easy to lose perspective in the noise. Be faithful to your goals, budget and values. Review the four variables that parents and their student identified as important. Parents have a budget in mind. They know how much they're able and willing to spend. This amount is your Affordable Family Contribution, the AFC.

Why do you need to know your Expected Family Contribution (EFC), also called Student Aid Index (SAI)? Once you've decided what is your Affordable Family Contribution, your AFC you have an amount that you can discuss with financial aid administrators if the award package they offer is hard for you to pay. In the next chapters, you will calculate your expected family contribution (EFC) under the Federal Methodology (FAFSA), and the Institutional Methodology (IM). You will know what is your EFC at FAFSA-only colleges and CSS Profile colleges.

To calculate your EFC before filing a FAFSA go to the College Board website and type "EFC calculator" to find their calculator. If the calculations seem complicated, you can bypass my next EFC chapters by going to the College Board website and use their EFC calculator. The questions you will answer here are the same as what you'll find on FAFSA and CSS Profile. You'll be able to estimate both your federal EFC and institutional EFC. For now, however, let's stick to figuring out your federal EFC, expressed in the FAFSA form. Click on Federal formula and choose the "Federal EFC". Here you can enter your information, in the privacy of your home. Remember, the more accurate the financial information you enter, the more accurate your EFC will be.

What does the EFC tell you? Your federal EFC is a minimum amount that colleges expect you to be able to contribute from your own resources. You may find this amount to be higher or lower than your Affordable Family Contribution. Typically, it's higher.

What does your AFC tell you? Your AFC is the amount you've calculated you can afford to pay and are willing to pay. It's made up of contributions from your current income, savings and borrowing.

Avoid Mistakes! When negotiating with FAAs, parents may make the mistake of asking colleges for help with paying their EFC. Be careful! This is an egregious mistake. This is like saying you are not willing to pay your share. The EFC is what you should have saved up and be able to cover by yourself. If you haven't, colleges will offer loans but not grants. They may assume you lived high off the hog, or indulged in consumer spending, or took too many vacations. They will offer you loans, the unsubsidized kind. Bottom line, calculate your Affordable Family Contribution based on a careful analysis of your income and assets. Regardless of whether colleges call your Expected Family Contribution "EFC" "or SAI," you will have records, budget sheets, and proof to substantiate your Affordable Family Contribution.

What is “demonstrated need?"

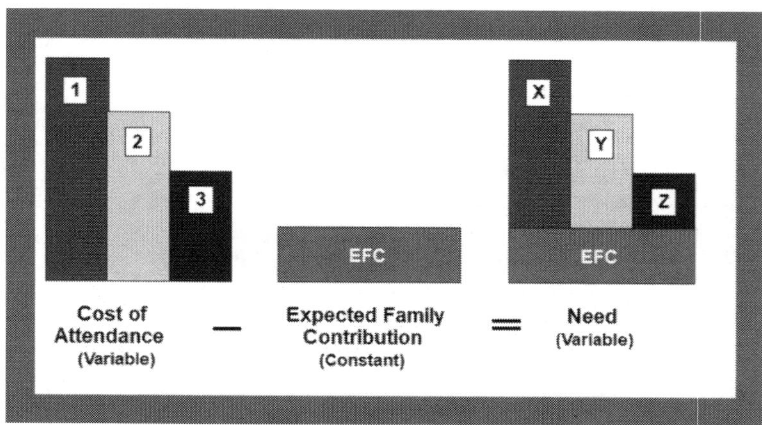

Demonstrated Financial Need = COA minus EFC (or SAI)

The higher the cost of colleges, the more likely are families to demonstrate financial need. For example, my student Jamie, who will be described in the chapter “Meet the Students", has a family EFC of $45,000. She has no financial need at her in-state institution that has a maximum cost of $30,000. However, if Jamie attended a higher cost college – she liked Wagner College on Staten Island, with a COA of $66.173 – she would have a demonstrated financial need of $21,173. Many colleges don’t fund this gap, yet this unfunded amount is the demonstrated need.

The parallel middle class of families and colleges.

Each family’s demonstrated financial need varies, just as each college’s ability to fund families’ demonstrated need varies. Just as there are “middle class” families that struggle to pay the college costs, so there are “middle-class” colleges that struggle to keep the lights on. This means that middle-class families often end up paying more than they can afford, and middle-class colleges lower their costs more than they can afford.

The parallel result is that families can end up borrowing excessively and jeopardizing their financial future. Colleges too risk going out of business if they discount so much that they can’t stay in business. It’s as if middle-class families and middle-class colleges need to join forces and look after each other!

The Coronavirus Pandemic

If the Coronavirus pandemic taught us anything, it's that more students began to appreciate the benefits of having the full college experience, the social exchange of ideas, feeling, values. Who would have thought that students would miss those conversations in the hallways, by the water fountain or in the residence hall?

College is more than going to class and taking notes. It's living with others in the same room, suite, or floor that helps students better understand themselves, their principles, and their place in the world.

The coronavirus meant that more students began enrolling at a college within commuting distance from home. Parents began to wonder if some colleges would go out of business. Local community colleges and public universities became more attractive.

Parents realized that although public institutions have suffered state funding cuts, they have more staying power than the smaller, liberal arts colleges with fewer than 2,500 students enrolled. Colleges with 900 to 1,500 students lack the critical mass to sustain a variety of majors and the funding needed to provide student services.

It will be a shame to lose the smaller colleges because they provide an ideal learning and developmental experience for many students. Public universities often have higher admission standards than small liberal arts colleges, that can pay more attention to the fewer students they have. In the chapter "Meet the Students" you'll notice that in Sonia's case, she was well-served at a smaller college than at the flagship university. Her perfect match turned out to be a private college, and the cost was about the same as that of her in-state public institution. Smaller private colleges can offer a nurturing space to students who might get lost at a big public institution or may have some learning style differences. Sonia's middle-class parents are making a substantial effort to pay for Sonia's college costs, but they feel it's well worth it.

Only a couple of dozen colleges meet 100% of the financial need of families, and they do so only after they've used their own formulas to make sure they didn't miss any funding the family could have provided on their own! The majority of colleges meet the demonstrated need with loans, mainly the Parent PLUS loan.

Middle-income and low-income families tend to be unaware of how financial aid works, and parents often end up borrowing more than they planned. Students whose parents have no income are exempted from reporting the value of their assets. These are students who qualify for "Automatic Zero Student Aid Index." If the parents earn less than $60,000 and don't file any schedules (Schedule A, B, D, E, F or H), or, if the net gain or loss from business on Schedule C is less than $10,000, they qualify for what used to be called "Automatic Zero EFC." Students will be able to obtain the maximum Pell Grant, which is slated to increase. If this comes to be, students could pay for public universities, like CUNYs, SUNYs, and others. Otherwise, the full Pell Grant still doesn't cover the cost of a four-year college, so the Parent PLUS loan remains the go-to source of funding.

Zero EFC students who have a "Zero Index" and are high-performing will still pay next to nothing at a college that meets 100% of need without loans. Public universities and community colleges will also be affordable.

Note that even when colleges say they meet 100% of demonstrated need, a dependent student is required to take out the full amount of federal undergraduate loans, which means they graduate with about $30,000 in debt after four years.

Unfortunately, there are so few colleges cover 100% of need, and these colleges have an admission rate of less than 10%, that it's next to impossible for a very low-income student to come up with the highest test-scores and grades needed to get in. These colleges are among the most selective.

These colleges that meet 100% of need do so only after examining the family's resources through a fine-toothed comb. You will see what I mean when you read Rebekah's experience. Very low-income students often end up at their local community college, which is a much better option than landing at a for-profit college, or a college that packages students entirely with loans.

If low-income students have average to above-average test-scores and grades, they often succeed at four-year, in-state, public institutions. African-American students are often recruited by HBCUs (Historically Black Colleges and Universities). These are much needed and excellent institutions, from Howard University to Morehouse, Spelman, Xavier U of Louisiana, Florida A & M, and many more. However, there are some smaller HBCUs that are costly, the education and training is questionable, and don't discount tuition sufficiently to make it affordable to attend without taking out large loans. Some are entirely tuition driven. I don't mean that they should fill 100% of need. I'd be happy if they covered 40% or 50% of need form their pockets.

Financially-strapped families can prepare to pay their portion plus a small gap, but I've seen some cases where the family paid the entire tuition. (Read Kevin's story.) So many families have saved a fair amount more than equivalent to their EFC but even then, parents must borrow more to cover the shortfall. The Parent PLUS Loan provides colleges with a means to get families to pay the funding gaps. These loans were never meant for low-income families when they originated in the seventies and eighties. They were meant for parents who may have investments in the stock market and didn't want to cash out or needed to adjust their cash flow.

I remember working in the student lending industry, when financial aid administrators weren't certifying the loans, and one company in particular would get the telephone number of parents and would call them. They would ask: "What's the maximum amount of loan do you need to pay for your son/daughter's college?" At that point, parents hadn't even received an award package, so they would quote the full cost of attendance. Then this loan company would say: "Ok, we will give you the full amount."

In those days, the loans were released to the parents, not the school. Some parents went out on a shopping spree or purchased recreational boats or vehicles. This type of lending came to a screeching halt when the amounts of loans had to be certified by the schools. Now Parent PLUS loan lending is entirely under the oversight of the U.S. Department of Education. Please note that colleges are not supposed to list the Parent PLUS Loan on an award letter, because it's not financial aid per se. It's no different than a commercial loan although the origination fee of 4% includes a type of life insurance provision whereby if the borrower dies, the loan is forgiven. This guarantee is absent from many private student loans. Families need to pay attention when a Parent PLUS loan is listed on an award letter in an amount to zero out the balance due. Sometimes parents catch on that it's a loan, but not always.

Mind the Gap (Unmet Need)

Mind the gap! Why is it important to know your Affordable Family Contribution? In case it's not yet clear, your assets are yours. Your income is your hard-earned funds, and you have every right to allocate what you think best to pay for college. You can spend them in whichever way you want, on whichever college you can afford, and is best for your child. By getting ready to make a fair contribution, planning to borrow specific amounts of loans beyond which you won't, by doing the best you can all four years, you will not be overextending yourself. Typically, parents spend every last cent on their first-born child and short-change the younger ones. If you know what you can spend, what you can borrow, you will know how to explain it to the colleges. If there's a disconnect, you will be able to ask the colleges how you're being assessed.

When you file the FAFSA and CSS Profile, the data points will calculate a Student Aid Index (SAI), formerly called an Expected Family Contribution (EFC), and, as we discussed earlier, families need to calculate their own **Affordable Family Contribution (AFC)**. You calculated your AFC from when you did your budget, assessed how much you can pay from current income, from savings, and from future borrowing.

The chart below shows that your family contribution is static. In other words, your EFC doesn't change regardless of where your student applies to college.

What changes is the cost of colleges. Assume that College #1 is a selective private college with a price tag of $80,000. College #2 is an out-of-state public university with a price tag of $50,000. College #3 is your in-state university with a price tag of $30,000.

You quickly notice that the amount of demonstrated need increases with the higher costs of attendance.

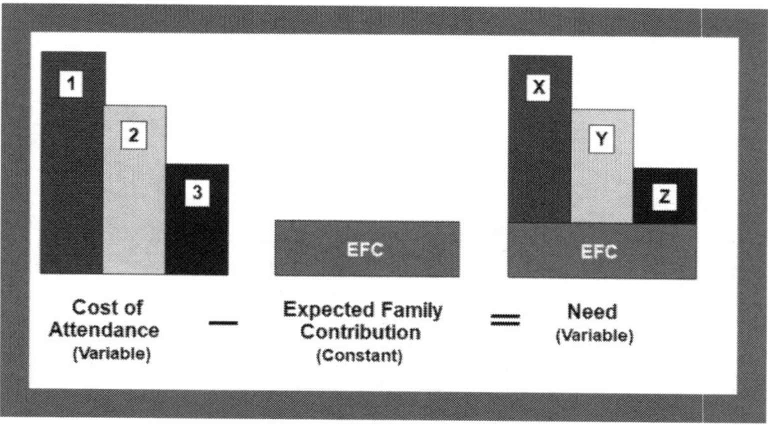

The amount on top of your EFC is the amount of demonstrated need at college X, Y and Z. You can see that the more costly the college, the greater the financial need. When this happens, students will be eligible for the Direct subsidized loan of $3,500 in first year, $4,500 in second year, and $5,500 in third and fourth year.) The additional $2,000 is always unsubsidized.)

If College Z fills 100% of your demonstrated need, your net cost will be only your EFC. If College Z meets only 40% of your demonstrated need, your net cost will be your EFC plus 60% of the demonstrated need the college doesn't meet. This unmet need is also called the "gap."

The "gap" is the area of negotiation that parents can engage in.

In the next chapter you will see the percentage of your income and assets the FAFSA formula and CSS Profile consider available funding for college. If your Affordable Family Contribution is similar to the EFC/SAI that the college calculates, you're on the same page. If not, recalculate the percentages of income the formulas consider in the FAFSA and CSS Profile.

You will be able to raise issues of affordability if you know your financial status, the percentages you're supposed to contribute from your own funds. You can ask the financial aid administrator how you are being assessed. You need to know your AFC to be able to calculate the size of the gap. The gap is the demonstrated need amount. This is the area where you can negotiate.

To recap: do calculate your AFC in an approximate way as the formulas do, so you can explain exactly how much you are able and willing to contribute from your resources. You'll know how to play your cards after you see what the colleges offer you in the award letter. You'll avoid the egregious, monumental mistake of asking colleges to help you with your AFC/EFC/SAI amount, which you should be willing to pay on your own! You may of course, ask to increase your Parent PLUS loan if you can't pay your EFC. Financial aid administrators qualify parents for loans every day. It's a seamless process.

Colleges will not pay your share of costs, like your EFC and gap. It won't ever happen, unless your student is a NCAA Division One recruited athlete, and the coach promises full funding for your student.

For example, if a college costs $60,000 and you have calculated that your AFC is $40,000, you need $20,000 from the college for it to be affordable. A financial aid administrator can certify you for the Federal Parent PLUS loan for that amount. But let's suppose that you don't have $40,000 to contribute, then the financial aid administrator can certify you for the expected family contribution of $40,000 as well.

Could you be denied for a Parent PLUS loan? Yes, if the parents have had a bankruptcy discharge, foreclosure, repossession, tax lien or already defaulted on student loans within the last five years.

To compare your college offers, you can use my excel worksheet which is available on my website (www.eduave.com). Another sheet is the federal "Shopping Sheet" (also called an Annotated College Financing Plan) designed by the U.S. Department of Education and the Consumer Financial Protection Bureau (CFPB) for colleges to use.

Unfortunately, the majority of colleges don't use the above Annotated College Financing Plan. But it's a good form for families gain a better perspective if they use it.

Note how clearly it presents a space to indicate your FAFSA EFC and the Institutional EFC. If colleges filled that line families would gain a much better understanding of their obligation. This would make so easy for families to calculate the gap and compare how different colleges assess them.

By using their own financial aid award forms, colleges don't have to enter the federal and institutional family contribution. It's why I emphasize their Student Aid Report or SAR. I printed one sample for "Sonia," one of the students I featured in the "Meet the Students" chapter.

I don't need to remind you to establish your Affordable Family Contribution based on your real data, such as your income, your expenses, your tax filing, your assets, ability to borrow and pay in the future, and more.

Regardless of whether the EFC is called SAI or some other acronym, your Affordable Family Contribution is the amount you can pay for college. It's like going to the grocery store with $100 and knowing that you can buy only $100 of groceries. The AFC is what you know you are able to contribute. It tells you how much college you can afford to buy. This base amount to contribute is under your control.

Another example of the gap: The college awarded your student a merit scholarship and the $5,500 Direct student loan. Let's say that the remaining balance is $54,500 and your EFC is $30,000. Your cost will be your EFC of $30,000 plus the gap of $24,500. The gap is the demonstrated need, the amount of funding you need to provide in addition to your EFC. If the gap is small, the size of a puddle, you'll be able to stretch and hop over that body of water. If the gap is the size of the Gulf of Mexico, you will need to navigate those waters in a raft, at least, you will need to be prepared, or you'll find yourself in rough waters. The gap is the area for negotiation. If your dealings with the financial aid administrator don't pan out, you and your student need to have other colleges in your pocket, and be willing to move away and look at those schools.

When the probability of employment is not a certainty in this new economy, especially if your student is going to major in the liberal arts and will need to go to graduate schools, your calculations need to be based on reality and not wishful thinking.

Your AFC will guide you to colleges where the net price is not much higher than your AFC. Cast a wide net at the start of the application process. Students need to apply to different colleges, from their in-state flagship to a regional in-state campus to a small liberal arts college that will discount tuition for the right student. You will find that the college fits you financially when the net price is within range of your AFC. In fact, in a perfect world, parents would pay just their AFC. But it isn't so. If you know by how much the college is gapping you, you can negotiate the amount. The gap is where appeals are filed and won. You will ask for what's reasonable to ask. It's why knowing your AFC backed by the evidence of your budget, pay stubs, mortgage payment all add up to facts that matter in the needs analysis.

To their credit, colleges try to meet your "demonstrated need" and minimize that gap to the best of their abilities. However, they are quick to say they are not obligated to meet all of your need. In fact, only a handful of colleges do, and that's after students have "self-helped" themselves to the full complement of the allowable loans. If you're unhappy with the amount of financial aid you received, you must have a plan before you talk with financial aid administrators. Otherwise, the solution will be easy for them, though not for you. They are more than willing to certify parents for Parent PLUS loans. It's their mantra: college is possible, but you have to take loans. Parents can get loans for up to the total cost of attendance minus any other aid given to the student.

Students from **wealthy families** with EFCs higher than the COA will need to seek out merit scholarships. They will find these at the colleges where they rank near the top or at least top quarter of the applicant pool.

Wealthy families find the best bargains at their in-state universities. The Honors programs rival those of elite universities. If their students have high grades and test scores, they may qualify for merit scholarships and state aid, making the cost of attendance extremely feasible. For example, South Carolina residents pay approximately $13,000 on average, at the public universities. The lottery-funded state aid can award from $5,000 to $7,500 each year to high-performing students regardless of whether they need financial aid or not. The price of in-state tuition is negligible for wealthy parents. The sad part is that poorer people buy lottery tickets and have lower grades and SAT/ACT scores. In fact, they are subsidizing the cost of public education for the wealthier.

The Covid-19 Effect. The pandemic has put a damper on students' trend of going far away for college. In-state flagship university and satellite campuses enjoyed record enrollment in 2020-21. It makes sense to shop for college in-state. What's the sense of paying for out-of-state tuition if their student is sitting at home and has to learn remotely? In addition, families breathed a sigh of relief on the assumption that online learning would be cheaper. But thus far, it's not. Colleges can rebate part of room and board if they have to send students home due to a virus outbreak. But, tuition and fees weren't refunded, to my knowledge. Online learning isn't all bad for some students. What they miss the most is the social contact with friends. Student development is curtailed when they can't be on campus, where they share a room, talk into the wee hours of the night, debate opinions, ideas and lessons learned in class.

SUMMARY: In this chapter, you learned how middle-income and low-income parents need to shop a variety of colleges and compare costs carefully. This is how they can gain better control over the current financial aid system. Wealthy families get discounts by shopping for merit scholarships. Families need to figure out what they can reasonably and feasibly pay. IECs and School Counselors can direct families to this process by either using these forms or giving this book to their clients. The family budget is especially valuable in figuring out what is left each month to pay for college. If parents have more than one child, they can plan an amount to pay for each child. If the college proposes a higher amount, families can raise issues of affordability by referring to their budget. They will be able to explain what they can pay from current income, savings, and borrowing. This will go a long way to ensuring that students will graduate and parents will control the amount of loan debt they take out.

QUIZ: Check Your Knowledge

How would you describe the EFC (which will be called the Student Aid Index (SAI) starting July 1, 2023)?

1) A minimum amount of money that both parents and student are expected to contribute from their resources. It's not the final amount families will pay.
2) The Expected Family Contribution/Student Aid Index is calculated when a student and one parent enter their financial information on FAFSA.
3) The EFC/SAI shows up on the SAR (Student Aid Report) after a family submits the FAFSA.
4) It's useful to know one's EFC/SAI to figure out how much more the college is charging.
5) All of the above.

What is the Affordable Family Contribution or "AFC?"

1) The AFC is a term the author coined to refer to an amount that families can afford to pay and are willing to pay. This amount is based on the family's budget, their savings, current income, and loans.
2) The AFC requires a careful examination of the family's resources.
3) It involves considering the family's budget, all resources, risk-tolerance for borrowing, in addition to considering the values that the family adheres to, along with the student's educational needs.
4) All of the above.

What makes up the Cost of Attendance or COA?

1) Direct and indirect costs.
2) Direct costs refer to tuition, room and board.
3) Examples of indirect costs are transportation, books and supplies.
4) All of the above.

Correct answers for above questions: All of the above.

How to Apply for Federal Student Aid

FAFSA stands for Free Application for Federal Student Aid. You must file the FAFSA each year to requalify for federal aid.

Changes are taking effect starting July 1, 2023 for academic year 2023-24. All changes to any Title IV federal funding for higher education must be approved by Congress. Many readers have heard of the Consolidated Appropriations Act, 2021, which is a 5,593-page bill approved on December 27, 2020. In it, there are 167 pages that "simplify" the FAFSA form, effective academic year 2023-24. It's arguable whether or not the changes actually simplify the form or clarify anything for families, though it does reduce the number of questions on the FAFSA.

The Expected Family Contribution, EFC, changes name to "Student Aid Index," or SAI. Apparently, families thought that the EFC was the net college cost but in fact, it's only an amount to qualify for federal aid eligibility.

I think an "Index" will make it a bit more nebulous for families to figure out their minimum federal contribution. It will be much harder for middle and upper-income families to qualify for any federal grant aid. It will be even more important for parents to establish their AFC, Affordable Family Contribution, if they want to take control of their college costs.

The changes show that the FAFSA will align more closely with the IRS Form 1040, which is programmed to download into FAFSA automatically via the DRT (Data Retrieval Tool). With fewer than 36 questions the FAFSA can be completed by kids on their iPhone in minutes. I'll add my comments as we go through each change.

The foundational computations behind the FAFSA form remained the same, such as the percentages for assessing parental and student income and assets.

There will be slight changes to the allowances, which are deductions that lower the expected family contribution, and certain changes in the amounts personal income allowance each year can be updated by U.S. Department of Education.

The major changes affect couples who are divorced or separated. Starting in 2023-24, the parent who must complete the FAFSA will be the one who provides more than half of the support for the student, not the parent with whom the student resides. Starting in academic year 2023-24, it no longer matters whether the student lives with one parent more than the other.

The amount of child-support received will no longer be considered untaxed income. Currently, it's added back into the parent's Adjusted Available Income (AAI) and typically raises the expected family contribution, thereby phasing the student out of Pell Grant range. Child support will be considered a parental asset, and assets are evaluated at the lower rate of 5.64%. The rationale for this change may be that by considering child support an asset, it will have less effect on increasing the family's federal EFC. Also, in many instances, child support and Social Security benefits end when a student graduates from high school or reaches the age of 18.

Allowances are deductions and these will be adjusted to the Consumer Price Index for All Urban Consumers (CPI-U).

State and local taxes will no longer be deductions on FAFSA, another indication that FAFSA is aligning with the IRS tax returns. (Families file separate forms to pay state and local taxes.) Most families take the standard deduction so the state tax is no longer deductible on FAFSA – and it makes the FAFSA calculations simpler. The allowance for state and local taxes was never all that accurate, anyway, and had a small impact on the EFC.

Asset Protection Allowance is a deduction that lowers the family contribution. However, these have steadily decreased over the years, and it will eventually disappear altogether.

It makes sense because assets are not reported on IRS Form 1040 except for contributions to retirement funds, which are never counted as funding for college. Also, any FAFSA grant aid is designed for very low- or no-income families who typically don't have assets.

The FAFSA fundamental formulas for contribution from assets of dependent and independent students will remain 20% Contribution from assets for parents will remain 5.64%.

The bit of good news is that the income protection allowance is increasing, probably because even the government can see that families can't subsist on the federal living allowances.

Considering the increase in food, housing. medical care and cost of living, the income protection allowance needed to be increased years ago. Allowances will be adjusted annual based on the Consumer Price Index (CPI-U).

Starting on July 1, 2023, the formula allows no EFC adjustment for families with multiple children in college at the same time. I feel sorry for those families who planned to have children close together, so the kids could grow up together, and now will pay more for college! Parents with twins and triplets will be affected the most in terms of cash flow issues and paying for college.

These changes also close the FAFSA loophole with respect to divorced/separated parents. As I mentioned, prior to July 1, 2023, the person with whom the student lives files the FAFSA. Often, this is the custodial parent who earns less. This has resulted in students obtaining more need-based aid than if the student lived with the parent with higher earnings who provided more financial support. This loophole will close on June 30, 2023. As of July 1, 2023, the parent who provides more financial support will be responsible for filing the FAFSA.

There will be some changes in the way the FAFSA will be designed. Feel free to check to updates on my website www.eduave.com for the Resource Library, which I will update if there are additional changes.

Cost of Attendance (COA) change: Another change that will take effect July 1, 2023 for academic year 2023-24 is that colleges will be required to list every single element of the Cost of Attendance, instead of listing room and board together, for example. The costs for board must be the equivalent to three meals a day.

Untaxed income: Child support and alimony received will no longer be considered untaxed income and added to the Adjusted Available Income thus raising the available funding for college.

Pell Grant: On December 27, 2020, the former President signed Consolidated Appropriations Act, 2021 which included a $150 increase to the maximum Pell Grant. The maximum Pell Grant award for the 2021-2022 award year is $6,495. The corresponding maximum expected family contribution (EFC) eligible for a Pell Grant is $5,846, which is 90% of the maximum Pell Grant. If the family's EFC is one dollar more than $5,846, there's no Pell grant.

A "Dear Colleague Letter" GEN 21-01 reports the Pell disbursement schedule and this: Section 401(b)(4) of the Higher Education Act of 1965, as amended (HEA), establishes the minimum Pell Grant award to be 10 percent of the maximum award amount for the award year. "Because we use mid-points in both the EFC columns and the cost of attendance (COA) rows in constructing the schedules, the actual 2021-2022 award year minimum scheduled award amount will be $650."

This is an improvement over previous years when students with EFCs nearing the $5,846 threshold received just a few hundred dollars. For low and zero-income students, the Pell Grant is slated to increase 35% in 2023-24 to a maximum of $8,768 regardless of how many students from the same family are in college at the same time. This will clearly benefit those students living on the poverty line. These students receive means-tested federal benefits, such as the free or reduced lunch program.

What will go away? The EFC reduction for parents with several kids in college at the same time. This will no longer provide a reduction of EFC, which is a shame for those families with twins or triplets, and those with children born close together that overlap in college by one or more years. However, the question about how many children in the family are enrolled in college will remain on the FAFSA. It may give financial aid administrators pause to consider the amount of aid to give out. I suspect some will go to bat for families with triplets, because they'd be paying for 12 years of college in four years!

Will there continue to be a subsidized Direct Loan for Undergraduate students? There were proposals in the House about stopping the interest subsidy on the subsidized Direct loan for undergraduate students and adding those funds to the Pell Grant program.

According to Mark Kantrowitz, "Cutting the subsidized interest benefit would yield about $2 billion a year, which could be used to fund increases in the maximum Pell Grant. President Biden has proposed doubling the Pell Grant. Republicans proposed cutting the subsidized interest benefit without increasing funding for other financial aid programs."

According to Mark Kantrowitz, "The Pell Grant program is overfunded because fewer eligible students have enrolled in college from 2018 to 2021. Also, the federal government biased it toward overfunding because in previous years it was underfunded, and they had to borrow funds from the next federal fiscal year to cover the underfunding. Academic years span two federal fiscal years: from July 1 to June 30, while federal fiscal years run from October 1 to September 30. The misalignment contributes to perennial underfunding until periodically, Congress increases funding to eliminate the accumulated deficit. Until Congress decides to make the Pell Grant program a true entitlement with 100% mandatory funding, as opposed to part mandatory and part discretionary funding, there will be a mismatch between the appropriated funds and the actual funding in the program."

If you're reading this book and going to college in 2021- 22 and 2022-23, the information and links provided are up to date. If you have any questions, feel free to email me at claire@eduave.com

Note that while IECs charge for their expertise in college guidance and advising, you won't have to pay for help with filing a FAFSA. IECs have never charged and continue to help without charging.

They will likely direct you to this federal website: FAFSA.gov. Don't accept any other solicitations for completing FAFSA. Make sure the URL has a .gov domain name, to be sure you're entering the U.S. government website when you file.

If you want to view the questions that will come at you on the FAFSA you can download a worksheet to get ready. Don't mail the worksheet though. Use it only to prepare to file the FAFSA online. I heard that H&R Block will complete FAFSA forms for free for low- and zero income families.

I recommend that parents let their students file the FAFSA form to make them aware that this is a financial transaction. By becoming aware of them, they will have skin in the game. First-year undergraduate students will be offered small loans that they're responsible for paying back. It's wise to let them know the amount they are borrowing and the responsibility they have to pay for part of their education.

The U.S. Department of Education has endeavored to make the FAFSA form easy for students themselves to complete. They produced an app that students can download onto their mobile phones, and students can complete the application. Students can download their parents' income tax returns by clicking on the DRT (Data Retrieval Tool). The income and tax information on the FAFSA will then be considered "verified" because the download comes straight from the IRS.

As the FAFSA form continues to align with the IRS tax forms, the number of questions will be reduced, as will the number of families that get audited.

Students who complete the FAFSA on their own, say on their phone app, still need parents' help to complete it. In case the DRT doesn't activate, you'll hear: "Mom, Dad, what's your income?" Oh, kids still need their parents, even if the U.S. Department of Education is trying hard to communicate with them directly.

There are other questions to complete, like mom and dad's Social Security Number, the name of the college parents attended, if any, or the date when parents got married, separated or divorced. The entire process of filing for aid can raise difficult conversations and emotional issues. The U.S. Department of Education may think that graduating high school students should be adults, but they still need mom and dad, and parental support of many kinds.

To register for access to FAFSA online, one parent and the student each need a Federal Student Aid ID, referred to as FSA ID.

These FAFSA moments can bring a dose of reality to the financial application process when parents can explain to their kids that by signing a promissory note, they promise to pay the loans in full. Although parents help out to the best of their ability, this is an investment students are making in their education. The results will yield good returns if the student takes responsibility for this investment in themselves.

FAFSA help, 24-7: What if you get stuck when you file the FAFSA? Each question has a check-mark. Click on it and an explanation pops out. If you get stuck after reading the directions, there is help on completing the FAFSA online at studentaid.gov/help-center/contact. You can also chat with a representative online, or call the FAFSA hotline by phone at 1-800-433-3243 (1-800-4-FED-AID). This is an important number to keep handy because you can speak with a real person, in real-time, who can clarify all steps from A to Z. Trouble obtaining your FSA ID? Trouble with the Data Retrieval Tool? The FAFSA support people are seriously there for you. They're open from 8 am to midnight eastern time on weekdays, 8 am to 5 pm on Saturday and noon to 6 pm on Sundays, except federal holidays, the day after Thanksgiving and December 24. The representatives will guide you step-by-step.

FAFSA's path: Where does FAFSA get processed once it's submitted? What path does it travel?

When you click on "submit," the FAFSA goes to a Central Processing Service (CPS) at the U.S. Department of Education.

Once processed, the student receives a Student Aid Report (SAR) via email.

You can view a real example of a Student Aid Report (SAR) on my website www.eduave.com.

Students should check the email they listed on their FAFSA for correspondence from the government.

The email from the U.S. Department of Education ends with a .gov domain.

Colleges receive a report similar to the Student Aid Report or SAR. It's a form called the Institutional Student Information Record (ISIR). It includes everything on the SAR except for the list of colleges receiving the student's information.

Your eligibility for federal aid depends on what's on the SAR.

Financial aid administrators examine the ISIR.

Hence it's important for students and parents to review their SAR to make sure the entries are correct.

If any mistakes were made, the SAR will say on the first page if it was flagged for verification.

To recap the FAFSA application steps:

- The student and one parent (either one if married) register for an FSA ID each. This is an electronic signature that allows both student and parent to sign and submit the FAFSA form.
- Student takes charge in completing FAFSA at https://studentaid.gov/h/apply-for-aid/fafsa
- Parent waits nearby with bated breath. Just kidding.
- The parent uses their FSA ID to provide personal data.

- If the Data Retrieval Tool doesn't download the prior-prior year Tax return on file, the parents will need to enter it manually.
- Then the student enters his/her financial information.
- Dependent Undergraduate students can earn up to $6970 in 2021-22 before any earnings will be counted in their EFC calculation.
- Earnings above the student's Income Protection Allowance of $6,970 are assessed at 50%.
- Once completed, student clicks on "Submit".

Student should print the last page, also known as the Confirmation Page. It has useful information, from the EFC to the list of schools that will receive the application. It also includes a record of the date the FAFSA was submitted.

The FAFSA travels to the U.S. Department of Education's Central Processing Service (CPS) where the computations spew out your info to your colleges on your list.

The CPS sends you a SAR (Student Aid Report) and the cycle is complete.

Now you will need to wait until each college sends you an award letter.

Compare your financial aid offers and focus on the net price of each college.

If the net price is very different between two similarly ranked colleges, you should call the financial aid administrator to ask why.

Some students are afraid that colleges can view where they applied. This is no longer so. Colleges can't view the other colleges who are receiving your application.

When you compare your award letters, you should notice that each college awards the same amount of Title IV, federal aid. Your federal aid eligibility and your parents' expected family contribution is a constant variable that doesn't change. The variables are the colleges costs. Grant aid from the government is based on the demonstrated financial need the family. Students can use their federal aid at any college they choose.

FAFSA FAQs

Financial aid has many abbreviations all of its own. By necessity, you need to familiarize yourself with the following definitions and concepts. If in the following chapters you forget what each acronym means, check the Glossary at the end of the book.

Students can apply as early as on October 1 of their senior year in high school. While colleges want to receive a FAFSA ASAP, and the U.S. Department of Education's Central Processing Service can process a FAFSA from October 1 of the student's senior year until June 30 of the following academic year. Families must adhere to the colleges' deadlines, but if something happens, they can submit to the federal government until June 30 and qualify for federal aid.

Federal aid consists of grants and loans. Grants are like gifts that you don't have to pay back. Loans are obligations that you will have to pay back with interest and fees. This federal aid is yours to spend at whichever college you choose. It's accepted by any college that admits you.

Who must file the FAFSA? The student and one parent. If parents are divorced, in 2021-22 and 2022-23, students enter the financial information of the parent with whom they live the most e.g., 51% of the time. If the amount of time is exactly equal, then student files with the social security number and financial information of the parent who provides more financial support. Starting in 2023-24, it's the parent who provides more financial support.

Divorced parents who remarry as of the date the FAFSA is filed must include the income and assets of both parties on the FAFSA. Those who fall in love again and plan to remarry the year prior to the student starting college may want to delay tying the knot, otherwise the income of the new spouse will be included in the EFC. However, if the student is not eligible for any federal need-based aid such as the Pell Grant or the subsidized Direct loan, it's a moot point. Go ahead! Tie the knot!

Is FAFSA complicated to file? According to the U.S. Department of Education, it should take approximately 25 minutes on average to complete it, but in my experience it takes longer. The U.S. Department of Education has a FAFSA Overview video you can watch before you go to the fafsa.gov website. Many families want to review the questions ahead of time and download the FAFSA worksheet, but it cannot be mailed or used officially. Have on hand: Social Security cards, driver's license, tax returns, bank records and asset information. Beware that the Social Security Number is the key identifier, and it's complicated to correct if it's entered incorrectly.

Can students pay for college by themselves? Not often. If students are independently wealthy or are going to a very low-cost school or certificate program, maybe yes. However, the majority of first-time undergraduate students are dependent on their parents, so the answer is no. First-year undergraduate students typically don't have enough funds to pay for a four-year public or private college on their own. Some students are in a court-ordered legal guardianship and can take out larger unsubsidized loans. Others may have a trust fund or inheritance. Few have worked and saved a substantial amount of money. All dependent students who file the FAFSA can borrow limited amounts of loans from the federal government. If they attend their in-state community college and live at home, such federal aid may be sufficient to cover tuition costs.

Who is Independent? Students can borrow more as independent students if they are 24 years of age or older, are married, have legal dependents other than a spouse, are in graduate or professional school, have served in the U.S. military, or are homeless or at risk of being homeless, or are orphans or wards of the court. These students can borrow larger amounts of unsubsidized federal loans. In effect, students who qualify for "independent" status borrow more loans and take on more debt.

Cost of Attendance (COA) as we've seen consists of direct and indirect costs. Direct costs are tuition, room and board, books, and supplies, fixed by the college, and billed to the parents. Indirect costs are transportation and personal expenses. (see the chapter on COA) The new Consolidated Appropriations Act, 2021, requires colleges to break down the indirect costs so that the consumer can better understand them.

EFC (Expected Family Contribution) is changing its name to Student Aid Index (SAI). Even though words change, the family contribution represents the amount that families should be able to contribute out of their resources. Federal aid is based on a review of the family's prior-prior year taxes and their current economic circumstances. The Coronavirus pandemic has affected many households' financial situation. In December of 2020 the Consolidated Appropriations Act, 2021, contained changes to the FAFSA that were approved by Congress. These changes will take place for the 2023-24 academic year. Overall, federal aid continues to provide more funding for families living around the poverty line.

Wealthy families with EFCs that are higher than the Cost of Attendance demonstrate no financial need. Therefore, all federal aid will consist of unsubsidized loans. For example, if a family's EFC is $90,000 and the college costs $80,000, the family doesn't qualify for any need-based federal aid. If the EFC is less than the COA the difference is the "financial need." For example, if the EFC is $50,000 and the private university costs $80,000, then the family demonstrates a financial need of $30,000. The student will be eligible to receive a Direct Loan for $5,500 in first year. Parents will be able to borrow the rest, which is up to the full cost of education minus the $5,500 or other aid already awarded. Most parents end up taking a federal Parent PLUS loan. The estimate of financial need can vary significantly among colleges due to COA (Cost of Attendance) and the institution's own policies for calculating eligibility. While federal aid, also called Title IV funding, is carefully regulated by the federal government, private colleges can set up their own criteria for calculating the Expected Family Contribution for their own financial aid funds. Some colleges create their own financial aid forms to collect any additional financial information they need. Others use the CSS Profile form.

Tuition-dependent colleges: Many colleges have no funding of their own and award only federal aid. These colleges are entirely dependent on tuition revenues. To appear generous, they may inflate the cost of attendance and then award scholarships to lower the tuition. At the other end of the spectrum, the elite and Ivy League universities have deep pockets and can fund any student of their choosing regardless of ability to pay.

First-generation college students who need financial aid are most likely to borrow excessively if they fixate on a "name" college. Students may be susceptible to recruitment practices and need to be aware of the colleges where they will pay less.

If families figure out their Affordable Family Contribution before their students apply, they can establish a baseline amount to pay each year that is affordable for them. They can compare their AFC with the results of Net Price Calculators to forecast their net costs. Net costs are the full cost of attendance minus the amount of grants and scholarships ("gift aid") you receive. It is not the price you pay after you accept loans. I don't consider loans "financial aid."

Wealthy families whose contributions are higher than the cost of attendance will need to look for merit scholarships. They may be able to size up the colleges' internal aid policies to better plan their cash flow.

Net Price Calculators "NPCs" are tools that can give you an approximate, personalized estimate of what it will cost to attend a particular college. It's the cost you may pay after scholarships and grant aid have been applied. If you know which colleges you're interested in, you can get a guesstimate of costs by using net-price calculators. By federal law, calculators must be available on each college's financial aid websites. You can enter your financial information into these Net Price Calculators. If you're unsure that the results are right, you can contact the college financial aid administrator and discuss the results. The better NPCs use the same information that you'd enter on FAFSA. The NPC is supposed to give you an idea of your EFC, your net cost to attend the college, and take you one step further by listing the federal aid you'd be eligible to receive.

The more NPC questions you can answer with accurate data, the more accurate will be your estimated costs. For example, if the NPC asks for the student's grade point average, number of AP and Honors classes, standardized test scores, and rank in class, it means it's programmed to determine your eligibility for merit scholarships at that college. The NPC will then subtract the estimated aid from the COA to determine an estimated net price.

Title IV funding consists of all federal student aid funds administered by the U.S. Department of Education. Title IV of the Higher Education Act (HEA) of 1965 (as amended) authorizes programs that provide financial assistance to students qualified to enter college. As long as students are enrolled and making progress, Title IV funding helps students pay for post-secondary education at accredited institutions. These include public, private non-profit, and proprietary for-profit institutions. Programs must lead to a degree or prepare a student for gainful employment in a recognized occupation.

If you demonstrate federal financial need, you may qualify for federal grants and subsidized loans. Even if you don't demonstrate need, the federal unsubsidized Direct loans for students and PLUS loans for parents are available regardless of demonstrated need. Students can borrow up to the aggregate limits. Parents can borrow up to the full Cost of Attendance (COA) minus any other aid awarded.

FAFSA myths: https://studentaid.gov/articles/breaking-down-fafsa-myths/

Glossary: As you read through this book, refer to the Glossary at the end for explanation of abbreviations and clarification of terms. Don't forget to check out what amount of aid may be available for high school graduates from your state of residence. The State Aid Sampler at the back of this book provides ways for you to contact your state office but be aware that since the Covid-19 pandemic, the aid eligibility may have changed.

College Scorecard: Best resource for parents, students, IECs who want to make decisions based on facts about the colleges that interest them. collegescorecard.ed.gov College Scorecard collects data elements from both the colleges directly and the National Student Loan Data System (NSLDS). Colleges are held to the highest standards when they report the role of Enrollment Management to the U.S. Department of Education (DoE). The DoE works to ensure the completeness and integrity of institutions' enrollment reporting data.

Definition of Terms

Dependency Status: Determining the student's dependency status is the first litmus test to establish aid eligibility. Is the student dependent or independent? Independent students can borrow larger amounts of unsubsidized loans. Typically, high school students entering college for the first time would like to believe they're on their way to independence. Not so fast. They are dependent on their parents, unless they can answer "Yes" to any one of the following questions.

1) They have completed a Bachelor's degree;
2) They have served in the military and were honorably discharged.
3) They are 24 years of age or older.
1) Are they married or are they supporting a dependent other than their spouse?
2) Are they legally emancipated minors?
3) Is the student an orphan, in foster care or ward of the court since turning age 13?
6) Is the student homeless or at risk of being homeless?

If all the answers are "No", the student is DEPENDENT. See additional details here: https://studentaid.gov/apply-for-aid/fafsa/filling-out/dependency#dependent-or-independent

You can see that Independent students are the neediest of young people. The Consolidated Appropriations Act, 2021, removed some of the need for homeless students to provide police reports and such legal documents. Also, they will not need letters from neighbors, guidance counselors, ministers or rabbi to prove that they cannot get parents to complete the FAFSA.

The FAFSA definition of family size aligns with the IRS that considers children and other relatives living in the household a dependent. Children must live with the parent for more than half the year and provide more than half the support.

In dire situations, the college's financial aid administrator can change the student status from "dependent" to "independent."

Independent Status: Independent students get larger unsubsidized federal loans. This isn't always the best thing for the student because it simply adds more debt to the amount that they have to repay. It's essential then that the independent student major in a field of study that will provide immediate employment upon graduation. The technical fields in computer science, engineering and nursing have the best outlook. Studies show that if students graduate with at least a certificate, or Associate's degree from a public community college, the costs will be minimal. A four-year degree will be achievable after their financial situation stabilizes.

Selective Service: Up until June 30, 2023, male students must register with Selective Service to receive federal student aid funding. Starting in academic year 2023-24 males will no longer have to register. It is possible that the U.S. Department of Education will implement this change sooner.

Student race and origin: FAFSA will have this new question starting July 1, 2023. We don't know what the U.S. Department of Education will do with this information, but I assume it's to help financial aid administrators in assessing which candidates are minorities and underserved students.

Data Retrieval Tool "DRT" and verification: Once students get to the parents' financial information questions, they are likely to call (or yell) for help. They don't know their "parents' Adjusted Gross Income" and may wonder whether or not to use the "DRT." For families that filed regular, straightforward taxes on IRS Form 1040, the DRT downloads the prior-prior year tax records directly from the IRS. The tax info is redacted, so students can't see how much their parents earned or paid in taxes. There are advantages to using the DRT: the parents' financial information is considered "verified" because it came straight from the IRS and the FAFSA will not be selected for verification.

If the DRT doesn't work: If for some reasons the download doesn't happen, it means you must enter your financial data manually and then send copies of your tax returns to each college. Reasons why the DRT won't download your prior-prior year taxes may be because you filed a Schedule 1, or Schedule A, B, C, or IRS Form 1040-X. You might also not be able to use the DRT if you filed your federal income tax returns too recently. Colleges will not award federal aid until they verify the original tax returns. They may require you to provide and IRS Tax Return Transcript by filing IRS Form 4506-T or using the online Get Transcript tool.

Taxes are from two years previous: Note that the tax information on your FAFSA is that of your prior-prior year. If you file in October of the student's senior year, let's say October 1, 2021 when the federal Central Processor goes online, the financial aid is based on tax returns of 2019. Hence the financial information is from approximately 18 months earlier. Colleges used to run into trouble requesting parents' previous year's tax returns in January because most families hadn't yet filed their taxes. Parents with relatively fixed income earn approximately the same amounts each year, and the "prior-prior" year tax returns are already on file with the IRS for most families. The Data Retrieval Tool downloads your taxes and populates the right FAFSA fields. It's super easy. Everyone is happy. Do a little dance. Unless. Unless the income from two years ago is different than your current income. If you won the lottery, let the college know you don't need aid anymore. Maybe you'll even donate part of your lottery winnings to help build a pool or new football field. Offer to build them a residence hall or new library. My neighbor donated enough money to build a bathroom in the stadium, and he was proud as a peacock that his name was on the door. All kidding aside, if the college awarded you any need-based grants, give them back with a "thank you, but no thank you" if your financial situation has improved.

On the other hand, if your financial circumstances took a turn for the worse, let the colleges know it. The **Covid-19 pandemic** resulted in parents losing their jobs, getting evicted, and dying from the coronavirus. It's written in the federal methodology that families' financial ability to pay must be evaluated as of the day they file the FAFSA. If your income took a nosedive on the day after you filed, do inform the colleges. Parents need to keep accurate records of unemployment benefits, costs incurred in finding a new job, and any financial information that substantiates their particular situation. There are no guarantees that a financial aid administrator will be able to increase the aid package, especially if the college doesn't have funds of its own to give out to needy families. Often, the increase in aid will result in more loans for parents, which are unsubsidized. Occasionally, if your situation is highly unusual, the financial aid administrator exercises "Professional Judgment" and can revise the FAFSA data points to change the index of need and provide additional aid. You may not be a lottery winner, but you will feel like one if a college funds your demonstrated need with their institutional grants.

U.S. Department of Education's Central Processing Service (CPS) is open from October 1 to June 30 of the following academic year. However, colleges want FAFSAs "as soon as possible," and it's good to adhere to their schedules. File as early as possible on or after October 1 of the student's senior year of high school. My experience is that the CPS tends to process slowly right on October 1 because too many people are on the server. Give it a couple of days. It's better to wait a few days and then file online at fafsa.gov. Remember that FAFSA is a free application: You should not have to pay anyone to file your FAFSA.

Ten is the number: Students can list up to ten colleges on FAFSA. If they want to apply to more than ten colleges, they wait until they're sure that at least one college received it – which means all ten received it – and then add more. When you receive the SAR, it means the colleges have received your ISIR. Why would a student apply to so many colleges? Maybe they want to throw everything up on the wall to see what sticks. Perhaps they want to go for broke. The truth is, they didn't compare their GPA, rank in class, and standardized scores to the colleges' admission requirements. Also, they didn't identify the values and variables that are important to them, and the impact of college. They need to go complete the "Value-Sort Exercise" posted earlier in this book and compare their personal values to the mission of each college. President George H.W. Bush said "Read my lips." I say "Read the Mission Statement of Each College!" "Read the catalog of classes, highlight the ones you like!" You need to study – yes, study – the colleges you've already applied to. You don't need to apply to ten colleges if you identify what's important to you. And, if you're reading this book, I assume that affordability may be one of those values and variables.

Students need to consider that it's not where they start college that matters. It's what they do when they get there. It's whether students graduate in four years instead of six, which is the national average. And now I'll get off my pulpit, but not before I've said what I said: it's tough to handle ten applications. The mantra of "four-to-eight" colleges is there for a reason. It's hard to juggle a few balls in the air, leave alone ten or twenty! Cut down the college list!

Verification: If your FAFSA is selected for verification, your SAR (Student Aid Report) will say so on the first page. Students and parents will be required to show the college more than the prior-prior year income tax returns. If you don't have them or can't find them, you can go online to www.irs.gov and, under the Tools heading, click "Get a tax transcript." Click "Get Transcript ONLINE." Make sure to request the "IRS Tax Return Transcript" and not the "IRS Tax Account Transcript". If you are a graduate student, and therefore, independent, submit your tax returns your and spouse's (if applicable).

If you're verified, the college will likely require the household information from July 1 of the previous year to June 30 of the current year. Keep your budget sheet updated.

A common issue with verification is that students or parents have untaxed income that is not reported on your tax return. These amounts increase your index of contribution. Effective academic year 2023-24, college Financial Aid Administrators will no longer ask for your untaxed sources of revenue. It was part of the Consolidated Appropriations Act, 2021. Therefore, untaxed income such as military BAS/Clergy allowances, disability/retirement (non-SSI) benefits, worker's compensation, Social security income of SSI disability, alimony and child support received will no longer be considered in the EFC. Good news for grandparent-owned 529 plans is that qualified distributions will no longer be assessed as income to the student.

Another change: if you are a graduate student or an undergraduate student who qualified for independent status, colleges will not require your parents' financial information.

Who is the Parent?

Who is the parent on FAFSA? When the student lives with both biological or adoptive parents either one can file the FAFSA. The first step to take is for one parent and the student to get one FSA ID each, and make note of it because it's attached to your Social Security Number. The FSA ID will allow the student and parent to sign and file the FAFSA electronically, for as long as the student is in college.

Divorced or separated? Who is the parent who should file the FAFSA when parents are divorced or separated? The law was confusing and it's about to change yet again. Up until June 30, 2023, the parent who files FAFSA is the one with whom the student lives the most. Even 51% of the time is sufficient to define which parent should file. If it's an exact and equal 50/50 amount, then it's the parent who provides more financial support. In the 2023-24 academic year, the Consolidated Appropriations Act, 2021, changed this definition and the parent who will file the FAFSA will be the one who provides more financial support. This could be the non-custodial parent who also claims the student and takes the exemption on tax returns.

Which tax year will be considered? Federal aid considers parents' prior-prior year income. It's a result of the FAFSA trying to align more closely with IRS forms. Hence, in July 2023, the parent who provided more support in 2021 will be the one to file. (The timing may change as the law is ambiguous with regard to the timing of the financial support of the parent who completes the FAFSA. Family size, however, is based on tax dependency status from the prior-prior year tax returns. Even with family size, however, changes subsequent to the prior-prior year and the treatment of multiple support agreements have yet to be determined.) This FAFSA change closes the loophole where the parent who earned less filed the FAFSA and demonstrated more need.

For example, I remember having lunch with a few Directors of Financial Aid at a Rhode Island Higher Education Meeting, and they were talking about this FAFSA loophole. One Financial Aid Director recounted this story: a very likable fellow was earning his work-study wages in his financial aid office. One day, this director of financial aid asked the student to cover the office a little longer until the staff returned from a break. The student replied that he couldn't, because he was meeting his dad. His dad? This was the first time this FAA heard of a dad. He peeked out the window only to see this student get in a late model Mercedes! In addition to Federal Work-Study this was a full Pell Grant recipient, a member of a program for first-generation, under-served students. He lived with his mother, and she had filed the FAFSA. The formulas had done their job correctly, but this Director nearly choked on a chicken bone when he was relating this story. I'm sure he will be glad that starting July 1, 2023, the parent who provides more financial support will be the parent on FAFSA! Some cases may still slip through, but the majority will end up paying their fair share. I bet that academic year 2023-24 can't come soon enough for FAAs who had such experiences.

Unmarried parents who live together under the same roof are considered the same as married parents.

Note that colleges that use the CSS Profile require both ex-spouses to provide their financial information. Financial Aid Administrators (FAAs) explain it this way: "You can divorce your spouse but not your children."

The mysterious case of disappearing federal free aid: I remember this dad who called me after his ex-spouse received a second financial aid award that had less aid than the first one. I receive these calls quite often form divorced parents, especially on weekends, when college financial aid offices are closed. This dad questioned why his daughter's aid decreased from the first award to the second and wondered if his ex-wife filed incorrectly. His daughter lived with mom, so at the time, the mom was "the parent," the right person to complete the FAFSA.

The dad explained that in the first award letter his daughter qualified for a Pell grant that disappeared in the second update, after the school put the ex-wife's information through "verification." The college wanted to know whether mom received any child support. She had. Child support is untaxed income and gets added to the Adjusted Available Income (AAI). The mom's contribution was below the Pell Grant phase out but the child support brought her EFC to $7,950. The student no longer qualified for any Pell grant. "What's worse," the father lamented, "my daughter also lost a matching amount of need-based aid from the institution." The dad was unhappy about the resulting cost and asked if he should file the FAFSA himself. I told him "NO" in no uncertain terms. There cannot be two FAFSAs per child! Also, he was not the parent on FAFSA because his daughter lived with the mom. To appease him, I reviewed his financial information and ran it through an EFC calculator. It turned out that his EFC would have been twice as high as his ex-wife's, and had he filed, the net cost would be even higher. He became quickly persuaded to leave well enough alone.

Starting on July 1, 2023, this dad will be "the parent" on FAFSA, because his child support payments were greater than the support his ex-wife provided to the student. Parents filing for the 2023-24 FAFSA will be under these new rules.

Changes in the Financial Aid Formula

There are several upcoming changes in the federal financial aid formula that will go into effect on July 1, 2023 for the 2023-24 FAFSA.

Child support: The amount of child support received has always been counted as untaxed income on FAFSA. (In the case above it pushed the student out of Pell Grant eligibility.) Starting July 1, 2023, child support received will be counted as a parental asset, and assets are counted at the lower rate of 5.64% instead of untaxed income, which could be assessed anywhere from 22% to 47%. By treating child support as an asset, it will have less of an effect on the federal aid eligibility of the receiving party.

Gifts to the student: For a student this can mean that if grandma or grandpa want to give their grandchildren $1,000 in cash for Christmas or toward college payments, the student will no longer have to report it as untaxed income. In the past, a qualified distribution from a grandparent-owned 529 plan was considered untaxed income to the student. In the future, it will be ignored.

Automatic Zero EFC/SAI will change to allow a negative amount up to <minus>$1,500. The new eligibility for the Pell Grant will also be based on a multiple of the poverty line. A student can still qualify for the simplified needs analysis and some Pell Grant funding if the family income is less than $60,000, and if the parents didn't file any schedules (Schedule A, B, D, E, F or H), or, if the net gain or loss from business on Schedule C is less than $10,000

Who else can be the parent on FAFSA? The term "parent" is not restricted to a student's biological parents. Adoptive parents and parents who are listed on the student's birth certificate are "the parents." A stepparent married to the student's biological parent is considered a parent for as long as he or she is married to the biological parent. If a parent is deceased (but not both), the student reports the living parent's information. If both parents were dead, then the student would qualify for independent status and no parental information would be considered.

Who is not "the parent" on FAFSA? Legal guardians, grandparents, aunts, uncles, siblings, other relatives and friends of the family with whom the student lives, are not the parent responsible for filing the FAFSA unless they have legally adopted the student. The FAFSA looks only for the biological or adoptive parents.

Multiple children in college at the same time? The discount for having more than one child in college at the same time ends June 30, 2023. On July 1, 2023, the expected family contribution for each will be the same.

Until June 30, 2023, the federal methodology allows a 50% reduction of the EFC if two siblings are in college at the same time and a 67% reduction if three siblings are in college at the same time. The parent contribution portion of the EFC is divided by the number of children enrolled at least half time in college at the same time. Parents often try to have children close together so they can grow and play together. It's quite common to have siblings overlapping in college for one or two years. More than half of families with two or more children have at least one year of overlap among their children. This reduces the expected family contribution during those overlapping years.

This discount is significant for families with twins, triplets and quadruplets. Apparently, they are more common nowadays when women have children later and with the help of modern medicine end up with multiple births. I cannot fathom why the change. Maybe, when the government approved this reduction in 1986, twin births were less common and even well-to-do families were experiencing cash flow difficulties. It seems plausible to me since the growth of federal student loans was initially due to families needing a "bridge loan" so they didn't have to cash out of their investments. No one could have predicted that Pell-eligible students would pay for college via student loans.

Effective July 1, 2023, families with more than one child in college at the same time will not receive this reduction of EFC.

Name change from EFC to SAI. Just as families got used to the concept of the Expected Family Contribution, or "EFC", the government decides to change its name. The EFC is an amount of money families are expected to contribute from their own resources. The FAFSA formula takes a percentage of income and assets of the parent with whom the student lives. It calculates a sum that parents and students can reasonably contribute to their education. I argue in this book that families at all levels of income are finding it increasingly difficult to pay their EFC. It's why I recommend that each family document and establish their own AFC, "Affordable Family Contribution," based on what they are demonstrably able and willing to pay.

Gap: Families pay more than their federal EFC because most colleges don't meet the demonstrated financial need. The amount of unmet need is referred to as a "gap." The gap is the negotiating zone because it directly affects the net cost.

Student Aid Index: Staring July 1, 2023, the EFC name will change to Student Aid Index or SAI. I believe that for awarding federal aid, the government doesn't need to have a specific number like the EFC, which some parents erroneously believe will be their net price. The EFC determines eligibility for federal student aid but it's not what the college will charge the family. Colleges cost more than families' EFC. For awarding federal aid, the U.S. Department of Education just needs to know if the student will be Pell eligible. It's why the FAFSA has long been called: "The Pell Grant qualifier."

Affordable Family Contribution (AFC): I use this term to refer to an amount of resources that families can afford to pay for college. Regardless of whether the federal government calls the EFC by another name like SAI, families want to be able to manage their resources and want to decide for themselves what's they are able and willing to pay. Families may have several children with different needs. Parents tend to spend the greatest amounts of resources on their first child, but not always. For example, I worked with a family that had three children and the youngest one had special needs. Parents were trying to set aside more funds for that youngest child. It looked like they were hiding something when colleges wanted to see the amounts of savings in the other siblings' name, but in this case, these parents weren't agreeable to using that nest egg on their first child.

Parents have every right to decide what amounts they can set aside for college for each child. Colleges want to know if siblings have funds because parents must provide their own funds first, then accept the federal aid offered, and last of all, accept any amount of institutional funds. Often, institutional funds are tuition discounts in the form of merit scholarships that students earn if they have good grades. Parents can gain control of college costs by shopping for a college based on what they can afford to pay that still fits their child's academic and social needs.

In the case of the family I mentioned, the youngest child was on the spectrum and the parents knew that this child would need a special pre-college program in "pragmatics" and eventually, would need to attend a small college that provided support for these students.

AFC: Families can calculate their Affordable Family Contribution by examining their budget, their income-to-expenses ratio, savings, and ability to borrow. There's a question on some college forms that require parents to say what they can pay for college. Many parents aren't sure how to answer. Some wonder if they should say "zero" in order to get more aid, or, print an amount that would wish to pay for college.

Parents may review the initial chapters that explain the family budget, at the beginning of this book. It will help define the "Affordable Family Contribution" Some parents already know their budget, cash flow, investments, but in addition, I recommend utilizing the Net Price Calculator of each college. The National Center for Education Statistics (NCES) also publishes the College Scorecard and College Navigator websites, which can show what would be the average cost for families in their income bracket.

Parents need to establish their specific amounts they can pay for college, without risking losing their home or other possessions. At the very minimum, parents who need affordable colleges should not send their children to colleges that gap them. If the cost of attendance is twice the family's Affordable Contribution (AFC) then it's time to cast a wider net and apply to different colleges.

Elite universities such as Yale, Brown, Harvard, Princeton, MIT, Stanford, Cal Tech and the other usual suspects all meet the demonstrated need of students. The problem is that these colleges typically accept less than 10% of their applicants.

Students who want to go to college without breaking their parents' budget should consider applying to lower-ranked schools. According to author Jeff Selingo, there are "seller" and "buyer" colleges. The sellers get more than a third of all applications though they can offer admission to fewer than 20% of students.

The "seller colleges" are still very good institutions that have to discount tuition to attract students. If students like the smaller setting of a private college, to pay less they need to target those "seller" colleges where students rank at the top of the applicant pool.

This means that students must **not get blinded by "name" colleges**. I know it's hard for a 17-year-old to understand the meaning of the world, the amount of time it takes to earn tens of thousands of dollars, and the return on investment.

To infuse some reality into the costs of college and the salaries associated with specific degrees, I refer my students and parents the College Scorecard from the National Center for Education Statistics (NCES). This website shows the salaries that graduates earn in specific fields. Graduates in computer science will earn good salaries whether they graduate from Podunk University or an Ivy League school.

Families who live paycheck to paycheck and "middle class" families that don't have discretionary funds are incredibly susceptible to borrowing excessively. These families end up with high debt burdens. Regardless of what colleges ask parents to pay, families need to know what they can afford, and this is why I start the book with a budget sheet so families can determine their AFC. The amount should be feasible and involve low risk. Affordable Family Contribution means making a measured, well-calculated purchase because what is affordable is "low risk."

Estimated Financial Assistance (EFA) consists of non-need-based federal aid. The Parent PLUS loan, the unsubsidized Direct Loan for undergraduate students, and the Grad PLUS loan are examples of unsubsidized loans. They are EFA funds because the borrowers will fully repay this funding with interest and fees.

References:

The Chronicle of Higher Education of 1/5/2021 further explains what the FAFSA simplification really means: Big Changes in the Federal Student-Aid System Are Coming. Here's Why They Matter. (Chronicle.com)

Kantrowitz, Mark: Pandemic Relief Simplifies FAFSA (Forbes.com).

Text of Consolidated Appropriations Act, 2021. The FAFSA changes appear in pages 5139-5307.

Federal EFC

The Federal Expected Family Contribution (EFC) is made up of four major financial elements: the parents' income and assets and the students' income and assets. These four elements are typically referred to as the "four-legged stool." The federal tables that explain how each element of a family's financial contribution is assessed is a publication updated each year and available on IFAP.ed.gov Look for the EFC formula guide in the section for "Worksheets, Schedules & Tables." There you'll find the EFC formula guide for various award years, such as the 2021-22 formula guide.

PRINCIPLES OF FEDERAL NEEDS ANALYSIS

**THE FAFSA FORM AND FORMULAS BEHIND IT:
THE FOUR-LEGGED STOOL**

The Federal Expected Family Contribution is often referred as the four-legged stool because it's the Sum of four Contributions:

1) Parents Contribution from income: **22% to 47%** of Adjusted Available Income (AAI)
2) Parents Contribution from assets: **5.64%**
3) Student Contribution from income: **50%** after a personal Income Protection Allowance (IPA) of $6,970 in 2021-22 for dependent students
4) Student Contribution from assets: **20%** (assets can be cash, savings, checking, trust-fund, net worth of investments)

Under the FAFSA families contribute 22% to 47% of their Adjusted Available Income (AAI.) This is a progressive rate, from Table 8 of the 2021-22 EFC Formula Guide:

- If the AAI is: - (minus) $3,409 to $17,400 then the formula takes 22% of AAI
- If the AAI is: $17,401 to $21,800 then the formula takes $3,828 + 25% of AAI over $17,400
- If the AAI is: $21,801 to $26,200 then the formula takes $4,928 + 29% of AAI over $21,800
- If the AAI is: $26,201 to $30,700 then the formula takes $6,204 + 34% of AAI over $26,200
- If the AAI is: $30,701 to $35,100 then the formula takes $7,734 + 40% of AAI over $30,700
- If the AAI is: $35,101 or more then the formula takes $9,494 + 47% of AAI over $35,100

The computations behind the FAFSA form happen automatically, and when the data is downloaded directly from the IRS website, the income and tax information on the FAFSA is "verified."

After students submit their FAFSA, the U.S. Department of Education sends a SAR, Student Aid Report. Students and parents must pay attention to the Student Aid Report, or SAR. This is a critical document to review, which unfortunately, many students don't know what to do with. The first page of the SAR lists the family's EFC. (In the future it will have the letters SAI for Student Aid Index.) Families need to know if they are gapped, and by how much. For example, if the cost to attend is $50,000 and your Affordable Family Contribution is $10,000, the difference, of $40,000 is the gap. A sample SAR is available on the IFAP web site.

Takeaways

What is Title IV funding?

Title IV funding consists of federal student financial aid, established by the Higher Education Act of 1965, as amended (HEA). The HEA is the primary authorizing legislation for post-secondary financial aid programs. Amendments must be approved by Congress. Examples of Title IV funding for undergraduate students include the subsidized and unsubsidized Federal Direct Stafford Loans, the Federal Pell Grant, the Federal Supplemental Educational Opportunity Grant (FSEOG), Federal Work-Study (FWS), and the Federal Direct Parent PLUS Loans. Graduate students can get the Federal Direct Grad PLUS Loan. There are no subsidized loans for graduate students.

What is the Expected Family Contribution (EFC) soon to be called the Student Aid Index (SAI)?

The EFC/SAI is an amount of funds that families should have saved and should be able to provide on their own. The eligibility for federal aid depends on the family's EFC/SAI. However, EFC/SAI is only a minimum that the family must pay. Most colleges don't cover 100% of demonstrated financial need, so many families will have to pay more than their EFC/SAI.

Who is responsible for paying for college?

Federal student assistance programs are built on the premise that funding a student's education is primarily the responsibility of the family. Eligibility for financial aid is based on ability to pay, not willingness to pay. To fairly and uniformly assess the families' need, Congress authorizes the Federal Methodology (FM) expressed in the FAFSA form. The formulas behind the form run a "needs analysis" to measure ability to pay for college. Each year, families must file the FAFSA. The "needs analysis" varies depending on each family's financial information. The formula is as follows:

Demonstrated Financial Need =
Cost of Attendance (COA) –
Expected Family Contribution/Student Aid Index (EFC/SAI)

Demonstrated Financial Need: Most colleges are not able to meet 100% of demonstrated financial need. They leave some students with a gap of unmet financial need. These colleges may award merit scholarships through the admissions office, to reward students who are high achieving. High grades and test scores help colleges provide a more competitive applicant pool and improve their rankings. While merit scholarships are a great way to reward students who performed well in high school, typically, these don't fill the full demonstrated financial need.

Gap: A gap occurs when the college doesn't fill the demonstrated need. The gap is the difference between financial need and financial aid. The family must then play their EFC/SAI plus the gap.

Net Price Calculators

Benjamin is a student who wants to attend a "Private" College, and his parents are wondering what it will cost. Let's assume that the total COA is $60,000. His family's EFC is $25,000, and his parents have saved this amount they are prepared to pay for the first year. Let's assume that when Benjamin gets his acceptance letter, it contains an offer of $15,000 worth $60,000 over four years. What is the real out of pocket cost for the first year?

Answer: The only "free" money is the merit scholarship of $15,000. The balance to pay is $45,000 each year. Parents have saved $25,000 and will need to pay an additional $20,000 for Benjamin to start college. The federal Direct loan for undergraduate students will allow Benjamin to borrow up to $5,500 in first year. Parents have good credit and can borrow the $20,000 from the Parent PLUS loan. Is this a good offer?

The rule of thumb or the accepted wisdom is that if the cost is more than $10,000 than you can pay, the cost is too high. In this case, Benjamin's college costs $20,000 more than his parents budgeted.

If they borrow similar amounts each year, Benjamin and his parents will be more than $100,000 in debt by the time Benjamin graduates.

Financial need is defined by this formula, based on the difference between college costs and the EFC or SAI:

Estimated Financial Need = COA minus EFC (or SAI)

Colleges make no promises they can cover the full need of families and, in fact, are not obligated to do so. If colleges are not obligated to cover families' financial need and keep raising their Cost of Attendance, then families should not feel obligated to enroll their child at such colleges. I realize that the student may not want to forego the college and parents may feel compelled to do everything possible to make sure Junior attends the college of his choice. If the student has special learning or social needs, parents may have to pay more. However, students are adaptable and after the initial disappointment recover quite well. The reality of the costs involved need to be discussed clearly.

Let's assume that Benjamin is thrilled with the $15,000 scholarship and insists of going to the college. There's nothing stopping Benjamin from negotiating directly with the financial aid administrator. Often, it's the only way students really get it. Let's say that the college decides to meet 10% of demonstrated need, which is $20,000 now because it was reduced by the scholarship. Now 10% of the $20,000 is $2,000. The formula would look like this:

(COA $60,000) minus (EFC $25,000 + Scholarship $15,000 + need-based grant $2,000) = Remaining need: $18,000

The remaining need is 90% of $20,000. The unfilled need is $18,000. This is the gap.

The Net Price to pay for this college is: (EFC) plus (GAP) = NET PRICE $43,000.

You can also calculate the net price by subtracting the grants and scholarships from the cost of attendance.

Net Price = COA ($60,000) – Scholarship ($15,000) – Need-Based Grant ($2,000) = $60,000 - $17,000 = $43,000.

CSS Profile

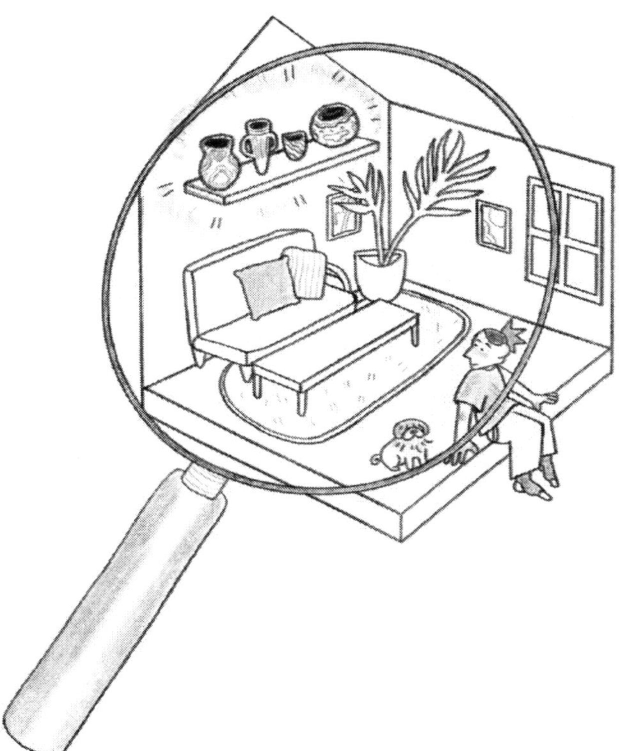

The CSS Profile: The Form and the Formulas Behind It

What is the CSS Profile? The CSS Profile is a form designed by the College Board to help colleges collect more financial information than the FAFSA does. Are you ready to be evaluated under a magnifying lens?

You'll recall that all colleges must receive a FAFSA in order to determine the type and amount of federal aid students are eligible to receive, based on the "Federal Methodology."

The CSS Profile form is supported by different formulas that make up the "Institutional Methodology." The formulas behind the form provide a more precise assessment of families' ability to contribute to their children's education, especially when families earn high incomes and own substantial assets.

You'll recall the FAFSA is a "student document." Not so for the CSS Profile. This is a "parent document." The parents are directly responsible for completing it. Students are involved to the extent that parents must use the same login as their child's College Board account. It's the account the student created to register for the SAT or AP tests. This links student and parents' identities.

In this chapter I'll be walking you through the forms you need to file in order to apply for non-federal, institutional financial aid. I'll discuss institutional grants, scholarships, and loans. Yes, there are some colleges that offer their own loans, so that parents don't have to apply for the Parent PLUS loan. There are also many private lenders that may offer better terms if you have a very high credit score.

Remember the budget you created in Chapter 2? Remember your affordable and workable family contribution? When you file the CSS Profile you're in unchartered territories. The colleges will know more about your potential sources of funding than you know for yourself. For example, a client of mine inherited a lot of land that was under water and unbuildable. She'd tried to sell it for years and never found a buyer even when she tried to give it away for pennies on the dollar. The taxes on it were more than they were willing to pay. She'd pretty much forgotten about this lot until she filed the CSS Profile form. Then it became something valuable. My client thought of it as a liability. The college saw it as an asset, so she had to spend time and money getting an appraisal to report the value correctly.

Your Affordable Family Contribution, AFC, is all the more critical when you're filing the CSS Profile, and much more if the costs are so high that you just can't afford them and need to file an appeal.

The AFC It's what you can reasonably afford, regardless of what the CSS Profile shows. It will take discipline to stay within your affordable, workable, realistic contribution. Use your budget sheet to raise issues of affordability.

A Profile school adds a level of complexity to applying for aid. The data points dig deeper into the family finances. The CSS Profile has more than double the number of questions on the FAFSA, and that's before the simplified FAFSA eliminates two-thirds of the questions starting on July 1, 2023. If the parents are separated or divorced, both will need to submit to the same scrutiny. If one of the parties refuses to submit the CSS Profile, or, submits it but then refuses to contribute, the uncooperative ex-spouse jeopardizes the enrollment for their student.

You may wonder why the student will miss out on any institutional aid. After all, it's not the student's fault if one of the parents or both are uncooperative. Well, it's not the college's responsibility's either. Financial aid administrators say that "you can divorce your spouse but not child."

There are a few dozen colleges that meet 100% of demonstrated need, and give only need-based aid, not merit scholarships. You can view them at MyinTuition.org.

They do so only after they've made sure the parents are contributing first, and the high-need student would raise the academic profile of the college. Ex-spouses with any funds who file the CSS Profile with no intention of contributing might as well not file at all.

Public universities that use the CSS Profile form are typically softer on their in-state residents. I'm thinking of the University of Michigan, which states on its financial aid page. "If you wish to be considered for U-M grants and merit scholarships that address need, complete the CSS Profile."

"The merit scholarships that address need" is a very confusing sentence for many families. A scholarship is usually an award for pure academic merit. What Michigan means here, the funds might be available if there's demonstrated financial need, and it's not for out-of-state students.

University of Virginia and UNC-Chapel Hill also award more merit aid for their in-state residents. They will try to fund the difference between the EFC and the COA (Cost of Attendance). They cannot make the same commitment unfortunately, for out-of-state students who will end up paying their EFC plus the gap. Remember, the gap is the unfilled amount between the COA and the EFC. Thus, if students are looking to attend an out-of-state university and need financial aid, they will get less funding.

Many students are lured by out-of-state public institutions, higher ranked in the U.S. News and World Report because they may be Research One Institutions. First-year college students are not yet scientists, and may learn more, get more teaching and support at a Research Two Institution.

One of my students already knew that his dad would not cooperate, and thought he could push his application through by himself. He problem is that few families can afford the costs of elite universities without their institutional financial aid.

The middle-of-the-road selective colleges award academic-merit scholarships before the college checks the financial situation of the family.

Parents who earn high income need those merit scholarships to bring down the price. If they apply to colleges that meet only demonstrated need and they have none, they will pay the full sticker price. However, this doesn't seem to deter them because they see high returns in having their kid graduate from the likes of Amherst, MIT or Stanford or Caltech.

You may want to file a financial aid appeal if two colleges rank in the same class of selectivity and that have similar admission requirements but have different net costs.

During the Covid-19 pandemic many financial aid administrators bent over backward to respond to families and come up with strategies for helping. Starting in 2023-24, the federal government will require that each and every financial aid appeal be evaluated.

Your take away from this chapter is that the elite, highly-endowed colleges that require the CSS Profile fill 100% of demonstrated need. If you don't file both the CSS Profile, you don't get the chance to obtain financial aid from the institution.

However, be prepared to have every financial resource combed through. In fact, some families didn't know that their collections and trinkets could be monetized and would be considered an asset!

By now the reader knows they have to file the FAFSA to get federal aid, and supplemental forms like the CSS Profile to get institutional aid. For those who want to dig deeper, the U.S. Department of Education explains how the federal expected family contribution is calculated in the EFC Formula Guide. The reader can add the equity in their home and business to the federal EFC to get an estimate of the Institutional EFC. They can also use the College Board's EFC Calculator for the Institutional EFC

Unfortunately, we don't know if the College Board will continue to update their EFC calculator. Mark Kantrowitz, the national financial aid guru, is planning to design an EFC calculator for the Student Aid Index, and I will post the link to my website www.eduave.com when it's ready.

If you're not able to pay for a first degree, you need to explore the least expensive educational options, and you know my now that your local community technical college will be a bargain.

According to a PayScale survey of 248,000 respondents in May 2019, 2/3 regretted their degree. Most respondents to PayScale's Salary Survey report having college regrets, particularly about their student loans. Older generations, those with higher education levels such as Masters and Ph.D.s in higher earning fields, had the lowest rates of college regret.

Graduate School debt is the largest part of the $1.64 trillion in 2021, a hot-button issue among politicians. The Biden-Harris administration is particularly worried and will incentivize parents and graduate students to pay off their loans.

FAFSA and CSS Profile Differences

This chapter takes a deep dive into the differences between the FAFSA and CSS Profile forms. You may skip it if your student isn't applying to a Profile school. However, you will find the differences fascinating in terms of how public education is focused on benefiting the public at large, whereas private education is more focused on benefiting the individual.

Both FAFSA and CSS Profile forms are supported by their own unique methodologies. The formulas behind the CSS Profile are tailor-made for private institutions to award aid based on their individual mission. While only elite private universities used the Profile, over last decade, several large public flagships, such as UNC-Chapel Hill, University of Virginia, and University of Michigan have started requiring the CSS Profile.

The institutional methodology is based on econometric models, such as the evaluation of horizontal and vertical equity. Horizontal equity means that families with similar financial strength will have a similar financial need and pay a similar amount. Vertical equity means that families in different financial situations will be evaluated in different ways appropriate to their situations. For example, families who rent may demonstrate more need than families who own their home. A family with a high income will be treated differently than one with moderate or low income. This is referred to as vertical equity.

It's not an understatement to say that the FAFSA figures out who is poor, and the CSS Profile figures out who is rich. The CSS Profile contains many more questions designed to collect more information about the parents' financial status. The rationale behind this methodology is explained in a seminal book by Dr. Sandy Baum, *Primer on Economics for Financial Aid Professionals.* According to Ms. Baum, an economist and policy analyst, colleges are not the only entities that sell the same product to different people for different prices. The airline, hotel and rental-car industries have done this all along. Colleges can better assess the many different and varied financial capabilities of individual families by using these precise econometric models than the formulas in the FAFSA.

Dr. Baum's "A Primer for Financial Aid Administrators" is a must-read for anyone who is interested in how living standards, income and necessities are defined in the institutional needs-analysis.

Is your student applying for admission to a college that uses an Institutional Methodology? If the college requires you to submit the CSS Profile form, you can expect that your income and especially your assets will be treated differently than in the federal methodology. Your family contribution will likely be higher because more assets are considered, assessed and seen as sources of self-funding.

An evaluation of the family's resources is in addition to a federal assessment produced by filing the FAFSA. Typically, the more selective, well-known, and well-funded colleges require the CSS Profile. Check here for the list of participating institutions on the College Board's web site.

Cost of CSS Profile form: Whereas the FAFSA is provided for free by the U.S. Department of Education, the CSS Profile form is provided and processed by the College Board. To send the first application it costs $25, then to send it to additional colleges it costs $16 each.

FORM AND FORMULA FAFSA and Federal Methodology	FORM AND FORMULA CSS Profile and Institutional Methodology
The federal formula must be periodically approved by Congress. Annual adjustments to the tables in the federal methodology are made by the U.S. Department of Education. Financial aid administrators also have a significant influence on the changes to the Federal Methodology in response to financial aid appeals, and, thereby, the financial aid that students get.	The Institutional Methodology is set by the College Board, revised annually, and driven by consumer data. It is revised based on the recommendations of established economists and financial aid administrators. Each college can customize the questions on the CSS Profile to suit their goals and purposes. This form is for parents to fill out. If they're divorced or separated, each parent must file one CSS Profile form.

References

Institutional Methodology Overview, College Board.

Completing the CSS Profile Form, College Board

CSS Profile and Institutional Methodology

Approximately 200 colleges require parents to file the CSS Profile, provided and processed by the College Board. The first application costs $25, each additional app $16. Review the CSS Profile Student Guide for instructions on completing this application. The list of colleges that require the CSS Profile form is also available on the College Board website.

Just like the U.S. Department of Education provides processing and distribution of FAFSA information to colleges, the College Board does the same and more for the CSS Profile, by customizing the CSS Profile to the particular college's requirements.

For example, some colleges have a minimum student contribution or summer work expectation or count all or part of the net home equity of the family home. The FAFSA has neither of these.

A college may want to know the religion or affiliation of a student. For example, a Catholic College may receive scholarships from certain dioceses. If there's a church or cathedral on campus, you can bet that the college started as a seminary or synod or some funds from a religious order.

Other colleges may have started out with seed money from a religious order but today, they may be totally unaffiliated. For example, Wake Forest University was founded in 1834 by Baptist State Convention of North Carolina, but today is nonsectarian and not affiliated with the Baptists.

Many of these private colleges are secular institutions nowadays, and as private entities, can decide who will get their funds, whether through scholarships, demonstrated financial need, demonstrated merit, or a combination of all of the above.

These colleges are bound to Title IV funding rules and regulations when they give out federal financial aid but they are entirely autonomous when they decide who will receive their institutional aid.

So, you can see that the Federal Methodology is a reflection of the American society, its generally approved values, principles and status quo, whereas the Institutional Methodology (IM) reflects the private mission of individual institutions.

Big "P" or Small "p." Colleges can use the CSS Profile in a big or small way. I learned this when I interviewed a Financial Aid Director and Former NASFAA president David Gelinas. Big "P" colleges use the CSS Profile in total compliance with how the College Board designed it, and then add more questions of their own. Other colleges use only certain parts, in a small "p" way. Still other colleges make up their own forms.

Priority deadlines: Filing the CSS Profile, your families will need to pay attention to colleges' own "priority deadlines" for a chance on institutional funds. Each college has its own priority deadline for receiving the CSS Profile. I tell parents to submit the form at least five days before it's due.

Home equity and student contribution: The CSS Profile includes equity in the home as an asset in addition to the income and assets of parents. There's no income protection allowance for students, and in fact, they must make a contribution from $2,200 to $3,500, depending on the college. You'll remember that under the FM, students have an income protection allowance of $6,970 in 2021-22, and it's slated to increase each year.

Another major difference is that if parents are divorced and remarried, Profile colleges require financial information from both biological parents and their respective new spouses, potentially examining the income and assets of four people (e.g., biological mom and step-dad, biological dad step mom).

The Consensus Methodology

A third methodology? There's yet another institutional methodology discussion taking place among the Presidents of the most prestigious universities referred to as the "Consensus Methodology."

There is a third group of private colleges, called the 568 Group, that awards need-based aid and deviates even further from the CSS Profile. This isn't really a methodology, but a method of meeting demonstrated need. It consists of a group of Presidents from the most elite colleges that committed to filling 100% of demonstrated need, so they say they offer true need-blind admission. Before you get excited, these colleges reject nearly 95% of all qualified applicants, so they have more students who can pay than students who are on full financial aid. Exceptions I have noted include Amherst and Swarthmore colleges.

The consensus methodology continues as a conversation among presidents who are committed to giving low-income students enough aid to be able to attend their colleges. They are listed here and below: www.myintuition.org Students with high financial need e.g., Pell-eligible students, who are exceptional students, will have lots to gain at one of the following 18 colleges:

Amherst College, Boston College, California Institute of Technology, Claremont McKenna College, Columbia University, Cornell University, Dartmouth College, Davidson College, Duke University, Georgetown University, Grinnell College, Massachusetts Institute of Technology. Middlebury College, Northwestern University, Pomona College, Rice University, Swarthmore College, University of Notre Dame, Wellesley College, Williams College, and Yale University. As you can see, these are among the most highly selective colleges in the country.

The www.myintuition.org website also provides a handy Net Price Calculator that with six questions can give families with financial need a quick and easy estimate of costs:

Who should apply to these colleges? Low-income and zero-income students, minorities, traditionally under-represented students who have exceptional grades, test scores, work or volunteer experience or achievements.

Let's clarify what meeting 100% of need really means: some of the colleges that meet 100% of demonstrated need do so without giving loans to students, not even the usual amount of $5,500 Direct loan for undergraduate student. I can think of a few colleges that do this, such as Amherst, Bates and Swarthmore colleges. Certain other colleges meet 100% of need but still expect student to take their allowed amounts of self-help, in the form or federal loans and federal work-study.

Families with EFCs higher than the Cost of Attendance (COA) will pay the list price at the above-listed colleges. These don't award merit scholarships regardless of how talented is the student. It doesn't seem to discourage wealthy parents, however, because the Ivies and Elites are perceived to provide a guaranteed Return on Investment (ROI)!

Middle-class families must seed a bit of this and that. Students fare better at private institutions or small liberal arts colleges that offer a sizeable discount of the tuition.

Comparison between FAFSA and CSS Profile

COMPARE FAFSA WITH CSS PROFILE

FAFSA vs. PROFILE	FAFSA	PROFILE
Which financial aid form do colleges require?	Colleges require the FAFSA to award federal and state aid. These colleges must be accredited and approved to receive Title IV funding.	About 200 use the College Board's CSS Profile to assess demonstrated need and award institutional aid.
Timeline for filing	Can be filed as early as October 1 of the student's senior year of high school, or soon after the student applies for admission. While the U.S. Department of Education keeps the FAFSA processor open until June 30 of the award year, colleges prefer to receive FAFSA as early as possible after October 1 of the student's senior year of high school. Some states award grants on a first-come, first-served basis.	File beginning on Oct 1 of senior year. It's important to file by the colleges' priority deadlines to make sure you don't miss out on their institutional financial aid.
How are parents' incomes assessed?	Progressive rate from 24% to 47% of AAI Adjusted Available Income	Progressive rate from 24% to 46% of Adjusted Available income
How are students assessed? Note the IPA, Income Protection Allowance Differences:	Students have a Personal Income Protection Allowance (IPA) which is an exemption of income not counted in the federal formula. The amount a student can earn is $6,970 in 2021-22.	Students have no IPA or other personal income exemptions. They are required to contribute approximately $2,250 up to $4,000 from their own funding. Then, 50% of any additional earnings are

	Earnings above the IPA are added to the student's EFC at the rate of 50%. The Consolidated Appropriations Act, 2021, increases dependent students IPA to $9,410 starting in 2023-24.	added to the student's contribution.
At what rate are parents' assets considered?	5.64%.	Typically, 3%, 4% or 5% and Institutions can decide.
How are students' assets considered?	20%	25%
How are the federal and Institutional formulas different?	The portions of Federal Aid, such as the Pell and SEOG grants are entitlements or gifts that don't have to be paid back. The subsidized Direct loan, veterans' benefits, Federal Work-Study are subsidies that involve self-help. Students have to find jobs earmarked for work-study to earn money. Loans have to be paid back with fees and interest. Students' federal eligibility for loans and grants is the same no matter where they attend college.	Colleges that require parents to submit the CSS Profile decide internally how much they want to give out in institutional aid. Some reward merit, others need, yet other colleges award a combo of both merit and need. Students receive different amounts from different institutions.
Cost for filing?	Free	The College Board administers CSS Profile, and each application has a fee. $25 for the first one and $16 for each additional one if filed at the same time.
Source of funding?	Federal and state governments	College's own funds

Which tax forms?	Parent with whom the student lives with, e.g., 51% of the time) until June 30, 2023. Starting July 1, 2023, the parent who provided more financial support files the FAFSA.	Custodial and Non-custodial parent(s) and respective spouses. Potentially, the income and assets of 4 parents and step parents.
Which formula considers the equity of the homestead?	FAFSA does not consider home equity of the family's principal place of residence.	Profile considers home equity (market value minus what is owed on it. Colleges suggest checking on Zillow to figure market value)
How is business or farm equity assessed?	No assessment if a family business or farm employs fewer than 100 employees. (This is changing on July 1, 2023.)	Considered in net worth, but there is no uniform formula.
Are there required filing methods?	Students and parents are required to verify their tax information by using FAFSA's Data Retrieval Tool (DRT).	Parents must send in their tax returns for up to three years. Some colleges require parents to transmit info through the College Board service called "iDocs."

I mentioned earlier that the FAFSA does a good job of figuring out who is poor, and the U.S. Department of Education needs to collect only enough information to determine Pell eligibility. Hence the FAFSA is known as "the Pell Grant qualifier."

Colleges that promise to meet a high percentage of demonstrated need collect more financial information to figure how much more of a contribution the family can make.

I hope that by now you will see that the government's grants and self-help aid can't keep up with filling the need of truly poor kids because the college costs have increased exponentially. The Pell grant and Supplemental Education Opportunity Grant (SEOG) are great help with funding community college and in-state public universities, but a far cry for funding out-of-state universities and expensive private colleges.

It's essential for School Counselors and IECs to guide low-income students to these less expensive colleges so that they will not take on the type of debt that will crush them. These students are particularly vulnerable to recruitment practices, for-profit schools, and "name" universities that will cost double or triple their in-state institutions.

I've come across too many of these students who are buried in debt after just the first year of attendance at a private, or, out-of-state public school, when they could have gone for free at a local school.

If the main source for college is the Pell and FSEOG grants, students truly need to humble themselves and start at the community college or nearby regional university to defray the costs of room and board.

I realize that these low-income students from families who live at the poverty level would benefit from staying on campus for all four years. The maximum amount of Pell Grant is $6,495 in 2021-22. I tell my students that it doesn't matter where they start, it matters that they graduate with a two or four-year degree with minimal debt. I tell them to get the most education for the least cost.

The Pell Grant phases out when the family has an EFC of $5,846 or more. The rest of the aid consists of federal loans. Every undergraduate student who files the FAFSA can receive the aggregate amounts of unsubsidized loans from the federal government, regardless of their family's wealth or lack thereof.

However, loans weren't meant as the way for the poor and working poor to fund the entirety of a college education. The Lumina Foundation explains that originally, in the 1970's, federal loans were offered to help families who didn't want to cash out of investments. "No one could have predicted then that federal loans and private education loans would become the main source of college funding."

https://www.luminafoundation.org/history-of-federal-student-aid/ (Scroll down to the video and further down for the written transcript.) https://www.luminafoundation.org/history-of-federal-student-aid/chapter-one/

Apparently, loans are a large source of revenues for the government, and if the U.S. Department of Education stopped making student loans, it would suffer a significant deficit. Imagine the number of employees hired to service federal loans. Incidentally, as bad as it is to have to borrow to get an education, federal loans offer reasonably low interest rates and offer more guarantees and flexibility in repayment. When parents don't qualify for the Parent PLUS loan, they end up taking more costly and less flexible private loans.

Undergraduate students who are dependent on their parents can borrow only limited amounts which is good because if they graduate after four years, their debt totals around $27,000 plus interest and fees. If they pay the interest each year and start payments as soon as they graduate, the debt is typically paid off easily on the ten-year standard repayment of approximately $250 per month. Parents who take out large Parent PLUS loan, however, take on larger debts and end up paying their children's education into their retirement years.

Graduate students borrow the largest amounts. They are eligible for the unsubsidized Grad PLUS loan, which must be repaid with interest and fees. It's as if the government helps with some subsidies toward gaining a first degree but after this, there are no more subsidies. If you consider the cost of medical school at $100,000 per year, you can understand why doctors can graduate with half a million or more in debt. Other graduate programs, from veterinary to law school can set these students back hundreds of thousands of dollars. You can see why graduate loans make up the larger portion of the 1.67 trillion dollars of debt.

What's unusual to me is that many borrowers default on their loans when the balance is a mere few thousand dollars. It makes me wonder if these people dropped out before earning any degree or certificate, or if they were poor to start with and remained poor even after going to college. I've come across families with zero EFC whose children were accepted to the likes of New York University and took out hundreds of thousands of loans, just because they believed the prestige of the university was going to be worth it for their child.
https://www.nytimes.com/2010/05/29/your-money/student-loans/29money.html

The Institutional Methodology

Colleges that use the CSS Profile know that paying for private colleges is not an amount that families can pay from one year's income. They expect families to pay a percentage of costs from savings, current income and future borrowing. They are experts at calculating the family's ability to absorb debt.

The amount that colleges want families to pay is just an offer. Parents can counter-offer or move onto other possible colleges. There are many colleges in the United States of America. Hence, it's even more critical that my readers return to their AFC (Affordable Family Contribution) calculations and proceed with this all-important educational purchase while staying within their budget.

When they buy a house, families can't buy more property that they can afford. The housing bubble of 2004 was caused by people buying houses on margin or with no money down and no way to pay for them. Some families are in the same predicament with buying a college education. Since the housing market crash, realtors are quick to ask the price range that families can afford and a lending company determines the maximum amount of mortgage that buyers can get.

I used to naively believe that the purpose of filing the CSS Profile was to see which scholarships students could get, because the name CSS stands for College Scholarship Search. In my experience, the primary purpose is to assess the family's willingness to pay. Colleges calculate the price they will require parents to pay, since students are limited in the amount of loans they can get from the federal government.

Colleges propose a price to pay based on their internal regulations, philosophy and mission. Likewise, parents can set a price to pay based on their values, expectations, return on investment, probability of employment upon graduation, and calculated financial risk to the family.

According to David Gelinas, financial aid director at Davidson College (NC), some colleges use the CSS Profile analysis in a big way, with a capital "P"; others use it in a small way, with a lowercase "p." By this he means that some colleges use the CSS Profile like the College Board designed it, in all its breadth and depth. Furthermore, colleges can choose additional questions to collect specific details they deem relevant for their institution. For example, if a college is religiously affiliated, it may care to know if the student is Lutheran, or Episcopal, or Catholic. When colleges can fill 100% of demonstrated need, they want to make sure that the financial need is real. If you have more assets than meets the eye, they want to know that too! After all the leaves are turned over, and families answer all the questions, the CSS Profile form ends with yet one more question: "Is there anything else we didn't ask?" "Are there any other assets we didn't think to ask?"

I remember hearing a discussion among financial aid administrators who couldn't agree on whether a man who owned a cow in Texas, had an asset or a liability. Some administrators said it was a liability because the man had to pay the rancher to provide feed for the cow. Others saw it as an asset because a man who owns a cow is better off than someone who doesn't. Yet other administrators claimed the cow should not be considered in the EFC evaluation until it was steak, on the plate, whether rare, medium, or well done!

Administrators try very hard to allocate financial aid to those families who really need it while keeping in compliance with federal rules. They also work hard to comply to the rules that their institution establishes. Schools that use the CSS Profile rake through a family's assets and income in great detail. Let's consider that CSS Profile schools collect families' prior-prior year income tax returns, just like the FAFSA. Then, they collect your most recent, previous year tax record as well as your current year financials. Some colleges expect to receive this information via iDocs, which adds another charge to the cost of filing the Profile. I really appreciate colleges that use the CSS Profile with a lowercase "p," meaning the level of investigation into families' finances is less intense, and they may create their home-made, in-house forms, that parents can mail out without going through the College Board and using iDocs. At the college I used to work at, the friendly financial aid administrator, Jim Canning, would simply send an email asking for the amount of equity in the home, or a few more questions, and that was enough.

The four-legged stool that makes up the Institutional EFC:

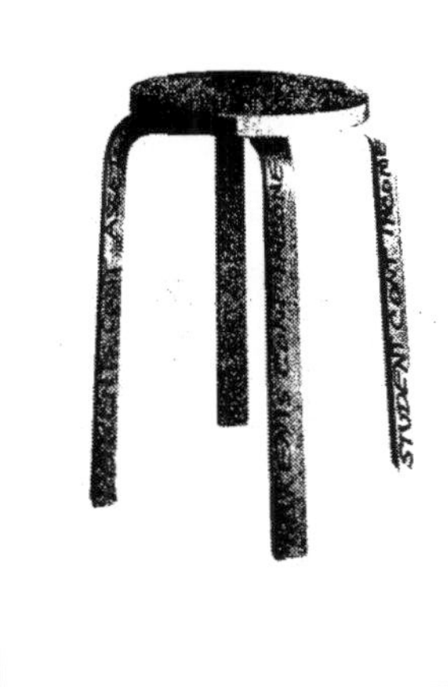

INSTITUTIONAL EFC is the Sum of 4 Contributions:

Parents Contribution from income: **22% to 46% of Adjusted Gross Income**

Parents Contribution from assets: **3% to 5%**

Standard Student Contribution: varies from **$1,800 to $2,500** (e.g., Princeton U requires $3,400.)

Student Contribution from income after contributing the above amount: **50%**.

Student Contribution from assets: **25%** (assets can be cash, savings, checking, net worth of investments)

You will recall that FAFSA computes your EFC by adding the income and assets of both parents and students. The metaphor of the four-legged stool is the same for Profile schools: parents' income and assets are added to the student's income and assets.

However, the Institutional EFC is different from your Federal EFC because the percentages are different and are at the discretion of the college. The needs analysis and data points considered are different. Although there are general principles of computing the EFC that are embedded in the College Board EFC calculator, in the final analysis, private colleges can award whichever amount they want. The funding is theirs, as opposed to federal funding which has to be awarded in compliance with federal rules and regulations. The government audits approximately 18% of FAFSAs. Colleges cannot award federal aid willy-nilly unless they can justifiably change the data elements by applying "professional judgment" or PJ. Colleges that award their own aid must simply comply with their internal rules.

After students submit the CSS Profile to the College Board, families do not receive a SAR report as they do when they file FAFSA. The Student Aid Report (SAR) that comes from U.S. Department of Education lists the Expected Family Contribution on the first page. It's more difficult for families to figure out their Institutional EFC, and this places them at a disadvantage when it comes to calculating the amount that the college is not funding. To remedy this, use the College Board EFC Calculator "with a grain of salt," because private institutions tweak the formula according to their goals. You can also try using each college's Net Price Calculator.

Divorce or separation: In the case of separation or divorce, both parents complete the CSS Profile. If they are remarried, the new spouses' financial information is required on the CSS Profile. This can result in the college collecting the financial information from the custodial parent and new spouse (if remarried), and the non-custodial parent and new spouse, potentially examining the income and assets of four people (e.g., biological mom and stepdad, biological dad and stepmom). Both households submit the same data points in a parallel fashion, although more weight is placed on the wealth of the biological or adoptive parents.

Divorced or separated spouses often worry that the financial aid administrator may reveal one's financial situation to the other. You can rest assured that financial aid administrators will never disclose the financial information of one ex-spouse to the other.

Are there any adjustments to income? Yes! Your EFC may be higher or lower at a CSS Profile college than at one that uses FAFSA alone. In my experience, the CSS Profile EFC is typically higher. For example, untaxed Social Security benefits are not assessed on FAFSA but they are on the CSS Profile. On the other hand, pre-tax contributions are considered in both forms. See the illustration below for the treatment of family income under the federal methodology vs the institutional methodology.

Total IM-EFC Contribution = (Custodial Parent Contribution) + (Non-Custodial Parent Contribution.) This Institutional Methodology can potentially produce double the family contribution if both households are counted. If any member of that foursome refuses to file the CSS Profile, the college will not award any institutional financial aid to the student. If one of the parents completes the forms and then refuses to contribute, again the student will likely have challenges paying for college. In difficult divorces, sometimes the student is stuck in a no man's land, like in the case of Rebekah, which you'll find in the next chapters.

How much can you pay? Parents will encounter this question on the CSS Profile more times than it's possible to imagine. It's as if the amount they can pay will increase by asking more often, or parents will be tripped up and answer they can pay more than they previously said. If you say "zero" the colleges will assume you're not taking responsibility. But, colleges do not specify how they use this figure. Do they add this number to what they calculate you are able to pay? Do they take the larger of this number and the calculated ability pay? They certainly don't use this number if it is smaller than the calculated ability to pay. Saying anything other than zero does not help you. If you don't want to say zero, then answer a minimal amount, such as $100.

Even after parents have listed their cars' make and year, after they've listed their motorcycles, bicycles, and canoes, collection of ceramic turtles or penguins, jewelry and watches, a question pops up at the end of the CSS Profile form: Is there anything else? After parents have listed the storage cabin in the backyard which they purchased at the Home Depot to hide the lawnmower and garden tools, the CSS Profile form has more questions, just in case parents forgot to list other resources. I wouldn't be surprised if a disgruntled parent wrote something silly like: "We have installed new carpet in our home and replaced the wooden floor in the kitchen!" Be sure to remember your AFC and not change it, because you'll be able to back up the amount you can pay by showing your household budget, receipts and bank statements, which you assembled at the beginning of this book.

If the price of the college is much more than your AFC, and your student really likes it, you can appeal. Starting in 2023, financial aid administrators will not be able to dismiss appeals out of hand. I suspect that more families will gain the confidence to reach out to college administrators. Mark Kantrowitz, our nation's foremost expert in federal financial aid, advises to not ask for a specific amount in an appeal. Let the college tell you. You may be underestimating the amount you could get. Who knows, the college might propose a higher amount than you thought possible. It's important to know that the financial aid administrator can adjust your EFC data points. Be sure to support your narrative with clear documents that show your income, assets and expenses. Colleges already have your prior-prior year income tax returns from FAFSA. In fact, Profile schools have three years of tax returns: prior-prior year, prior year, and the current year. Review your returns before talking with a financial aid administrator. Be sure to ask how they arrived at the cost and how you're being assessed.

IM/FM Data Points

How EFC is assessed under the <u>Institutional Methodology (IM)</u>

Income (including)	**Assets (including)**
Taxable income Untaxed income & any other benefits	Cash, bank accounts Investment equity Home equity Business/Fam net worth Other real estate equity Assets in siblings' names 529 Plans
LESS Income Allowances Mandatory taxes Medical and dental expense allowance Employment expense allowance Annual Education Savings Allowance (AESA) Income Protection Allowance (IPA)	**LESS Asset Allowances** Emergency Reserve Allowance (ERA) Cumulative Education Savings Allowance (CESA) Low Income Asset Allowance

Elementary/Secondary tuition allowance	
= Contribution from Income	+ Contribution from Assets
Assessment rate: 22% to 46% (progressive)	**Assessment rate 3% to 5% (graduated)**

= EXPECTED FAMILY CONTRIBUTION (Institutional Methodology)

Similarities: Both Federal and Institutional methodologies deduct the mandatory federal and state taxes, an annual education savings allowance, and an income-protection allowance from the gross income of a family.

In 2020 there was discussion about increasing funding for the Pell Grant for very low-income families by removing the interest-rate subsidy on the subsidized Stafford loan for undergraduate students. However, the Pell Grant program is over-funded, which would mean that not enough needy students have used it because they haven't gone to college. The Biden Administration will need to review this funding, especially because the federal methodology is due for a process called "Reauthorization." This means that a lot could change in the federal methodology and the institutional methodology could also change to follow suit.

The percentage of the Adjusted Gross Income (AGI) added to the EFC is only one percent lower than in the federal methodology. The institutional methodology assesses income at the incremental rate of 22% to 46%. There are other deductions, such as uncovered medical/dental expenses, a small employment expense allowance, and a possible deduction for elementary/secondary private school tuition payments.

How much are you expected to contribute from assets under the Institutional Methodology?

A family's contribution will be higher the more assets they have, such as a second home, boat and cars. Savings, investments, 529 plans, grandparents' assets, assets in the siblings' name, trusts, annuities, and business/farm equity will be considered. Often, colleges will ask to review the trust fund documents to see who is the designated beneficiary.

Add Home Equity and Business Equity.

The major increase to the EFC results from the amount of equity in the home or business, of parents who own one. The institutional formula considers that families who own a home are in a much better position to pay for college than families who rent. Say that two families have the same income: renters don't get the mortgage interest deduction or stable monthly payments. Owners can borrow from the equity built into the house. Counting home equity as a source of funding for college has raised many parental eyebrows. If you borrow from your home, you may risk losing it. According to Mark Kantrowitz, a national financial aid guru, "they can repossess a house but not an education!" Whether or not you live in high-cost, real-estate areas like California or in the Midwest, houses are our home, our residence, a roof over our heads.

You may have a substantial amount of equity in your house, but if you sold it you may not be able to buy another home. If you use it to pay for college, you may actually not be able to remain in it. Parents may be counting on their home equity for retirement. Under the institutional methodology, the home is considered a potential asset and a possible source of funding for college. Some colleges substitute an imputed home value and adjust it for inflation, Many cap home equity as a multiple of income. They will limit home equity to 1 to 4 times your annual income, depending on the college. Colleges advise families to use Zillow to figure out the current market value. they may use the lesser amount: the value of your home minus what's owed on it, or your annual income (multiplied by) 1 to 4. Some colleges like MIT and Stanford don't use home equity. If your home equity affects your EFC you can appeal (see the chapter on appeals).

Families with significant amounts of home equity need to know how the college will assess it. For example, some colleges consider only a portion of home equity or twice the salary. Log onto my website to download a chart provided by Paula Bishop, CPA, which lists which CSS Profile colleges include your home equity in your ability to pay. For example, Cal Tech and Cooper Union don't use it at all whereas University of Michigan considers 2.5 times the earned income. Download a copy of Equity in Home used by Colleges (2019 latest) by going to www.eduave.com

Treatment of Retirement Assets

Both Federal and Institutional methodologies don't consider any retirement assets such as pensions, IRAs, 401(k),403(b), SEP, SIMPLE or Keogh plans as *assets*. But, they count the amount deducted from taxable income in the year when the contribution is made as untaxed *income*. But, once the funds are in a retirement plan, they no longer count. The cynic in me wonders why, then, if they don't count, do CSS Profile colleges want to know it? Perhaps it's an indication of how well-off families are. Or maybe they want to know if the family has an unusually high amount of retirement assets.

I remember talking with a young father who kept his money in regular, non-IRA accounts. He wanted to have that liquidity before age 59½ so he wouldn't have to pay the 10% early withdrawal penalty. This liquid cash increased his EFC considerably. The financial aid administrator at his son's school, Princeton University, told him that if those funds had been in a retirement account, none of it would have counted. However, I wonder what a financial aid administrator would think if a family happened to have millions in retirement accounts and still qualified for financial aid. I suspect it's not a common occurrence!

What does this formula include into the EFC from the parents' assets? There are three allowances or deductions, similarly as in the federal methodology: Emergency Reserve Allowance (ERA); Cumulative Education Savings Allowance (CESA), and Low-Income Asset Allowance.

How Is the Family Business Treated?

The equity in the family business or family farm is another component of the institutional expected family contribution. The Federal Methodology does not consider a family business an asset if it employs fewer than 100 employees. Likewise, a family farm is ignored if the family lives on the farm and materially participates in the operation of the farm. But, the Institutional methodology does. The business equity adds 3% to 5% to the asset side of the EFC.

References: The formulas behind the form: The Institutional Methodology explained, College Board.

Rebekah's Story

Rebekah's favorite college uses the CSS Profile form in the uppercase "P." Rebekah was a straight-A student at a very rigorous high school. She took many AP classes, 32 ACT, and was involved in many activities, from the student council president to leader of the largest regional Jewish Youth Groups. She had more than a working knowledge of Hebrew and tutored children after school at her synagogue. She studied both Spanish and French in school. She would start and end her day in French by setting her morning alarm to French music (she was a big fan of French techno) and tackled Harry Potter A L'École Des Sorciers before bed. When she was not trying to pin down Spanish grammar, she worked on her senior thesis project, which dealt with "pragmatic failures in interpreting."

She created a supplement for her school's French curriculum, based on the immersion programs she had experienced for two summers at the Monterey Language Academy. These summer programs influenced her appreciation for foreign languages and fueled her desire to become an interpreter. Rebekah had come to love the College, where the summer program took place. The campus was beautiful, the students were as hard-working and intellectual as she, but the cost of attendance was steep. Rebekah knew her mother wouldn't be able to pay $71,830 for her first year, not when she had two younger siblings also wanting to go to college. Rebekah's mother worked full-time and received some "forced" child-support from her rather uncooperative ex-spouse.

Rebekah got into this college and was on cloud nine. She basked in the feeling that her college dream was becoming real and spread the word among her friends and relatives. Then came the process of filing for financial aid. Rebekah's mother was divorced. She revealed to me that it had been a very long, bitter legal battle. The divorce decree stipulated joint custody with the girls living primarily with mom. In actuality, this mom said the father didn't call the girls but once or twice a year. "The only reason he's paying any child support is that he'd be put in jail," said Rebekah's mother, who had called the financial aid administrator to explain she was not on speaking terms with her ex. She explained that her ex-spouse would not contribute anything to the children's college education. He was marginally involved in their life. The Rabbi sent an email to the financial aid administrator explaining the father hadn't even shown up at Rebekah's bat mitzvah. Nevertheless, there was no way around it. The college required the divorced father to file the CSS Profile or, there would be no aid.

Rebekah called her dad, who had refused to file the form. Rebekah insisted, and finally, he relented. She was ecstatic! Again, she felt like her dream was coming true.

After the college received the father's CSS Profile, Rebekah and her mother received a financial aid award with no aid other than the usual $5,500 unsubsidized Federal loan. The dad had the financial wherewithal to contribute, but he refused. Rebekah was crushed and decided to travel to visit her dad and meet with him in person. Dad took Rebekah out to a fancy restaurant, and over dinner, he made it clear he would not be able to contribute. The mother's lawyer contacted the father to let him know he needed to contribute.

Then the father's lawyer pointed out that the divorce decree made no stipulation for college support, and besides if it did, it would probably refer to a "public institution" and not one that cost over $70,000 per year. The college explained to Rebekah that she wasn't eligible for need-based aid. The college also said to Rebekah that not only would she receive no aid in the first year, but she wouldn't be able to apply for financial assistance in future years. Rebekah could borrow the usual $5,500 in Direct federal loans for first-year students, but it was a drop in the bucket when the cost was over $70,0000. The mother could borrow from the Parent PLUS loan for parents, but she wisely declined. Rebekah could afford to attend her in-state public flagship university in the honors program.

This is an example of a college that practices the Profile with a capital "P". It does meet 100% of financial need after the parents have contributed their share. Had the father been estranged from the children a case might be made that Rebekah had no contact with her father. Even then, it's not easy to prove. Her father paid child-support to the mother. This amount would be reflected on FAFSA as the mother's untaxed income, and added back to the adjusted available income (AAI). A college financial aid administrator would find it difficult to believe that a student who is receiving child support doesn't know the whereabouts of her parent. An ex-spouse's unwillingness to contribute doesn't result in the college giving out more funds. Financial aid is based on the parents' ability to pay, not their willingness to pay.

Colleges view divorce as a break between two spouses but not between biological or adopted parents and their children. Dean Gelinas from Davidson College says: "You can divorce your spouse but you can't divorce your children."

Rebekah didn't want to create any further conflict between her mother and father. She reacted with surprising maturity and moved on to other colleges on her list. She was an excellent student and was accepted in the honors program at her in-state flagship institution. Her tuition was covered by state and local scholarships. In effect, the cost came down to that of room and board.

In addition, Rebekah was accepted to several other private colleges that also required the CSS Profile, and one did accept her without the non-custodial parent's CSS Profile. The financial aid award was based only on the mother's income, home equity, and child support received. You might say that this particular college practiced the Institutional Methodology (IM) with the lower-case "p". It filled 80% of her financial need. Rebekah received a small amount of Pell grant and work-study, and she borrowed the $5,500 in federal loans for first-year, undergraduate students. Mom paid her EFC of $3,500 and took out a small Parent PLUS loan. This was a relief given that Rebekah's younger siblings would soon graduate from high school and mom would need to fund them as well. Rebekah was able to attend this lovely private college that essentially cut her a break. This private college and her in-state university were her two "financial safeties." If these had not been affordable, Rebekah said she would have gone to the local community college.

Community colleges fill a huge community need for many reasons, not just economically for those who want to keep costs down. During the Covid-19 pandemic the cost-value relationship of expensive colleges came under scrutiny when students were taking classes completely online from their dorm room, at the cost of $70,000 per year. The semester was cut short and the number of contact hours seemed less. A student can attend a community college for $5,000 a year. Even if they don't want to attend community college, they could enroll at a public or private university and live at home, thereby saving in the neighborhood of $15,000 a year.

More Need Analysis Differences

These are the Different Data Points between FAFSA and CSS Profile

FAFSA: Adjusted Available Income (AAI) of prior-prior year	CSS Profile: Adjusted Available Income (AAI) of 3 years: prior-prior, prior, current year estimate.
+Plus: untaxed income	+Plus: untaxed income
+Bank accounts (checking, savings, CDs, MMs)	+Bank accounts (checking, savings, CDs, MMs)

+Education savings accounts (529, Coverdell plans)	+Education savings accounts (529, Coverdell plans)
+Liquid investments (stocks, bonds, EFTs, mutual funds)	+Liquid investments (stocks, bonds, EFTs, mutual funds)
+Principal residence does NOT count	+Equity in the home/principal residence counts
+Real estate investments other than home	+Real estate investments
Family business/family farm do not count if fewer than 100 employees.	+Trust funds, Non-retirement annuities, 529 Plans
	+Medical Spending Accounts (FSAs, HSAs, Dependent Care FSAs)
	+Siblings K-12 Private school tuition
	+Total retirement savings (not considered but required to disclose)
	+Siblings' assets in parents' name (Coverdell, 529s)
	+Other assets: cars, motorcycles, boats, jet skis
FM Income +Assets = EFC (FAFSA)	+Any other valuables: Farm animals, collectibles, jewelry. **IM Income + Assets = EFC (CSS Profile)**

"Allowances" are deductions or exclusions. These are subtracted from the total income.

FAFSA: Allowances against income	CSS Profile: Allowances against income
Mandatory Taxes: federal, state, FICA	Mandatory taxes as in federal formula
Formula set by Congress and revised with each reauthorization.	Additional deductions are set annually, consumer data driven.
Employment expense	Excessive medical dental expenses
Income protection allowance	Private school tuition
	Income Protection Allowance
Adjusted Available Income= (income - exclusions)	Adjusted Available Income= (income - exclusions)
EFC FAFSA: 22% to 47% of remaining income	EFC Profile: 22% to 46% of remaining income

Student Contribution from Income and Assets

The student's income and assets are assessed at a higher rate than parents. The rationale is that students don't have to pay bills and maintain a household. Their focus is on saving for their education. Profile institutions typically require students to contribute anywhere from $1,800 to $2,200 from their earnings each year. Princeton University requires a higher student contribution. This amount is added on the income side of the student contribution, whether or not the student earned it. Consequently, parents end up paying it. In the second year, students are expected to work in the summer and earn a bit more, since they now have one year of college under their belt. If they don't have it, once more parents come to the rescue.

What If Parents Have More than One Child in College at the Same Time?

The FAFSA formula for calculating the EFC of families with more than one student in college at the same time remains as I explained until June 30, 2023. The formula recognizes parents' hardship when two or more kids are in college at the same time. Just because they have two children in college doesn't mean they have twice as much money available to pay the college bills.

Under the Federal Methodology, (FM) the EFC per child is halved. If the family's EFC is $42,000, then each student's EFC would be $21,000. This would result in each student demonstrating a higher level of need.

Under the Institutional Formula, the parent's contribution with two students in college is supposed to be 60% of EFC per child or 120% of EFC for both. With three kids in college at the same time, the formula calculated 45% of EFC per child, for a total 135% of EFC. However, if kids were spaced four years apart, then parents' ability to pay would start at 100% of EFC for each child.

Sometimes, parents are successful at getting the college to consider their additional costs if they help support another child in graduate school, though this is not the rule. Graduate students are considered "independent" and can borrow larger amounts of funds on their own.

Over the years, since many colleges don't fill 100% of a family's demonstrated need, the EFC reduction for families with more than one child in college at the same time hasn't really reduce their costs significantly. The EFC being a baseline for what parents can afford is less meaningful, because in the final analysis, colleges charge what they want.

Starting on July 1, 2023 academic year, having more than one child is in college at the same time doesn't reduce EFC per child. And, the EFC is regarded more as an index of the aid a family needs, than a hard and fast number.

However, I believe that families' demonstrated need does matter, and parents can raise issues of affordability by talking with financial aid administrators, writing letters, or filing an appeal. Starting July 1, 2023, financial aid administrators can no longer dismiss all financial aid appeals.

Families and IECs who are reading this book already know that families need to review their budget. Families meeting with a financial aid administrator need to provide evidence for what they're saying. The initial chapters are about the "Affordable Family Contribution," or "AFC," as opposed to the "Expected Family Contribution" under the Federal and Institutional Methodology shows how to prepare a budget and show what the family can pay from current income. If families have studied their budget and can substantiate what they can pay and the maximum amount they can borrow, they are ready to talk about their "AFC.'

FAFSA Changes in 2023-24

The Consolidated Appropriations Act, 2021, included changes to the federal methodology meant to simplify and amend the FAFSA form. The changes will take effect on July 1, 2023. The high school graduating class of 2023 will file the new FAFSA after October 1 of 2022. The income used will be from the year 2021.

Name change: The Expected Family Contribution "EFC" changes name to **"SAI" for Student Aid Index**. The rationale was that families tended to perceive the EFC as the net amount to pay. But, colleges can up and change tuition costs every year, and the federal expected family contribution is unrelated to what colleges do with their Cost of Attendance. By changing the name to Student Aid Index, the U.S. Department of Education can be more nebulous and still get their job done, since FAFSA simply needs to target the students eligible for the Pell Grant. Other subsidies and self-help aid follow if a student qualifies for the Pell Grant (e.g., FSEOG Grant, Federal Work-Study, and the subsidized loan).

Reduced number of questions: The FAFSA form itself will have fewer questions: from 108 to about 36 questions. The DoE is working on the implementation of these changes.

Simplified Needs Analysis: Those students who receive federal means-tested benefits, from free school lunch to Temporary Assistance to Needy Families, will qualify for the full amount of the Pell Grant. Other low-income students will be evaluated by a precise formula tied to a percentage calculation of the poverty level. These are the students that receive pro-bono services from Independent Educational Consultant.

No EFC discounts for multiple children in college. One of the most controversial changes is the treatment of multiple children in college at the same time. Parents who have children that overlap in college by one or more years or parents with twins or triplets will no longer have their federal EFC divided by two or three. If parents have two children in college at the same time and their EFC is $30,000, the EFC per child is $15,000. After July 1, 2023, the expected family contribution will be the same for each child. This means that if your expected family contribution was $30,000, your minimum baseline for two children would be $60,000 per year or $90,000 if you have triplets. I dare not think what it would be if you had quadruplets!

Affordable Family Contribution: Regardless of whether the EFC is called SAI, or whether the college makes allowances for parents with more than one child enrolled in college, the Affordable Family Contribution can be the lighthouse in a storm. Parents cannot fall prey to the bumper sticker mentality. As explained in the "Budget Sheet" chapter, they need to calculate a possible amount they can pay from current income, an amount they can pay from savings, and an amount they can borrow via federal loans.

Families can do their own math: The Federal Methodology assesses parents' available income (after paying taxes and deducting a personal income protection allowance) under a progressive rate from 22% to 47%. Parents' assets are considered at the rate of up to 5.64%. Student assets are considered at the rate of 20%, and students have a personal income protection allowance. If families use these percentages, they can calculate their own EFC and gauge whether it's similar to their Affordable Family Contribution.

Under the Institutional Methodology, expressed in the CSS Profile, the percentages change slightly, but the examination of everything a family owns is exhaustive. CSS Profile schools are super-adept at assessing middle-class and wealthy families.

I post this chart below, to show the percentage amounts calculated in the two forms. Things change, but families know what they can and cannot afford. They need to keep records, judge the college's merits analytically, and consider the price-value for the student over the four years.

Assessment Comparison

CSS Profile **Institutional Methodology**	**FAFSA** **Federal Methodology**
<u>Parent Income Assessment</u> • Progressive rate from 22% to 46% <u>Parent Asset Assessment</u> • Graduated rate structure of 3% to 5% of net worth (assets less allowances)	<u>Parent Income Asessment</u> • Progressive rate from 22% to 47% <u>Parent Asset Assessment</u> • Up to 5.64% of assets less allowances
<u>Student Income Assessment</u> • From \$2,000 to \$4,000 (regardless of earnings), plus 50% of remaining earnings (no IPA) <u>Student Asset Assessment</u> • 25%	<u>Student Income Assessment</u> • 50% after Income Protection Allowance (IPA) of \$6,970 <u>Student Asset Assessment</u> • 20%

The Consolidated Appropriations Act, 2021, allocates slightly more aid for low- and middle-income families, closes the divorced parent loophole, and gives those with 529 plans a valuable advantage.

For example, in divorce or separated situations, the parent with whom the student lives with the most files the FAFSA. Starting with the 2023-24 FAFSA, the parent who provides more support is the parent who files. This closes a loophole where the parent with less income filed and received more aid.

Other changes apply to untaxed income and benefits that will no longer become potential funding for college:

Child support received, workman's compensation, veteran's education benefits, housing, food and other allowances for military and clergy, cash support to the student, disbursement of funds from 529 plans paid on the student's behalf and other untaxed income will not become part of the student's ability to pay for college.

For example, the Income Protection Allowance for students increases from $6,970 2021-22 to $9,410 in 2023-24. This benefits high-school and college students who may be working to support their parents or other family members.

Male students will no longer need to register for Selective Service to obtain federal aid. Incarcerated individuals and those with drug convictions will be able to get federal aid. Homeless youths will be able to prove their case more easily, without having to provide police, hospital or restraining order reports.

The U.S. Department of Education will require that the Cost of Attendance (COA) that typically lists room and board as one fee to be split into clearly defined costs for the room, and clearly defined costs of meals.

Parents need to figure out the round-about amount of EFC/SAI under the Institutional Methodology. Whereas the FAFSA produces a SAR which lists the family's EFC on the first page, the CSS Profile doesn't produce an equivalent estimation of an amount that would be the families to pay and an amount that the college would contribute. Parents still need to know a rough estimate of what would be reasonable for them to contribute. This can be done by using the EFC Calculators on the College Board Website, and compare it with what they can actually pay, which means they need to review their Affordable Family Contribution, AFC. They are required to come up on their own. This is the only way to figure out by how much the colleges are gapping. Then, the parents and student need to decide if it's worth attending the college, because costs will only increase of the four years, or whether it's worth it to file an appeal. The negotiable amount is the gap. Remember that you should not ask to pay less than your reasonable amount. "Reasonable" of course, is debatable. What families consider "reasonable" to pay can be vastly different than what colleges bill for. Colleges don't meet your EFC with grants. But if your out-of-pocket cost is way above your EFC, it means the gap is large. Call the financial aid administrator to understand how you're being assessed and refer to your budget and AFC (Affordable Family Contribution) to raise legitimate questions of affordability.

File the FAFSA in the first year of college even if you don't need money. In case your financial situation changes, the college will have your FAFSA already on file. Also, if students don't apply for financial aid in the first year at some colleges, they may not be able to apply for aid later in the following years. If your family becomes unable to pay due to unforeseen circumstances, you would be able to get the Federal loans with which to pay your bills.

Who determines the final amount you will pay? It's the financial aid administrators. They know that no formula, however precise and extensive, can cover all the individual situations in which families find themselves. According to Mark Kantrowitz: "When it rains, it pours. The hardships usually come in three: the major wage earner suffers a job loss, the economy takes a downturn, then the car or house is repossessed." During the Covid-19 pandemic, many people working in the restaurant and service businesses lost their jobs, if not their lives. These financial aid administrators have heard it all. Fortunately, they can exercise "professional judgment" to better meet each family's unique needs.

Your family must keep an updated budget, unemployment records, death certificates, testimonials from trusted figures, or any other piece of evidence that shows you're telling the truth and substantiates your facts. If you decide to appeal, you'll want to see what type of documentation financial aid administrators need to see. To learn more about specific cases, review the Professional Judgment Tip Sheets that the College Board' makes available to financial aid administrators who use the CSS Profile form.

Filing deadlines: Pay attention to the priority filing deadlines at Profile schools. Many colleges need to plan how much they can award in aid by their "priority deadline," and may refuse to consider a late applicant for financial aid. Sometimes these dates come before a student knows if they were accepted. It does happen that some parents completed the CSS Profile and in the end, the student wasn't accepted. Some parents wonder if their high financial need had something to do with it. Many colleges will accept full-need students if they also have full-pay students to balance off the revenue. At colleges where admission officers can view the amount of financial aid the student needs, the academically borderline applicant who needs a vast amount of financial aid may end up on the "deny" pile. Potentially even worse is when the college admits a student, but then denies them the financial aid they need to afford the college costs.

State aid programs: Don't forget to check how much aid the student would be eligible to receive from the state. In many states, once students file the FAFSA, the state awards need-based or merit-based aid. However, do check the deadlines for applying for state aid in your state of residence. The list of state FAFSA deadlines is available on the FAFSA web site. Also, note that in many States, if the student attends a public university or a private college that is out-of-state, the student loses the state aid.

Case Studies

Meet Kevin

I've said it earlier and will say it again: if students have a large amount of demonstrated financial need, they will pay less at colleges that meet 100% of need. Kevin started college at a school that didn't meet his demonstrated need. I assumed that college that require students to file the CSS Profile do so because they have funds to give out. I'm discovering that many colleges, including some HBCUs, require the CSS Profile form yet not be able to meet the full need of students. Before enrolling, students and parents need to check the College Scorecard provided by the U.S. Department of Education for graduation rates and average costs.

In South Carolina, where I live, more than 40% of residents, age 25 and older, have a high school diploma or less. This is a level linked to low earnings and the risk of poverty. It's an achievement when these students, against all odds, are able to graduate from high school. Although they are motivated to get a college education, there's little financial aid guidance for them, and they don't have the experience to shop wisely for colleges. They take it for granted that the college they attend is the least expensive and when I asked them to cite the cost of their nearby institutions they are clueless. I don't mean to discredit colleges and much less HBCUs which are so needed to encourage, support and validate the African American student. I am saying that families need to look at the facts on "College Navigator" and the "College Scorecard." Students need to be informed about the graduation rates, earning potential, and four-year costs. If the eight-year graduation rate of the college is 50% it reveals the uncomfortable truth that one out of two students drops out. It's good to know this before enrolling.

At the AME Church where I volunteered, I've personally come across recent high school graduates who were paying close to the full price of out-of-state public and private institutions. I remember Kevin, who attended an HBCU, three states over, who was front-loaded in the first year and then packaged essentially with loans. This means he was given more aid in the first year to entice him to enroll and less free aid in the second year. His mother pulled all stops to make it possible for Kevin to go to the college that recruited him, believing that the best institution was going to be the best insurance policy. She took the Parent PLUS loan for his first year and was having trouble paying it back. Kevin's mom paid her bills and had good credit. The financial aid administrator approved her for more Parent PLUS loans, but she refused. Since Kevin was a "dependent" student, he couldn't take out additional loans beyond the aggregate amount of Direct loans. Kevin looked for relatives and friends who would cosign on a private loan. Since he couldn't find anyone, he could not go back to school in the fall.

At first he was angry at his mother and it took him some time to realize that it was the right financial decision for both of them. Once I got to know Kevin, I persuaded him to show me his high school and college transcripts. He was above what I call an "emerging learner". He had mostly As and Bs in high school and three Cs in the first year of college. I thought he could have used a year or two at a community college to rack up some credits but Kevin looked crestfallen when I mentioned the word "community college." He said the kids who went there had a GED and he seemed proud to have graduated from high school. I realized then that no amount of persuading would have changed his mind.

I asked: "Are you ready to work your butt off?" Then I told him to visit three smaller, in-state, public universities. Kevin agreed to visit and decided to apply to Francis Marion University, where he was accepted immediately. He is passing his classes thus far, and I couldn't be happier for him. His Pell Grant and state grant cover almost all the tuition, and his federal loan and work-study covers the room and board. I believe in this kid. I want him to be successful. What I learned from this experience is that underserved kids may be more at risk at community colleges if they feel stigmatized by it. If they want a four-year degree, they are better off starting at a four-year college because they may encounter more motivated students on the four-year path. I hope this will turn out to be Kevin's story.

Let me make this comment about Kevin: his narrative is only too common with first-generation and under-resourced students. They want to go to college, but like many others, are susceptible to recruitment practices. The admission reps don't know who can afford their college and who cannot. If the student pulls at their sleeve, they will encourage the student to enroll. Students can be so easily sold on the name of the college, the reputation among friends, the emails and virtual invitations they received. Many students and parents don't realize that it's marketing, no different than when students market themselves to colleges by boosting the number of extracurricular activities they list on their application.

I believe in getting the most education and training possible for the lowest price and lowest possible debt. Too many adults carry student loan debt. Maybe fifty or a hundred years ago if you worked hard you could achieve the American dream. Today, the economy, skill-set needed and employment landscape are very different. Technology plays a role in most jobs. If Pell-eligible students don't start at community colleges or in-state colleges that fill their financial needs, they are more likely to take on "excessive" debt. For students who are Pell-eligible, any debt beyond the aggregate federal loan limits is likely "excessive." If they get themselves and their family into high debt starting in the first year, they may never get out of it. A high debt burden will limit their upward mobility.

High need families: If you work with families that have a high financial need, they will get "preferential packaging" at colleges that meet as close to 100% of their financial needs as possible. Typically, these colleges are very selective, but not always. Wofford College in SC meets 100% of need. Thank goodness for these colleges. They have endowments and other sources of funding that allows them to meet the entire financial need of each student. The challenge here is for these underserved students to work hard enough in high school so they can gain acceptance to these colleges.

Community colleges offer viable options: If students are not competitive in the applicant pool of colleges they want, they are aiming too high. They may need to humble themselves and start at the community colleges. If they are Pell-eligible, the Pell Grant could cover the costs or they may pay next to nothing. Students who transfer from a community college have the highest rate of success at four-year colleges and graduate school.

Need-blind explanation: Note that the expression "need-blind," doesn't mean colleges can fill demonstrated need. In fact, it's easy to be need-blind if a college doesn't meet financial need. It simply means that an admission decision will be made before the college knows the financial need of the student. This is the general rule anyway. The expression "need-aware" is more useful because it means the college will consider the student's financial need when admitting the student. This doesn't necessarily mean that the college is able to fill a large demonstrated need, such as a "zero EFC." As callous as this sounds, it's better than to admit students who can't possibly meet the price. Many colleges, especially on the for-profit side, from University of Phoenix to DeVry to Capella Online University to University of Arizona Global Campus in San Diego run their schools on the amount of federal aid that students bring to the college. The for-profit colleges typically attract adult students who are looking for an accelerated training to enter a specific industry. High school graduates are often unprepared for these schools as they are still trying to figure out what they should major in and which career will be suitable for them.

Get the facts: All families, whether their EFC is high or not, need to know the facts about the colleges they are considering by checking the college's scorecard at collegescorecard.ed.gov. Students, parents, and IECs, School Counselors should become familiar with this wonderful tool by U.S. Department of Education. Simply, type the name of the college and "score card." For example, if you search for

"College of Charleston scorecard" you will find https://collegescorecard.ed.gov/school/?217819-College-of-Charleston. The College Scorecard shows you the average cost, the graduation rate, and the average salary upon graduation.

Use the College Navigator: Another website I use frequently is the College Navigator from the National Center for Education Statistics at the U.S. Department of Education. It provides you with the tuition, fees, retention statistics, crime report, as well as the four-year costs at each college. Check also the colleges' websites under the tab "financial aid" or "admission and aid" to explore that institution's policies.

QuestBridge: Low-income students need to move away from high-cost colleges that are not meeting the family's financial needs. Pell-eligible students, under the best scenario, can try to get matched with colleges that partner with QuestBridge for full scholarships. High school counselors have information about the TRIO program which they give out to students who qualify for the free or reduced lunch program. If they leave their state, they could miss out for their in-state grants or merit scholarships. The U.S. Department of Labor has a free scholarship search tool as part of Career One Stop. Best of all, they can get matched to colleges that meet demonstrated financial need through QuestBridge.

AFC: All families, regardless of the ability to pay or lack thereof, need to review their financial aid award letters very carefully. They need to calculate their EFC under the federal and institutional methodology by using the EFC calculator on the College Board website, land compare the results to their **Affordable Family Contribution, the AFC**.

Take away: Colleges that use the CSS Profile form use an Institutional Methodology (IM) to assess families' EFC. This amount is different from the FAFSA EFC because it considers more resources. If students have a high demonstrated need and are super-achievers, they should apply to those colleges that meet 100% of demonstrated need. Middle income students need to cast a wide net by applying to various types of colleges that award both need and merit-based aid. Students whose EFC is higher than the cost of attendance (COA) should apply to those colleges that award merit-based aid primarily, regardless of demonstrated need. All families must compare award offers carefully, to discern which college is offering the best educational value, for the best price.

Meet Jacob

The 2020 academic year was anticlimactic for many students, especially for graduating high school seniors. Because of the Covid-19 pandemic and the need for social distancing, all graduation ceremonies were canceled. Jacob (not his real name) had been the captain of his frisbee team, lead actor in the school plays, treasurer for student council, and played an unusual instrument: the bagpipe. He felt he was getting no recognition for all his hard work.

He agonized over his decision whether to attend an out-of-state university or a private college about an hour from his home. "He became emotional," dad said. "Well, as emotional as a 17-year-old boy is capable of being" added mom. Jacob's parents had dutifully completed both the FAFSA and the CSS Profile in the fall of senior year. The financial aid administrators had been so nice to them. The price of both colleges was steep, though they had a good reputation and ranking. Then, in February of senior year, the Covid-19 pandemic took hold. By March, Jacob and his friends were home, studying online and playing video games the rest of the time. Jacob's dad, a marketing manager, was working part-time now and collecting unemployment.

The out-of-state university was well-known for its program in business and finance. The private college near their house offered excellent liberal arts classes. They examined their awards and noted that by attending an out-of-state university, Jacob would lose his in-state, lottery-funded scholarship of $5,000. The parents pointed this out to the out-of-state financial aid administrator, and she quickly added $5,000 as a scholarship into Jacob's package. This brought down the cost in line with the nearby private university.

Now, both Jacob and his parents were conflicted because both colleges were affordable. They talked, and talked, and talked. They thought of flipping a coin. Heads for the nearby private college, tails for the out-of-state public university. Parents became worried about having Jacob out-of-state, in case the virus raised its ugly head again. Immunologist, Dr. Fauci, Director of the National Institute for Infectious Diseases, was warning the public that the coronavirus could return in winter of 2020-21. Jacob's parents thought if schools closed again, and students were dismissed and sent home, as in early March 2020, wouldn't it make more sense to have Jacob attend a college closer to home? Besides, the coin landed on heads! Jacob and his parents agreed to send the commitment deposit to the private college that was less than an hour away. Jacob ended up taking human biology science classes with a few to going to med school. He discovered many of his peers were on the same path. This became the "Fauci Effect" that inspired a young generation to study the human sciences.

References

Baum, S. & Little, K. (2019). *IM: What Is It?* (download through www.eduave.com/resourcelibrary)

The College Board. (2020). *How to Complete the CSS Profile*

The College Board. (2019). *Tools & Calculators*

The College Board. *Institutional Methodology* (2021)

529 Plans Latest news from Mark Kantrowitz

Baum, S. (2004). *A Primer on Economics for Financial Aid Professionals* (download through www.eduave.com/resourceLibrary)

529 Plans

529 Plans: I get a lot of questions about 529 Plans from parents and grandparents. I'm not a financial planner and don't know which 529 plans are the best. I hear that states offer various deals but I have no idea whose is best! There's a huge amount of literature available. Morningstar publishes a white paper based on industry surveys on College Savings Plans. The website Savingforcollege.com publishes quarterly ratings of 529 plans. For the purpose of college financial aid, it matters whose name is on the 529 plan. Many grandparents have a 529 in their name that they have earmarked for a grandchild. There are ways to disburse the amounts to the colleges in a way that reaps greater financial benefit for the student.

Currently, money in a grandparent-owned 529 plan is not reported as an asset on the FAFSA, but distributions count as untaxed income to the student on a future FAFSA. Untaxed income can reduce the student's aid eligibility by as much as half the distribution amount.

Contrast that with money in a student or parent-owned 529 plan, which is reported as a parent asset on the FAFSA. This reduces financial aid by up to 5.64% of the asset value. Distributions are ignored.

There are several workarounds, such as:

- Transfer the money to a parent-owned 529 plan after the FAFSA is filed. Wait until after the FAFSA is filed because parent assets are reported as of the date the FAFSA is filed. If this money is spent before the next FAFSA is filed, it will have no impact on the student's financial aid. Be sure to use a parent-owned 529 plan in the same state as the grandparent-owned 529 plan, as some states have recapture rules if you rollover funds to an out-of-state 529 plan.
- You could also change ownership of the 529 plan to the parents, if this is allowed by the 529 plan. Not all 529 plans allow a change in ownership, except if the current owner dies or becomes incapacitated.
- Wait until after January 1 of the student's sophomore year in college to take a distribution from the 529 plan. This assumes that the student will graduate in four years. If the student will take five years to graduate, wait until January 1 of the junior year in college. Since the FAFSA uses prior-prior year income, waiting will prevent the distribution from being reported as untaxed income on a subsequent year's FAFSA.
- Wait until after the child graduates, then take a distribution to pay down up to $10,000 in student loans.

The good news is the Consolidated Appropriations Act, 2021, has changed the rules concerning untaxed income. Starting July 1, 2023, the FAFSA will no longer have a question about "cash support" (untaxed income). So, distributions from a grandparent-owned 529 plan will no longer reduce eligibility for financial aid on the FAFSA. It will probably still affect the CSS Profile form.

Parents must also consider when to disburse any 529 Plans to pay for qualified expenses. Aside from the sophomore year timing issue for grandparent-owned 529 plans, you also have to consider the impact of 529 plan money on the tuition tax credits, such as the American Opportunity Tax Credit or Lifetime Learning Tax Credit. These tax credits are based on amounts paid for tuition and textbooks. You can't also use the same tuition and textbook expenses to justify a tax-free distribution from a 529 plan. You can use each dollar of tuition and textbooks to justify only one tax break. Since the tuition tax credits are worth more per dollar of tuition and textbook expenses than a tax-free distribution from a 529 plan, it is best to carve out some tuition and textbook expenses (e.g., up to $4,000 for the American Opportunity Tax Credit and up to $10,000 for the Lifetime Learning Tax Credit) to justify the tuition tax credits, if you are eligible. Then, you can use the 529 plan distribution and student loans to cover the remaining costs.

Meet Luke, Jamie, Sonia and Tyler

Luke, Jamie, Sonia and Tyler are rising high school seniors preparing to go through the college admission and financial aid process! These four high school seniors couldn't be more different from one another! Each one worked hard in school; each one is seeking to find the best college major that will take them to a successful career. Luke, Jamie, Sonia and Tyler come from very different families and economic backgrounds, so each student has a different Expected Family Contribution (EFC). By now you know that that is, but if you want to double check, look it up in the "Glossary" at end of book. You know the Affordable Family Contribution (AFC) is a workable amount of money that student and parents can pay, regardless of what the college says you need to pay. Let's get to know Luke, Jamie, Sonia and Tyler. Let's give them some strategies they can use to minimize costs at the colleges that meet their academic and social needs.

Luke, Jamie, Sonia and Tyler present different grades and standardized test scores. They come from different socio-economic backgrounds. Luke, Jamie and Sonia are applying to colleges that use the FAFSA form only. Tyler is applying to colleges that use both FAFSA and CSS Profile. The CSS Profile form changes the financial aid calculations and EFC. One of these students' stories hopefully will resonate with you, your academic performance, and your financial situation. If not, there are more real student examples in future chapters.

Luke comes from a well-to-do family where both parents have Doctoral and terminal degrees and both have high-level employment. They have saved money for college for Luke and his younger sister. Luke's federal Expected Family Contribution (EFC) is $96,000. As of 2021-22, no college costs that much in the U.S. but it's not unconceivable that costs will break the $100K barrier in the next decade. This means that Luke doesn't have a financial need at any college. However, his parents' Affordable Family Contribution or AFC is different. They would like to find a college that fits Luke's personality and learning style AND costs between $30,000 to $40,000 per year. The amount they are willing to pay for Luke's four-year, undergraduate degree ranges from $140,000 to $160,000.

Jamie comes from a non-traditional family of artists, innovators and creative thinkers, who are technology and computer savvy. Dad is a multi-tasker and can write software manuals. Mom is a free-lance website developer. Their work is not steady. They may find well-paying assignments and then non for the rest of the year. They budget their finances carefully to make up for those months when they have no revenue. They have a daughter and younger son. Jamie attends a charter high school known for the strength of the arts in the curriculum. Jamie loves theatre arts and lives for those moments when she's on state, where she can let her words and emotions come alive in the characters she plays. Jamie's family's EFC is $45,000 but they want to spend much less. Their AFC is roughly $12,000 each year.

Sonia is the daughter of Hispanic parents and will be the first one in her family to attend college. Her father is the wage-earner and works as the head groundskeeper for a large company. His earnings range from $100,000 to $115,000 each year. Their EFC is $20,000, and it's going to be hard for this family to pay that much because Sonia has two younger siblings who will want to go to college in a few years. Their AFC is $10,000.

Tyler is an excellent African American student, and a gifted tennis player with a Zero EFC/SAI. Tyler takes two buses to get to his high school, which has the strongest academic curriculum in the state. Tyler lives with his grandparents who have raised him since birth. His mother was 16 when she had him, and she knows who the father is but he's married and has a large family of his own. After working in dead-end jobs, Tyler's mom moved to NYC to take a job as a nurses' aide. Recently, she started to attend the community college there where she is trying to get into the nursing program. On the FAFSA, Tyler's parent is his mom, because his grandparents did not adopt him legally. If they had, then they would be the adoptive parents who would file the FAFSA and CSS Profile. Tyler's EFC is zero, which means that he needs to apply to colleges that meet as close to 100% of demonstrated need as possible.

Let's take a look at the academics and expected financial contribution of each student's family. Also, let's consider the amount they can pay, their AFC.

Luke

Luke's Academic and Financial Stats.

Luke	GPA	SAT	ACT	EFC	AFC
Full I B	4.5/5	1470	35	$96,000	$35,000

Luke's parents earn well over $250,000 and Luke's Expected Family Contribution (EFC) is $96,000. We've established that Luke isn't a candidate for need-based financial aid. But, what if Luke's sister was old enough to enroll in college at the same time? In past decades, the CSS Profile EFC would be roughly more than half, or 120% divided by two ($96,000 x 1.20 divided by 2) = $57,600 for Tyler and $57,600 for his sister. If they both attended colleges that cost more than $57,600, and, if those colleges filled 100% of need, then Luke's family would demonstrate some financial need. For example, if Tyler and his sister's colleges cost $60,000, the amount of demonstrated need would be the difference, or $2,400. A merit scholarship or the federal Direct Loan would more than cover that amount. The reality here is that even when using these calculations, due to phase out in 2023-24, the cost of attendance is not significantly lower. The Consolidated Appropriations Act, 2021, took up 167 pages of the 5,593-page bill and changed this federal rule for parents paying for multiple kids in college at the same time. Families in this situation have until spring of 2023 to take advantage of this rule.

I hope it's clear that Luke demonstrates no financial need, so he will pay the full cost of attendance. A sample of these colleges is Davidson (NC), Amherst (MA), Williams (MA), the Ivies. The MyinTuition.org website will give you a list of colleges that meet 100% of financial need. These are highly selective colleges and many families do pay the sticker price because they know that the students will be well prepared to enter the workplace or continue to graduate school.

To get any discounts, Luke needs to look for merit scholarships. He needs to apply to colleges where he ranks at the top of the applicant pool **and** award merit aid. Do you see how many parameters students must look for? Then, Luke will be competitive for merit scholarships. There are many colleges that award more merit aid than need-based aid. These are excellent schools that have figured that scholarships are more effective ways to recruit students. The get students with better grades and test scores when they offer higher scholarships. Luke's academic performance is so high that at some of the smaller, lesser-known colleges he might receive a full-tuition scholarship. Luke would likely benefit from such a smaller college environment where the faculty members teach smaller classes and have time to interact with students, provide them individual support and mentoring. The professors would particularly appreciate a student as laid-back yet as high performing as Luke.

It's not unusual for high-income families to balk at the cost of elite colleges, when the sticker price is $80,000 per year, or $320,000 over four years. They may discuss this with their financial planner to see how they can best come up with a plan to pay. Some financial advisors may try to shift assets or investments in order to reduce the family's tax burden, but in some instances, this could backfire because maneuvers that would lower taxes often increase the Expected Family Contribution.

Besides, some shifting of assets could be dishonest if not illegal. There's a $20,000 fine and jail time if families file the forms with the intention of trying to hide income and assets. Financial aid administrators evaluate family's income tax returns day in and day out. They have more experience identifying fraud than parents have in perpetrating it. For example, financial aid administrators can impute the amount of investments by looking at the amount of interest or capital gains generated and reported on tax forms. They will know if you didn't report all your assets on the FAFSA.

If you work with financial planners relative to lowering your college costs, make sure that they understand how college financial aid works **at the particular colleges** where you're applying. For example, on FAFSA and CSS Profile any untaxed income is added back to the Adjusted Gross Income, thus increasing the EFC. Does your financial planner know how the federal and institutional aid formulas work, and the awarding policies of the colleges? Do they visit college campuses and work with students day in and day out to figure out who they are and where they will grow and thrive?

As mentioned, the best way for Luke to pay less for college is to seek out scholarships based on pure academic merit. The best scholarships will come from the college he applies to. These will be renewable each year, provided Luke maintains a specific grade point average. If Luke files the FAFSA, every college will send a financial aid package that will contain the unsubsidized Direct loan for $5,500. Parents may decide to let Luke take these loans just so he has skin in the game and to gains some financial literacy. Currently, the 2020-21 interest rate for undergraduate student loans is 2.75%, which is the lowest it's been in decades. Luke's parents are not interested in loans, not for themselves nor for their son. Other parents may want to invest in the stock market and let their student borrow since the rate is so low.

Compare Luke's college costs at his in-state public university, out of state public, elite private college:

In-State Public U.	**Out-of-state Public U.**	**Private Elite College**
Tuition 2021-22 $16,558	Tuition $38,390	Tuition $59,960
Room and Board $13,250	Room and Board $15,147	Room and Board $14,500
Books and Supplies $900	Books and Supplies $1250	Books and Supplies $800
Cost of Attendance $30,708	Cost of Attendance $54,787	Cost of Attendance $75,260

Luke's colleges with the school names:

College Type	In-State Public Univ	Out-of-state Public Univ	Private Elite College
Choice College List	Clemson	UCO-Boulder	Colorado Coll
Tuition	$16,558	$38,390	$59,960
Room and Board	$13,250	$15,147	$14,500
Books & Supplies	$900	$1,250	$800
Cost of Attendance	$30,708	$54,787	$75,260

(Data obtained from the National Center for Education Statistics and real colleges' websites.)

As you can see, if Luke attends his in-state institution he will pay $30,708 minus any available state grant. If state aid is awarded based on the family's demonstrated need, Luke will not receive any. In South Carolina, it's awarded based on test scores, GPA, and rank in Class, and Luke will receive the maximum amount. Thus, the amount of state scholarship depends on the state you live in. See the section on State Aid at the end of this book. If Luke attends an out of state public university his cost will be around $54,787. If he attends a private college that awards aid based on financial need only, the cost could be $75,260 on up.

State Scholarships: (See the Sampler in later chapters of this book.) Depending on which state a student lives in, the state may award aid based on demonstrated need, or merit alone, or a combination of both. Most states have no "free" aid. They offer loans which may/may not be competitive with federal rates and lending terms. Luke lives in South Carolina, and the state aid is awarded based on grades, test scores and rank in class. Because Luke is an excellent student, he would be eligible to receive the highest level of state scholarship. Other states that award aid without checking the FAFSA are South Carolina, which offers the Palmetto and Life scholarships; Florida, which offers the Bright Futures; and Georgia, which awards the HOPE scholarship. Most other states do require students to file the FAFSA.

For more information, check the section of this book under "State Aid." If Luke majors in the STEM sciences, he could obtain additional scholarships from the state in later years. The in-state university is a financial safety for Luke, whose parents want to spend around $30,000 per year. In fact, their net cost per year will be less due to the state scholarships. If Luke leaves the state, he will lose those funds. Other states, such as Vermont, allow residents to use some of the state funds to pay for out-of-state tuitions, although this policy is being debated in the State House with some representatives proposing that Vermont state funds should remain in Vermont and spent on Vermont colleges.

Out of state public institutions seldom offer generous scholarships to out-of-state students. Public universities are supported by the taxpayers of their state and their first priority is to educate its residents. Public universities are increasing costs of attendance across the nation because they have suffered major funding cuts. They relied on out-of-state students and international students to bolster revenues and keep afloat. When the pandemic hit and international students couldn't get visas to enter the United States and students went to college closer to home, these colleges, and especially the smaller ones with fewer than 2,500 students, struggled to stay afloat. Out of state universities don't have much "gift" aid to give out-of-state students, other than the federal aid. Students end up paying more at out-of-state public universities. Students like them because they want to get a change of scene. Maybe they live on the east coast, enjoyed skiing in Colorado, or Vermont or New Hampshire, and want to go to college there.

Are we all in agreement that at private colleges Luke will pay the sticker price? His EFC is higher than the cost of attendance at any U.S. college. At Colorado College, Luke's parents will pay $75,260 minus any merit scholarship. This college's top merit scholarship is $10,000. The net cost will be $65,260. Most IECs and School Counselors can't spend hours upon hours researching scholarships within each university department to identify a few options that the student or parents may dismiss. Since Luke was most interested in Colorado College, I encouraged him to research whether the department of his interest offered any internal merit scholarships. His interest in the sciences helped because fewer students are highly competitive in the STEM areas of chemistry, physics and biology. I knew he had some chances of finding scholarships to apply to may increase.

By driving the price down through the careful selection of colleges, Luke's list underwent several face-lifts. The starting list contained over 30 colleges from Harvey Mudd to Cal Tech to Olin School of Engineering in MA. But, these colleges awarded aid based on financial need, not merit. The second list targeted colleges that awarded substantial aid based on merit. These were: Purdue U. (IN), Worcester Polytechnic Institute, Wittenberg (OH); Duquesne, Creighton U (NE), Hope College (MI). Lycoming (PA), Providence College, Washington & Jefferson (PA), College of Wooster (OH). The parents said some on this list of colleges weren't "competitive" enough." The next list consisted of colleges that still awarded significant amounts of merit scholarships and were more selective: Gonzaga (WA), U C Boulder, Santa Clara (CA), SUNY Stony Brook, Colorado College, and Claremont McKenna. The rationale for selecting the last college was that the five-college consortium of the Claremont Colleges held a good deal of appeal.

The possibility for cross-registering at the other colleges was attractive to Luke. He initially was interested in Harvey Mudd due to its strong sciences program, but this college only awards need-based aid. Claremont-McKenna also offered majors in the sciences and liberal arts. The subjects from political science to Chemistry were taught in a practical, methodic way. The motto was "Learning for the sake of doing" and this suited Luke's personality and learning style. Claremont-McKenna was slightly less competitive to get into than Harvey Mudd. Claremont McKenna College would likely find a prospective student like Luke, who was planning to major in Chemistry or Biology, more interesting than Harvey Mudd College would. Claremont-McKenna seemed to offer more merit aid, especially for applicants headed for the sciences.

As Luke redefined his college priorities, he gained more insight into each college and the social life. Whereas the initial variables that were driving Luke's college search were large out-of-state public universities, now he focused more on identifying those private liberal arts colleges with excellent science programs that might have individual departmental scholarships.

This involved lots of research and pouring onto the National Center for Education Statistics examine the average amount of possible scholarships, scouring each college website for departmental scholarships in the sciences, and checking the Net Price Calculator on each site. This college list kept mutating. On the final list remained his two in-state universities which were "safeties" in terms of admissions, affordable for his parents, and well-fitting academically. The new choices were private colleges located throughout the United States, from Colorado, Washington, California and New York. Some of them touted a tad more diversity than he'd been exposed to at his primarily white, suburban high school. It was looking like a list of exciting colleges where Luke would find the classes, social life and academic challenge he wanted, and his parents would pay the price they wanted.

Jamie

Jamie's Academic Record and Her Story.

Jamie	GPA	SAT	ACT	EFC	AFC
Hon Track	3.4./5	0	21	$45,000	$12,000

Jamie's mother, Mrs. Johnson, called me when her daughter, Jamie, was in the junior year at a private high school. She wanted to make sure Jamie did everything right to get ready for college. She'd heard that the financial aid piece could be tricky and wanted to find out more about this.

I told Jamie's mom to compute her EFC by going to the College Board website, search for "EFC calculator," and bring me the results. It looked like Jamie's EFC was $45,000 under the Federal Methodology (FAFSA) and $52,000 under the Institutional Methodology (CSS Profile). Mrs. Johnson was less than happy. She was flabbergasted. She and her husband were in their early 50's and wanted to start saving for their retirement. After they examined their family budget, they decided their Affordable AFC was $12,000. The same amount was going to be allocated for Jamie's young brother in a few years.

At this beginning point, there was a problem. It was that Jamie had only one college on her mind: The Toronto Academy of Acting and Film & Television School. Her parents rolled their eyes. Mom raised the concern that Jamie was already having trouble getting up in the morning and often was tardy for school because she overslept. Mom had to prod her to get up and get ready for the carpool. Same story when it came to studying and doing homework. "How would you function in another country when you can't even manage life at home?" asked mom. Jamie gave a long and loud sigh and said: "I feel constantly under pressure, with homework I can never finish and meet all those strict deadlines." I made a mental note to remind myself that Jamie did not need to go to a cut-throat competitive school. This vivacious young woman was burning out with the amount of work she had to do for school. She needed to find colleges where she could enjoy a balance between study and social life.

In my subsequent meetings, Jamie's college list became quite large. I guided her to research colleges that offered theatre programs in the U.S. for students with her C, C+ grades. This was the starting list: Alfred University, Brevard College, Catawba, College of Santa Fe, Columbia College (Chicago), De Sales University; De Paul University, Emory and Henry, High Point, Keene State, Oglethorpe University, McDaniel College, Moravian, North Carolina School of the Performing Arts, SUNY Purchase and Point Park College.

Jamie diligently explored each one online and became especially interested in Oglethorpe University and SUNY Purchase because they had strong Drama/Acting/Theater Arts programs. This exploration turned out to provide an emotional growth process. As Jamie researched colleges, I encouraged her to correspond with the admission representatives. She began to see the differences between the programs along with the varying admission requirements. She grew to understand which college was a reach, a possible, or a safety school. She also checked the price tag attached to each.

Compare Jamie's college costs at her in-state public university, out-of-state public University and private college below:

College Type	In-State Public	Out-of-State Public	Private College
College List		SUNY	Oglethorpe U
Tuition 2012-2022	$15,946	$19,690	$41,370
Room and Board	$9,968	$14,548	$13,500
Books & Supplies	$1,200	$1,250	$1,200
Cost of Attendance	$27,114	$35,488	$56,070

***Data obtained from the National Center for Education Statistics and real colleges' websites.**

All three colleges were likely acceptances for Jamie because her grades and test scores ranked in the middle of their listed admission requirements. One additional cost of the public universities was due to the fees. Public universities don't charge a high tuition for its residents, so they make up for financial shortfalls by charging fees. You will notice that some public universities, such as UMA-Amherst, have fees that are as high or higher than tuition. The fee at the in-state university was $3,120, and $3,750 at the out-of-state university. The private college started to look good when Jamie read on the website that it would match the tuition of the student's in-state flagship institution. It did not specify whether it was with or without fees, but it sounded good enough. Jamie's in-state tuition was $15,946 and with fees it came to $19,066.

This college's website indicated that "over 90% of their students qualified for merit scholarships worth $18,000 per year." One would assume they were quoting averages. Jamie saw that the drama department offered an additional scholarship for theatre majors: one full tuition scholarship along with an internship with a professional theatre company. Jamie and her parents really liked this small private college located in a big, thriving city. "But wait, wait, there's more!" Jamie chanted. "If the student is eligible for state aid, the college matched it!" The family got in the car and drove to the college for "Scholarship Weekend", to see if they could get Jamie in for the price of their in-state tuition minus the state aid, and possibly, a drama scholarship as well. Jamie added the amounts in her head and wondered if she could get paid to go to college!

This private college that according to Jamie, was "it", required all drama scholarship applicants to audition. Jamie's eyes lit up. "I have auditioned many times already. I know what to expect and I already know which monologues I would choose." The college fit her perfectly, she claimed, and the swath of liberal arts classes would provide her with the general exposure to the humanities and social sciences as well. This way, she would continue to develop as an actor and gain valuable learning in other areas.

The visit to the college during the "scholarship weekend" proved to be extremely instructive for both Jamie and her parents. Apparently, you could not double up on scholarships. You either won one or the others. Jamie didn't win the full-tuition scholarship for Drama and the cost of attendance at the private college was well over $40,000. Following more visits, her eyes lit up when she visited the Theater Arts Department at Winthrop University, which was only 20 minutes from Charlotte in NC, but still located in SC where she could pay in-state tuition and obtain the LIFE state scholarship for $5,000 each year. Upon further inquiry, it turned out that Jamie could get an additional $2,000 merit scholarship if she brought up her ACT by 2 points.

This brought out the competitor in her. She re-took her ACT and improved it! It went from a 21 to a 24! The $2,000 scholarship was renewed each year and saved her $8,000 over the four years. It was lucky that Jamie started researching her colleges at the beginning of her junior year because it gave her time to re-take a standardized test and grow in her ability to assess colleges relative to her personal needs. Her explorations gave her a clearer picture of reality, and all thoughts of the Art School in Toronto disappeared. Jamie confessed that each of the college visits was a real eye opener. The college she chose matched up with what she dreamed of and met her parents' Affordable Family Contribution, AFC.

Sonia

Sonia is an 18-year-old in her senior year of high school. She lives in New Jersey with her mom, dad, and two younger siblings, Megan, 14, and Jason, 13. Both parents completed high school but did not attend college. Sonia will be the first child in their family to start college. Sonia is both friendly and quiet. She doesn't care to lead and does well if she can follow a strong leader. In the past, she's followed a friend or advanced in school because of the nurturing and support of a teacher. Sonia likes sports, music, children, and people, especially her friends. Her mom says Sonia is a natural with younger kids. From the age of 12 Sonia could be trusted to take care of her younger siblings. She gets many requests for babysitting and children love her. For this reason, Sonia considered becoming an elementary teacher.

However, she also wants to find a job that pays well when she graduates. She learned that teachers don't make much money and so she's exploring other majors. She said she was interested in forensics because her favorite TV show is Forensic Files II. Most of all, Sonia wants a career that will make her financially independent. For this reason, the college counselor encouraged her to explore more lucrative careers, such as business administration, accounting, health services.

Academics: Sonia attends a public high school in New Jersey with 1,100 students, of which 309 are seniors. She ranks in the middle 50 percent of her class (#150 at the end of junior year). She has taken college preparatory classes and will take one AP class, AP Human Geography, in senior year; her unweighted GPA is 3.4. She's not a good test-taker: her ACT is 19 and her SAT is 1050. The scores are too low to get her into her state flagship institution, Rutgers in New Brunswick, which is the most selective campus, and costs $36,120 for nearby residents. Sonia heard that she could go "test optional," especially during Covid-19 pandemic because the testing services cancelled the test dates. Sonia and her college counselor are looking into schools that are test-optional or are waving the requirement. Meanwhile, the admissions rep from a private college in New Jersey had been talking with Sonia. He invited Sonia to visit the campus, and she really liked it.

Sonia started out interested in several colleges for Speech and Drama primarily, Math and Science secondarily. In High school she was in the "College Prep" track and had taken a few honors classes. She said she enjoyed Biology and Earth Science. She liked them because "I'm good at them"! Here's a bit of background you need to hear from Sonia's mother: "She's truly is an inspiration! When she was a baby, just three months old, I knew something was off. When she turned two, she rarely spoke, and we began early intervention. When she turned three our school district took over. I fought for my child and finally, in third grade, we received a diagnosis: autism. I fought for her needs daily and came close to suing the district several times for not following her IEP. I never thought Sonia would go to a regular high school, have friends, learn to drive, or go to college!

Well, she is doing all that and more! She's gotten involved with the theatre group and has performed on stage. She's high functioning. Sonia has anxiety but many people suffer from anxiety. Since 9th grade in high school, she would go to meet college representatives at lunch time. I was thinking about RCBC (Rowan County at Burlington County Community College) or TCNJ, (Rowan College of South Jersey Cumberland Campus). Sonia didn't like it. Mom told Sonia that whatever she chose, she was behind her a thousand percent! Mom told her that regardless of how well she did on her SATs, she'd go to college. But mom meant "community college!" Sonia was very stubborn.

Mom worried that Sonia might not be able to handle a college she was not into. Mom wanted Sonia to be mainstreamed in a place where she'd be accepted for who she was. "Many people don't know she's on the spectrum." said mom.

Sonia	**GPA**	**SAT**	**ACT**	**EFC**	**AFC**
CP track	2.9/5	1050	18	$20,000	$10,000

Sonia's family used the EFC Calculator on the College Board site and saw even before they filed the FAFSA, that their federal EFC was roughly $20,000. You can review and download Sonia's SAR from my website: www.eduave.com/libraryresources, as well as a mock SAR provided by the U.S. Department of Education.

Sonia's Student Aid Report:

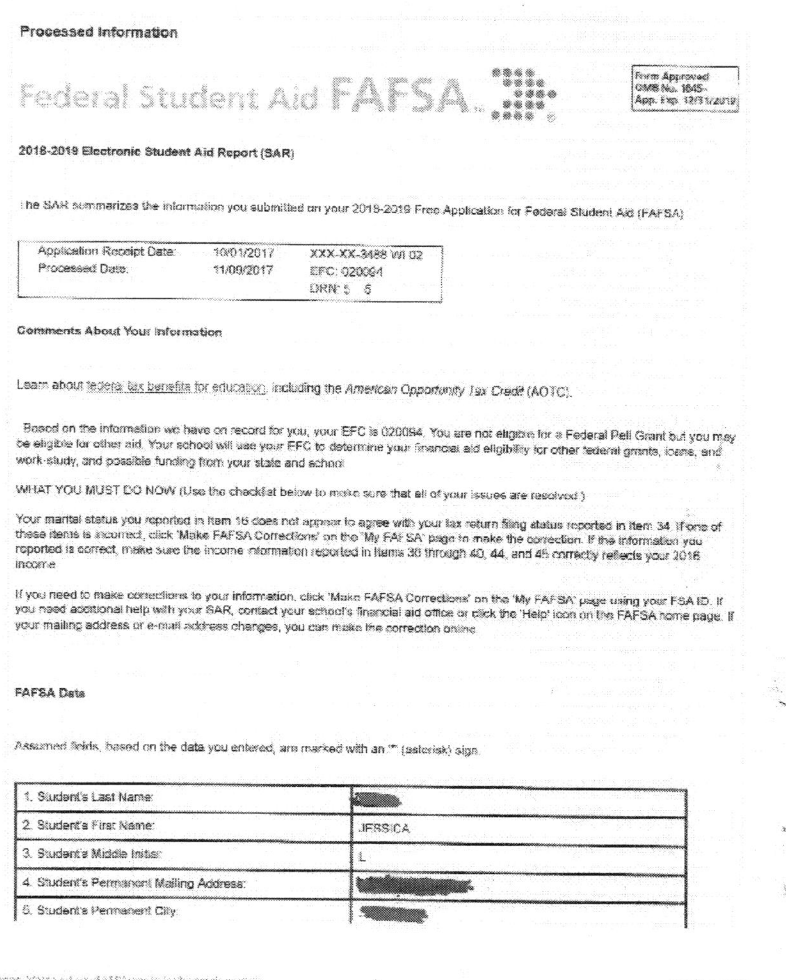

Processed Information

Federal Student Aid FAFSA

Form Approved
OMB No. 1845-
App. Exp. 12/31/2019

2018-2019 Electronic Student Aid Report (SAR)

The SAR summarizes the information you submitted on your 2018-2019 Free Application for Federal Student Aid (FAFSA)

Application Receipt Date:	10/01/2017	XXX-XX-3488 WI 02
Processed Date:	11/09/2017	EFC: 020094
		DRN: 5 6

Comments About Your Information

Learn about federal tax benefits for education, including the *American Opportunity Tax Credit* (AOTC).

Based on the information we have on record for you, your EFC is 020094. You are not eligible for a Federal Pell Grant but you may be eligible for other aid. Your school will use your EFC to determine your financial aid eligibility for other federal grants, loans, and work-study, and possible funding from your state and school.

WHAT YOU MUST DO NOW (Use the checklist below to make sure that all of your issues are resolved.)

Your marital status you reported in Item 16 does not appear to agree with your tax return filing status reported in Item 34. If one of these items is incorrect, click 'Make FAFSA Corrections' on the 'My FAFSA' page to make the correction. If the information you reported is correct, make sure the income information reported in Items 36 through 40, 44, and 45 correctly reflects your 2016 income.

If you need to make corrections to your information, click 'Make FAFSA Corrections' on the 'My FAFSA' page using your FSA ID. If you need additional help with your SAR, contact your school's financial aid office or click the 'Help' icon on the FAFSA home page. If your mailing address or e-mail address changes, you can make the correction online.

FAFSA Data

Assumed fields, based on the data you entered, are marked with an '*' (asterisk) sign.

1. Student's Last Name:	
2. Student's First Name:	JESSICA
3. Student's Middle Initial:	L
4. Student's Permanent Mailing Address:	
5. Student's Permanent City:	

Sonia's dad has an Adjusted Gross Income (AGI) of $115,338. Sonia's mom has no earned income. They had $10,000 in savings and nothing in retirement. Upon learning that most colleges "gap," which means they don't fill 100 percent of need, Sonia's mom was distressed. The EFC of $20,000 alone was high for her family, and she worries about funding colleges for Sonia's 14-year-old sister and 13-year-old brother. Their AFC price point for each year is $10,000.

Middle-income families are hard hit in the college search because they don't qualify for federal grants, such as the Pell Grant while the EFCs are high as a percentage of their available income. Consider that most residents at their in-state public institutions will pay nearly $15,000 for tuition and nearly the same for room and board. For example, in-state Cost of Attendance (COA) at Rutgers (New Brunswick) was $ 33,457 in 2019-20. The net price by income, as reported on the College Navigator website, is as follows:

Full-time beginning undergraduate students who paid the in-state or in-district tuition rate and were awarded Title IV aid by income.

AVERAGE NET PRICE BY INCOME (Rutgers, NJ)

INCOME	2016-17	2017-18	2018-19
$0 – $30,000	$11,640	$12,108	$13,545
$30,001 – $48,000	$13,839	$13,671	$15,779
$48,001 – $75,000	$20,201	$19,727	$20,935
$75,001 – $110,000	$26,280	$26,305	$26,914
$110,001 and more	$27,819	$28,187	$29,335

You will notice that families with zero to $30,000 in income pay $13,545, which is a huge amount if the student has a zero EFC. The Pell Grant would cover up to $6,430 that year so the financially viable option would be the community college for the first two years. A family with adjusted gross income between $75,000 and $110,00 pays a net price of $26,914 on average. This is a quarter of the annual income that Sonia's family brings in. Rutgers is an obvious bargain for those who earn more than $110,001 because $29,335 becomes an incrementally smaller portion of their income.

Sonia's College Selection

College Type	Community College	In-State Public	Private College
Choice: College List	RCBC	Rowan U	Rider
Tuition 2021-2022	$5,159	$14,000 Fees: $5,328	$44,460
Room and Board	N/A	$17,961	$14,390
Books &Supplies	$1,200	$1,850	$1,500
Cost of Attendance	$6,359	$39,139	$60,350

***Data obtained from the National Center for Education Statistics and real colleges' websites.**

At the two-year public community college, the costs for Sonia's family were about half their AFC. Most community colleges don't provide room and board. Sonia didn't drive and her mother would have had to take her. If one were to calculate the costs of housing and feeding a student at home and apply them to the cost of Room and Board, the end cost would be the same. If Sonia went to community college and lived at home there would be costs for transportation to and from the college, food, usage of water, electricity, and heating/cooling.

Sonia's in-state public university cost is nearly double this family's EFC. When the private college gave Sonia a $25,000 scholarship and another "Campus Connection Grant" for $3,000, the private college became less expensive than the in-state university (Private College $60,350 - $25,000 - $3,000 = $32,350.) It pays to shop these smaller, private colleges and compare their net costs to those of an in-state public university. If you looked at the sticker price of the private college without considering what might be your net cost, you'd think it was out of Sonia's reach. In fact, it was less expensive than the public university!

On a rational level, Sonia should be going to her local community college, but her parents saw a huge benefit in Sonia living in a residence hall, learning to share space with roommates and make friends. She would be able to continue taking speech and drama classes to continue practicing her speech-language skills. The learning specialist at the learning center reviewed Sonia's educational evaluation and assured this mom that Sonia's academic support would be available and provided on a regular basis. After much debating, where Sonia almost ended up at RCBS, her parents asked their relatives to chip in and help. Grandpa stepped up to heed the call. Against all odds and costing more than their "Affordable Family Contribution", Sonia is attending this private college. To this date, she's been able to keep up her grades and maintain the scholarship.

This is a case where the "Affordable Family Contribution" was met with the help of relatives. The most important variable was placing Sonia was a small, nurturing environment with friendly and supportive peers who would be accepting of Sonia's "quirky" ways. She is being successful there and is keeping up her grades. Granted, if grandpa hadn't stepped in to meet Sonia's college costs, the parents would have sent her to RCBS.

If families are on the cusp of qualifying for Pell Grant funding, adding any small amount of earned income or untaxed income will likely move them out of Pell Grant range. For example, when a parent receives means-tested aid such as social security or child support, these amounts are added back to the Adjusted Gross Income and increase the EFC. **In 2023-24 however**, the new FAFSA rules approved by Congress in Dec of 2020 will go into effect: child support or alimony received will no longer count into the assessment of the EFC. This is a huge break for those low-income families whose student is eligible for the Pell grant but loses it once the child support received is added back "above the line." This untaxed earned income will no longer increase the family's EFC, and will apply to those parents who separated or divorced after 2019.

Tyler

Tyler's Story

Tyler	GPA	SAT	ACT	EFC	AFC
Academic Magnet	5.312/5	1510	36	$0	$0

Tyler is a high achieving student at one of the most highly regarded public schools in the state. He lives with his grandparents who have taken care of him since he was born. His mother was unmarried when she gave birth to him at 17 years of age. The family figured out who the father was but he went on to get married and now has a large family of his own. He doesn't come around to visit Tyler nor does he provide any support. Tyler's grandparents didn't adopt him, so according to the federal methodology, they aren't the ones to file the FAFSA. Had they adopted Tyler, then they would be adoptive parents and would be financially responsible for contributing to Tyler's education.

Tyler's biological parent is his mom, 34, and she is "the parent" according to FAFSA rules. Mom lived in New York City, where she had found work as a nurse's aide at a retirement center. She was taking classes at a community college toward a degree in nursing. Tyler completed the FAFSA with his mother's financial information and his EFC came out to zero. To gain more information about "zero EFC" assessment for the 2021-22 federal methodology, you can review the EFC Formula Guide.

Tyler was now a rising senior. He was a delightful, if quiet, young man, top student and especially gifted in Calculus. I could see that a top college would not question his academic ability. He was also a gifted tennis player and earned some pocket money by giving private lessons. Tyler, however, was without any means to pay for college.

Tyler's Personality and Learning Style Preferences: Tyler has a slight preference for Introversion, though you'd never know it because he can be gregarious, entertaining with his friends.

His early years were marked by the loving stability of his grandparent. In recent years he became very aware of his financial situation, especially because most students at his school came from wealthy homes. During his initial meetings with me, Tyler tended to keep his thoughts to himself, no matter how important. He didn't reveal more than he had to. I wondered why he didn't volunteer more information about himself, his family and his grades.

Eventually, I realized he wanted to be accurate. He paid careful attention to details and he naturally came up with correct answers. When asked about his feelings relative to entering a major and a career in which he would feel happy, he tended to focus more on what he could do right here and now versus exploring future possibilities. He was an excellent student but never thought of graduate school for himself. He was the top tennis player on the school team but never thought to leverage that skill in college.

In the following one-on-one meetings, we began to explore more general fields of study where he could apply his strengths for details, accuracy. and preference for practical information. We looked at such majors as applied science, finance, securities, and statistics. Tyler had real strengths in organizing the external world with logical categories, putting facts into an orderly sequence, and paying attention to detail. He loved Excel spreadsheets, crossing off items on a daily to-do list, and keeping a physical notebook planner to manage every hour of his time. We checked out the Bureau of Labor Statistics Occupational Handbook, to find out what careers have the best salaries and futures.

Tyler started out with a long list of colleges that met demonstrated need. He spent much time on College Navigator, comparing colleges and learning about the retention rate. His preference for analysis and logic, facts and figures helped him to sort out what he wanted in a college. He relied on his internally stored information to test reality and actual events. At first we looked at small liberal arts colleges, and as much as he liked them, he felt that they classes focused much more on the process rather than the destination. Tyler liked binary answers because they gave him immediate feedback as to whether the answer was right or wrong. In choosing a major, Tyler wanted to carefully evaluate all the facts relative to eventually finding a job that would enable him to support himself and live a financially comfortable life. Hence his choice of major changed from liberal arts business, finance, and even engineering.

Tyler's initial college list: Swarthmore, Trinity College (CT); Amherst College, Cooper Union, Wake Forest, Morehouse College, Howard U, Georgia Institute of Technology, Northwestern University, Duke, NYU, and Columbia. As we continued to work together, it became evident that Tyler was gaining insight into issues of affordability concerning his race. It wasn't an easy discussion especially the one about loans. Even at colleges that meet 100% of demonstrated need, a student must take out the "self-help" portion of federal aid. This consists of work-study and loans for undergraduate students.

I explained that in first year, the amount of federal Direct loan is $5,500, and of this, $3,500 would be subsidized because Tyler demonstrated financial need.

Tyler thought about this and learned that Black students default at five times the rate of white Bachelor's degree graduates. He learned that the Black borrowers get hit especially hard. He quoted Julia Barnard, a student debt expert at the Center for Responsible Lending. "There's structural discrimination, and it's a larger civil rights issue."

He watched a webinar by Dr. Dominique Baker, Assistant Professor at Southern Methodist University. Her research and statistics showed that Black students are still not benefiting from their graduation as much as white students. "It's not just about completion. It's about race. Black students are struggling to pay even though they got their degree."

Tyler wasn't one to make a snap judgment and continued to explore the financial aid not only at the HBCUs on his list but also the "elite" liberal arts colleges. I reassured him that even if he had to take out the federal student loans for undergraduate students, he wouldn't be a statistic.

Compare Tyler's college costs at his selected colleges:

College Type	HBCU	In-State Public	Private College
Choice: College List	**Howard U (FAFSA only)**	**UNC-CH (CSS Profile)**	**Columbia U (CSS Profile)**
Tuition 2021-22	$27,206	$8,950	$61,788
Room and Board	$15,147	$14,276	$16,670
Books &Supplies	$1,900	$972	$1,294
Cost of Attendance	**$44,253**	**$24,228**	**$79,752**

***Data obtained from the National Center for Education Statistics and real colleges' websites.**

This exercise persuaded Tyler to consider taking a calculated risk. As his search continued, Tyler realized that although the first three liberal-arts colleges on his list met 100 percent of demonstrated need, they didn't offer the depth of programming in science and engineering that he wanted. He moved on to research the Historically Black Colleges such as Morehouse, Hampton and Howard University. These schools did not meet his demonstrated need and his bottom-line cost would have resulted in borrowing a significant amount. He realized that the regional public and small private institutions often do not have that lifeline to support their neediest students.

Tyler kept his public, in-state university top of mind as a financial safety. He knew he'd get the state scholarship, which was funded by the state lottery. *

After all colleges on his list were considered, Tyler understood that his minimum cost would be the federal direct loans of $5,500 in first year, $6,500 in second year, and $7,500 in third and fourth year. This would mean that he'd graduate with roughly $27,000 in debt, regardless of where he attended. The benefit here would be that his mother would not need to take out any Parent PLUS loans.

The choice became clear when Columbia University in NYC offered him a financial aid award which made it the least expensive. The graduation rate there for Black or African American students there was 98%, which was even higher than the graduation rate at the HBCUs Tyler considered. At Columbia, he'd join the Black Alumni Council where he might make connections with his own people and find mentors. He was excited about going to NYC which meant that he would be able to see more of his mom.

Footnote* The ironic part is that many state lotteries are funded by people buying lottery tickets, and poorer people buy them more than the wealthy. State scholarships based on academic merit benefit students with high SAT scores. Well-to-do families can afford to pay for their students to get test prepped or get tutored. Tyler discovered that lotteries are supported by poor families but benefit the wealthier students. Students with high scores end up securing those scholarships more often than poorer students.

Footnote** What is a quick way for parents to gain an estimate of their Expected Family Contribution before filing the FAFSA? Launch a browser and type "EFC calculator" or use the College Board's EFC calculator.

Reflections and Considerations

Luke's EFC is higher than the Cost of Attendance "COA" of all colleges because both parents have high-earning jobs. It doesn't mean that his parents can afford to pay $320,000 over four years. Where can Luke find money to lower the costs? Luke needs to apply where he can get merit scholarships from the colleges. Scholarships from the colleges that accept Luke will be the most valuable. These are renewable each year for four years, provided the student maintains a specified grade point average. Luke could seek outside scholarships from various companies and organizations. He can contribute his own money, saved from work and from birthday gifts. Luke can apply to colleges where he ranks at the top of their applicant pool and award merit-based aid. At the private colleges that interest him, Luke can search for STEM scholarships offered by the individual departments.

Jamie's Expected Family Contribution "EFC" of $45,000 is way over the amount the family wants to pay. Her Affordable Family Contribution "AFC" is roughly $12,000. What can Jamie do to find colleges closer to her AFC? Jamie can apply to her in-state regional colleges where tuition is less than at the "flagship" institution. Jamie can search for private colleges where she ranks at the top of their applicant pool. Jamie can audition for merit scholarship from the Theater/Drama department.

Sonia and her parents are shocked at the net cost of attendance at the private college, until they compared costs with the state university. What did they find? When they compared costs, they found that the net cost of the private school was slightly less than the cost of the in-state private university. Sonia would not get into the public flagship in her state. It turns out that the private college is also better match for Sonia because of the learning support and social opportunities that will enhance Sonia's development.

Tyler's takeaway is that financially needy students need to apply to colleges that award aid primarily based on need. There's a future for those academically high achieving students whose parents earn less than approximately $65,000 a year (for a family of four with minimal assets.) When students have a zero EFC as Tyler did, they need to identify those colleges that have deep pockets. Some colleges like Amherst College in Massachusetts are need-blind. If you're admissible on the basis on your academic and extra-curricular performance, you will graduate with no loans.

The Ivies and these elite colleges are looking for students just like Tyler, who showed extraordinary academic ability despite his financial difficulties. These are students who may be the first in their family to attend college. They may have maintained a part-time job to help their families pay bills. They may have distinguished themselves in volunteer work in or outside the classroom. There are programs like QuestBridge that identify underserved students and match them up with colleges. The QuestBridge website includes a list of colleges that meet 100% of demonstrated need. Tyler's award from Columbia University had no loans, no work study, and opportunity to walk onto the tennis team.

Not all students are as high performing as Tyler who took four AP classes in Junior year and four in senior year. All students need to check out their in-state universities and local community colleges. It's not where you start college that matters. Graduating with an Associate's degree from a community college or a Bachelor's degree requires motivation, hard work and belief in oneself.

There's no shame in attending a community college. Many wealthy families enroll their children at these institutions because they pay less and offer excellent education and training. In fact, community colleges are wonderful places to start college. If students complete the Associate's degree, they can transfer to a four-year college and get credit for the first two years of a four-year degree. Community colleges offer many support services, from writing centers to study skills classes to special help for students with learning disabilities. For these and other reasons, community colleges are a best kept secret!

The "Higher Education Community Forum" presented in April 2020, by Dr. Dominique Baker of Southern Methodist University, researched the effects of student loans on low-income and minority students. These students drop out before earning a degree. They take out larger loans than non-minority students. Even when they graduate they are less likely to find work and earn less than non-minority students. This means that first-generation and minority students must be even more careful before accepting loans and must be ready to start at the community college to lower the costs for the first two years.

Tyler circled round to his public, in-state university, and kept it in front of mind as a financial safety. He knew he'd get the state scholarship, which was funded by the state lottery. Depending on whether the lottery had money, students received more or lesser amounts. Tyler discovered the ironic part about state scholarships funded by lotteries: poorer people who tend to buy the tickets. State lottery scholarships benefit students with high SAT scores. Who has high scores? Those students who can prep for them. Studies show that these students come from the wealthier families who can afford the price of SAT prep programs.

Key Takeaways

- Families with high EFCs: Luke's EFC is higher than the Cost of Attendance "COA" of even the most expensive colleges in 2021-22 need to look for merit scholarships.
- Families with middle of the road EFCs like Jamie's need to identify their AFC, an amount that is workable and feasible for the family to pay.
- Families with lower EFCs: Sonia and her parents need to cast a wide net and apply to many different colleges. They will qualify for both merit and need-based aid.
- Why is it important for families to calculate their EFC? They need to gauge if the EFC is similar to their AFC. They need to view if there's a big gap between their EFC and what the college offered in financial aid. Parents need to know what is their EFC under the Federal Methodology (FAFSA) and the Institutional Methodology (CSS Profile) compare them to the amount the colleges offer. Which award package is closest to their "Affordable Family Contribution" or AFC?
- Families with zero EFCs need to be careful about taking on debt. Students who have excellent grades and test scored should apply to highly selective colleges and universities that meet as close to 100% of demonstrated need as possible. For example, Davidson College in NC meets 100% of demonstrated need. The net cost could be the same or less than at a public institution. If students' grades are not stellar, they should carefully evaluate the options at their in-state universities, regional campuses and community colleges. See the appendix for more detailed information.

References

Accurate Statistics on student retention, graduation, employment: collegescorecard.ed.gov

Baker, Dominique J., *When Average Is Not Enough: A Case Study Examining the Variation in the Influences on Undergraduate Debt Burden,* AERA Open, June 27, 2019.

Baum, S., Ma, J., Pender, M., Libassi, C. J. (2018). *Trends in Student Aid*, College Board.

Blagg, K., Chingos, M. M., Graves, C., Nicotera, A., Shaw, L. (2017). *Rethinking consumer information in higher education.* Urban Institute.

Cattaneo, M. D., Idrobo, N., Titiunik, R. (Forthcoming). *A practical introduction to regression discontinuity designs* (Vol. 1). Cambridge University Press.

Dixon-Roman, Ezekiel J.; Howard Everson and John J. Mcardle, *Race, Poverty and SAT Scores: Modeling the Influences of Family Income on Black and White High School Students' SAT Performance,* Teachers College Record, April 2013.

Figlio, D. N., Lucas, M. E. (2004). ***What's in a grade? School report cards and the housing market.*** American Economic Review, 94, 591–604.

National Center for Education Statistics, *College Navigator*

Occupations that are in demand: https://www.onetonline.org/

U.S. Department of Education, Office of Postsecondary Education . (2019). *College affordability and transparency explanation form: Summary guide to college costs for the 2018 collection year.*

Strategic Enrollment Management and You

Why do we need to pay attention to Strategic Enrollment Management? It has to do with how much you will pay for college. It has to do with merit scholarships, preferential packaging, and the man behind the curtain.

The history of "Strategic Enrollment Management" started in the 1970's when Jack Maguire, then Dean of Admissions at Boston College realized that if he were to take in financially needy students he also needed students who could pay the full amount.

As the inquiries and applications filled the enrollment funnel, he intentionally selected students who were both academically and financially strong. Then in the 1980s they built up their football team and applications started pouring in after Doug Floutie won the Heisman trophy. One wonders what the football team had to do with the quality of education, but it just so happens that students and parents enjoy those tailgate parties at Notre Dame, where "touch-down Jesus" is a revered event along with other traditions. Boston College became more selective and financially wealthy as more students arrived with higher credentials and more family funding.

Maguire Associates was the trailblazer who opened the practice of enrollment management for other colleges to establish marketing as a field of its own. Then came Noel-Levitz, Ruffalo-Cody and many other groups that continued to open the field and take it to a new level, with ways to leverage financial aid to build and shaper the class that colleges want. Here's a picture of the traditional enrollment management funnel:

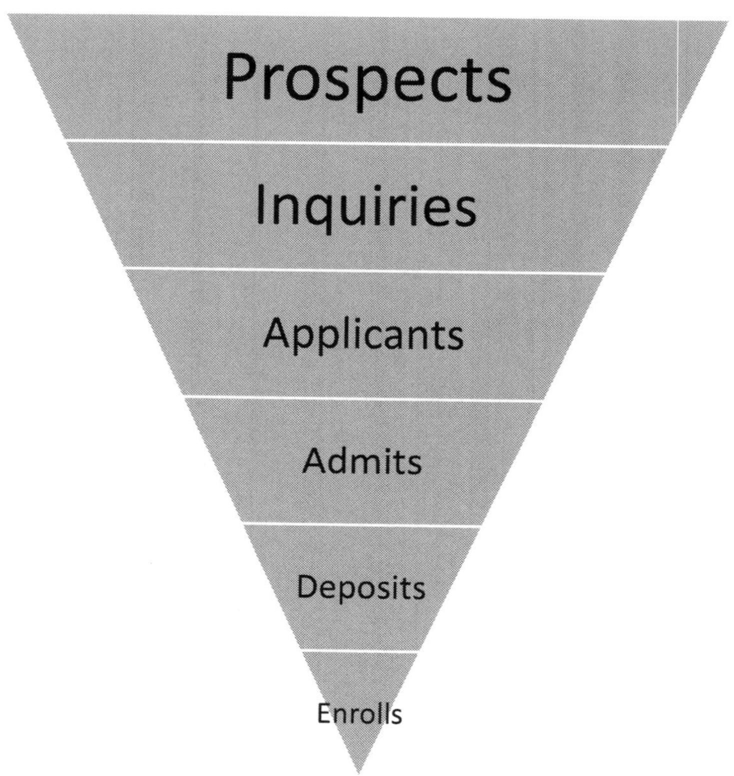

Colleges have weathered many ups and downs over the twentieth and twenty-first centuries, also affected by whether or not there were enough students to go around. In 2021, colleges are facing a demographic cliff: the pool of college-age students is smaller, and the Covid-19 pandemic put another nail on the enrollment coffin.

Many students postponed starting college, or took virtual classes from home, thereby shorting the income colleges expected to receive from room and board. Current students took leaves of absence to wait out the pandemic. Low-income and first-generation students were also much less likely to apply for admission. Students who did apply for admission were staying closer to home.

Due to Covid, colleges haven't been able have students visit their campus, which remains the most promising way to recruit. However, I found that one of the best sites to visit colleges virtually is https://campustours.com/. The "Open House" events have gone virtual, which cannot replace having parents and student visit in person, take a guided tour, eat in the cafeteria, sit in on classes, stay overnight in the dorms and meet an admission representative or a member of the faculty.

The coronavirus has prevented college admission representatives from traveling to high schools in person, to meet students in person or participate in college fairs. It's harder for colleges to get across the particular flavor of what they offer, their sense of their community, and what they stand for. This has affected the way colleges recruit, manage student services on and off campus, and teach classes.

The pandemic will have lasting effects in the way that colleges will deliver education. Although the on-campus experience is beneficial, online training can only get bigger and better.

Most colleges went test optional, since many SAT and ACT test administrations were cancelled due to the pandemic.

Enrollment management will adapt to the new landscape, and will continue to be the science of probability and statistics.

Consultants and college advisors are well aware of the "grids" that each college uses to award merit scholarships. They correlate students' GPA and scores with specific amounts of scholarships.

These merit scholarships usually are part and parcel of the acceptance letter. Students are ecstatic to get admitted and they feel good because they also received a merit scholarship. They certainly earned them by studying hard, but colleges use them to leverage their costs and enroll them.

Not many enrollment managers believe they are rewarding students' pure academic efforts. (Read Maggie McGrath's 2014 article, *The Invisible Force Behind College Admissions.*) However, if this is the game they play, then students too must partake in this game.

No doubt good students deserve scholarships and more. But, the reason for awarding them is disingenuous and self-serving on the part of the colleges, when these scholarships are recruitment tactics.

Typically, the amount of scholarship is a very small part of the cost of attendance. The higher the cost of attendance, the larger possible tuition discount. Very few exceptional students will receive enough merit scholarship to pay the entire bill.

The colleges' intent is to attract a student, persuade parents to pay the rest of the costs and enroll the admitted student. According to Christopher Hooker-Haring, Dean of Admission at Muhlenberg College, "if a student doesn't receive any discount and still wants to enroll at an expensive college, it must mean that the student really values the school, and the parents are willing to pay the full price." (Download the full article from my website www.eduave.com/affordability.)

What's wrong with this, you may ask. The problem is that by categorizing students by their ability to pay, and by incentivizing those who can pay, students who need more than a merit scholarship end up not enrolling, or worse, not going to college at all. We know that students in low-income families don't perform as well on SAT and ACT tests. They don't receive the level of tutoring and test prep that well-off students do. To restrict admission to just those students who can pay results in a waste of potential and talent.

Those who cannot pay and take out mega-loans end up in financial ruin. Consider the uninformed, first generation student who heard all along that college is a must in order to get ahead. If these students enroll at a college where they barely scrape in, they end up paying an inordinate amount that is not sustainable for four years.

Many students are susceptible to recruitment practices. They may persuade their susceptible parents to stretch and pay more than they can afford, at a time when parents are usually trying to save some money for retirement.

These are the students who most need the advice and guidance of Independent Educational Consultants and college advisors who know colleges, the aid award policies and get to know the family's financial situation. They can position to the student to gain an affordable college education without jeopardizing the future.

These students must apply to a range of different colleges, from their in-state university and its satellite campuses to their local community college. It's not where they start college that matters, it's where they graduate from.

There's a zero-sum game in college admissions, where every seat taken by a wealthy student denies admission to a talented low-income student. By rewarding students with high test-scores who can pay, those without funds have less access to higher education. These can be unintended effects of enrollment management.

Let me tell you about Oliver: his parents didn't go to college but are doing exceedingly well for themselves. They own a large profitable marine business. Oliver works a few shifts each week and already knows how to run the manufacturing side of the company.

He's not particularly interested in academics due to learning disabilities but he's obviously smart about concrete matters. He will go to college because his parents want him to. Even though they are doing very well financially, socially and otherwise, they've bought into the idea that they somehow missed out on something because they didn't go to college. So now college is everything.

They are looking at the U.S. News and World Report rankings and hope that Oliver will be able to attend a well-known, high-ranked university. Their choices are liberal arts colleges where students are required to be intellectual book-worms and geeks, in the best sense of the word, which isn't Oliver. Reading comprehension is an issue for Oliver. The world of abstract and theoretical thinking isn't his strong suit.

It will take me some time to disabuse these parents of the notion that Oliver's superpowers lie in the technical and applied areas of study, and that even if he doesn't get into the ranked colleges, he will be more successful at a college where he can learn concrete subjects, from business to manufacturing to engineering, that he can apply to the real world.

Through enrollment management, colleges can advance in the rankings and gain more notoriety. Their goals can be very different from the needs of students.

In the 1980s and 1990s, the mantra was that colleges wanted well-rounded students. Now it looks like colleges want to be well-rounded themselves. They want racial, ethnic and geographical diversity. In order to fit into the well-rounded college, students need to be angular.

This means that if they play three sports in middle school, they need to pick one and specialize in a single sport if they want to be more attractive to colleges.

If they enjoy a variety of extra-curricular activities, it's better to invest more years into one particular volunteer effort that demonstrates the depth of the student's commitment.

If students try to prepare themselves for what colleges want, they risk losing their soul. High school students are still developing their sense of self and efficacy. They may need to explore, try various activities, subjects and fields of study.

The more desired qualities that colleges want in students may not be what's best for students. Not all can define who they want to be and focus on such a direction by the time they reach college. Some students aren't angular and don't fit into the pie chart that colleges desire for their class.

It's why students shouldn't take personally any college rejections.

The effects of enrollment management on families may be subtle but it's deep. By knowing the forces behind the admission process, students can feel better about themselves and make better choices for themselves.

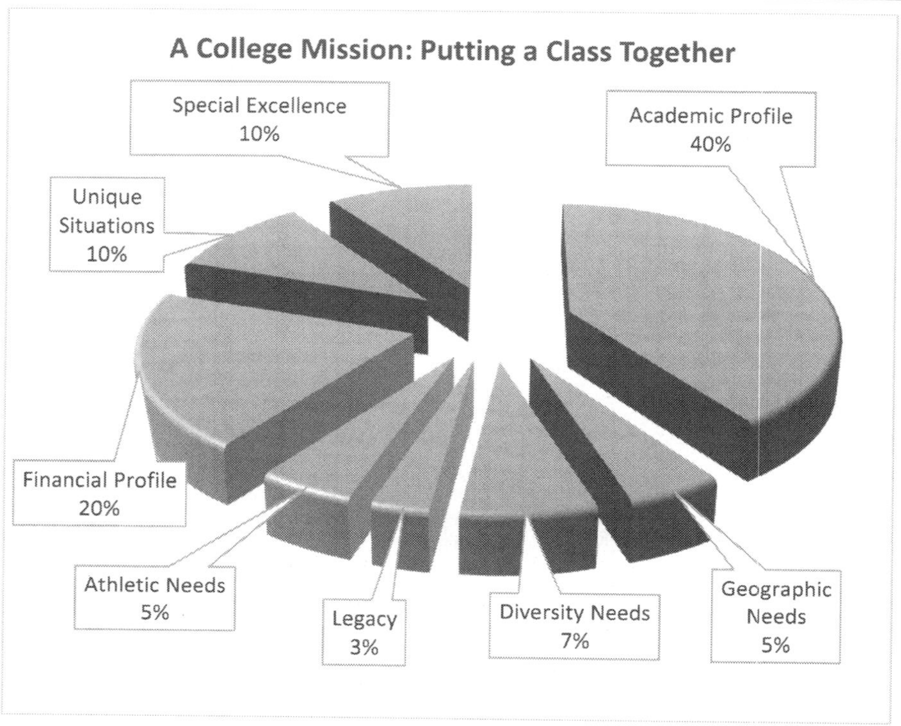

Strategic enrollment management enables colleges to build and then shape their class. Selective colleges don't just want to fill their dorms and classrooms with just anyone. They try to enroll students with good grades and scores, and a "hook" or something else. The majority of colleges need revenue each year and therefore need students who can pay the COA or at least the greater part of it. A diverse population is attractive to students so colleges strive to provide a well-rounded social environment by recruiting students from various geographies, cultural, ethnic and economic backgrounds.

Strategic enrollment management enables colleges to monitor all those variables. Sometimes, colleges will accept students who cannot pay, if they are highly-qualified and can help raise the overall academic selectivity of the college through their high test scores and grades.

Low-income students need to apply to colleges that award aid based on demonstrated financial need.

High-income students need to apply to colleges that award merit-based scholarships.

Middle-income students need to search for both merit scholarships and need-based aid.

All students need to be aware of what is marketing and advertising as opposed to real value for them.

Enrollment management includes marketing and advertising, which accounts for some of the mountains of mail and email students receive. After they take the first standardized test their email address and other contact information will be available for purchase by colleges.

I have worked in college admissions and on the SEM side of the desk, I can tell you SEM strategies are very effective in attracting students. SEM uses data mining and regression analysis to help colleges leverage financial aid and better predict the probability of student enrollment. These mathematical principles and statistics are what businesses do to attract customers and position themselves for success.

Students and parents are not aware of these forces at work behind the college admissions and financial aid offices.

I would prefer to see enrollment strategies used to identify campus issues. As mentioned, parking, upgraded dorms, and the quality of food are common issues for students. SEM can provide information that can help improve the first-year experience so students will return for sophomore year. This would be beneficial to the college because students would persist longer and graduate.

However, when enrollment management leverages the amount of financial aid to reel in the students most useful to the college, it starts to feel like a transaction, instead of the start of a symbiotic relationship. SEM can cause unsuspecting, need-sensitive students to enroll and take on an excessive debt.

Through these strategies, colleges leverage financial aid. They can calculate the minimal amount of discounts that hit the sweet spot with parents and students and produce a larger probability of enrollment.

By examining previous years' financial aid awards, the students' test scores and families' EFCs, colleges can predict how much financial aid is sufficient to persuade families to enroll their students. SEM provides the calculus for helping colleges meet their financial goals.

Although colleges need to recruit paying students to stay in business, **institutional interest is not the same as student interest.**

In fact, when colleges accept low-income, undergraduate students and then package their parents with Parent PLUS loans or private loans, they are harming the family. Who would have ever thought that you could go to college and instead of advancing your position in life you could end up in debt for decades or more?

I hear faculty members saying that colleges have suffered cuts in funding from the state, government and other sources. But, endowments have increased because the stock market has done well in the last few years, and many CSS Profile colleges could admit more low-income students without charging a penny.

When students and parents are saddled with student loan debt, they have limited ways to get back on their feet.

Colleges on the other hand, receive money from alumni donors, corporations, the federal and state government, research grants, dividend and capital gains from investments, endowments, not to mention tuition revenues, room and board payments from parents of in-state and out-of-state students, not just for one year but for four years.

Furthermore, since traditional colleges are not-for-profit organizations, they don't pay any tax. I remember the colorful Mayor Cianci, in Providence, RI, inaugurating some Johnson & Wales buildings at the Old Train Station downtown, and jovially pointing out: "Brown University, RISD, Johnson and Wales, Providence College have taken over the city, and don't pay any taxes!" It drew laughter, but there was a serious message there. The higher education industry gets many breaks. Colleges are far more impervious to pandemics, natural disasters, and the economic ups and downs than families.

Merit aid supplants need-based aid.

This shift to strategizing enrollment to attract students who pay more has resulted in merit aid supplanting need-based aid. Colleges use their institutional aid to attract better students who can also pay. Claire Gaudiani, former President of Connecticut College, provides this example: imagine that you have a student who needs all $60,000 to attend. What would happen if you parceled out the amount and gave $10,000 to six students as a "merit scholarship?" Now the college has six families who will pay the balance of the Cost of Attendance, which over four years will add up to more than $200,000 per family or $1.2 million from all six families. In addition, such families could become alumni donors and refer other well-to-do families. Download the article from www.eduave.com/resources

When higher education becomes a business, it disadvantages everyone because a highly-trained and informed society is essential for maintaining an educated electorate.

The public needs to accept that higher prices don't necessarily correlate with higher educational quality. The match between the student and the college is the most important variable.

If colleges are run like businesses, students are more likely to be treated as a product, a commodity, an item to be won over the competition.

As colleges spend an inordinate amount of funds on marketing and advertising to attract students and parents, I wonder if some of those funds wouldn't be better invested in paying salaries, to adjunct professors, for example, who sometimes carry an entire department, yet are the first to be laid off when funds run short.

When colleges are run like businesses, it's less profitable to fund low-income students, especially when funds are tight. Yet under-served students often add a distinguishing character, ethos and pathos to the entire community of scholars and faculty.

I have worked on college campuses and noted that students who come from underprivileged backgrounds work quite hard to improve themselves. They don't squander opportunities and tend to act with both passion and caution.

These under-privileged students put some fire in the belly of indulged and entitled students. I remember a student who worked in my admission office and was punctual and dependable in carrying out his work. The other work-study students worked harder when he was on shift. I realized he was trying to save money because he remained on campus over the weekends and holiday breaks.

Another Pell-Grant student was a mover and shaker when it came to social justice issues. A nation needs an educated populace that can sort truth from lies, facts from fiction, critical thinking in essence. He set a valuable example for how to contribute to the campus community.

My hope is that both public and private institutions will provide access to those who can't afford higher education. When colleges leverage financial aid, they fuel inequality.

By becoming informed shoppers, students and parents can exert consumer pressure on colleges and actually improve the quality of education.

Students must avoid becoming blinded by a "name college." I explain to my students that they will pay less at colleges where they rank in the top 25% of the applicant pool or higher.

While students' grades, test scores and rank in class are like money in the bank, the other side of this equation relates to the financial position of the family. Don't apply to an expensive tuition-driven school if you need financial aid.

If you don't qualify for financial aid, don't apply to those colleges that award need-based aid only. Shop for a variety of different colleges or consult with an Independent Educational Consultants or school counselor who can spend sufficient time with you and your parents.

Remember that Independent Educational Consultants accept students who are receiving federal means-tested benefits on a pro-bono basis.

Merit Aid vs. Need-Based Aid

Merit aid is often associated with scholarships and academic achievement. But, does it purely reward only academic achievement? Colleges reward the more desirable students with scholarships at the same time as they are admitted. Students receive admissions letters containing the specific amount of merit scholarship whether they applied for financial aid or not. Since the 1980's, colleges offer "preferential packages" to the students who rank at the top of the applicant pool, in the hope that students will get the message: "We want you!" Preferential packaging awards the same amount of need-based financial aid, but shifts the mix to more grants than loans, reducing the student's net price.

In the following article, the writer Maggie McGrath discovers the role of merit scholarships at a conference of 1,500 top notch admissions and enrollment managers. Not one of them raised a hand in answer to this question: "How many of you would say that the primary motivation for offering students merit scholarships is to reward academic achievement?"
https://www.forbes.com/sites/maggiemcgrath/2014/07/30/the-invisible-force-behind-college-admissions/

Merit scholarships are in essence tuition discounts for those students the college wants to treat "preferentially." Financial aid administrators recognize that the funding for scholarships often takes away from need-based funds, but can't break away from awarding scholarships which are so effective in reeling in students. Merit Scholarships provide that positive reinforcement that makes students (and parents) feel good about themselves. The recipients don't know how the funding came about, can't be blamed, especially because they probably deserve every bit of that reward.

If you read Maggie McGrath's article cited above, *The Invisible Force Behind College Admissions*, you will get the full deal.

For now, I want readers to notice that the cost of room and board, meaning room and meals, ranges from $13,000 to $17,000, and these indirect costs seldom discounted. Merit scholarships lower the cost of tuition, which is a "direct" cost.

A subtle point to note is that if the Cost of Attendance (COA) is higher, then the scholarship can be larger, because there's more playroom for discounting. For example, a college with a COA of $75,000 can offer a $25,000 scholarship and still bring in $50,000, a sizeable chunk of money. A school with a COA of $55,000 is less able to offer such a large discount. A scholarship for $10,000 at such a lower-priced school could be just as valuable, especially when the college is a good fit.

It's like buying a sweater that had a list price for $99 and now it's on sale for $49, and contrast it to buying a newly arrived sweater that costs $40. Which one fits you better? I've purchased the first sweater thinking it to be of better quality, since the original cost was higher, only to find that it didn't fit me as well on the shoulders. It's useless to buy a pair of Manolo Blahnick designer shoes if they don't fit. (Substitute Blahnick, a designer for women's shoes, with a coveted brand of male shoes.) Give me sneakers and I'll run a 10K race under one hour!

The bigger scholarship makes a bigger impression, but the educational experience may be very similar, or, worse, if the match between student and college is not there. Another subtle point to notice is that discounting through scholarships applies to the costs of tuition, not meals and housing. I can only think of recruited NCAA Division One athletes possibly getting the full ride.

Even with the bigger scholarship, the net price of the higher-cost college may still be higher than the net price of the lower-cost college with the smaller scholarship.

Anecdotally, I've noticed a trend toward need-based aid at the more selective colleges. The Amhersts, Williams and Ivy League universities of this world awarded need-based aid all along. Any student who gets into these colleges is meritorious enough, considering how smart and talented you have to be to gain acceptance into these famous halls of higher learning.

Anecdotally, again, I see a trend even among less wealthy colleges, toward giving more need-based aid to low-income students, minorities, and traditionally under-served students. Public institutions have always tried to meet the need of the poor, and even more so in recent years.

The Covid-19 pandemic has affected more blue-collar workers than those who work in an office in front of a computer. The internet and meeting platforms help get the job done in a virtual environment. Restaurant workers on the other hand, provide in-person services, and they are affected the most.

Colleges have pivoted to accommodate incoming students, by going test-optional, and evaluating them more holistically. It was a relief for many of my students to not have to sit for the ACT or SAT and risk exposure to the virus. Some were incredibly relieved because they don't do well on these high-stakes tests.

I don't mean to belabor it, but going back to the analogy with shoes, some students are more comfortable in elegant shoes, some prefer sneakers, others love wearing boots. I don't know what would be the college correlative of flats, sneakers, or high fashion shoes, but you get the metaphor.

Ideally, students would be well-paired with the colleges they attend. On the other hand, colleges would help students improve their listening skills, critical thinking and impart an ability to understand the practical and theoretical worlds.

The "Harkness table" educational philosophy is more common in secondary school than in college. This is an oval table that seats 12 students who listen carefully to one another's views. Students learn to debate respectfully as they explore various notions and different ideas proposed by people who think differently. No one is right or wrong. The group collaborates in finding solutions to the problem or issue at hand. The Harkness method effectively develops critical thinking in students. It promotes listening, oratory, and thinking skills.

I've placed many students in many colleges, and the most remarkable student-college-match occurred most often at small, liberal-arts colleges. I saw these students develop into their best selves, as a result of the relationships they developed with their professors and peers, and the improvement in their ability to think objectively, and sort out fact from falsehood. Students who strive to get into the most selective college can often end up biting more than they can chew. Highly selective colleges will test students' mettle when often, they would find enough challenge at a lower-ranked school, or a small liberal arts college where there's lots of personal interaction, activities and discussion between teachers and students.

I've also worked with students who were accepted to a college that matched their learning needs and social style perfectly, and yet decided to try for admission to a much more academically selective school. I remember one particular student who had told me how she felt constantly anxious in high school because of all the assignments she couldn't complete on time. She said she was exhausted by that constant pressure. I reminded her of her own words and finally she relented. Other students may not have a coach or parent who reminds them of what they said and persuades them to choose a college where they can feel less stressed, and enjoy a balance between study and social life. If by chance they get accepted, they would be at the bottom of the applicant pool, would struggle to keep up academically, and could end up paying the full cost.

Students and parents can fall prey to thinking the more expensive colleges and larger scholarships are a better value. It could just be that through enrollment management (SEM), the college was able to raise the price while the educational programs, quality of room and board, amenities and athletics remained the same. Marketing and advertising can change perceptions. We've all watched ads on TV for items we never knew existed or thought we needed.

A college education on the other hand, is imprinted in the minds of parents as the ticket to success. College is perceived as an absolute necessity, not as an option. In fact, as the world of work and employment continues to change, workers need highly developed skills and training. Occasionally, we have a Mark Zuckerberg who drops out of Harvard University and starts an online platform called Facebook. However, Zuckerberg graduated from a most prestigious independent school, Exeter Academy. Clearly, he learned what he needed to learn there. Some students gain enough knowledge in high school to become entrepreneurs.

Meanwhile, I ask my college bound students to read the course catalog of each college that interests them, and highlight the classes they like. Some students are surprised at how many interesting classes they find. There are so many they can't choose just a few. Others find the description of some courses aren't at all what they thought they would cover. This type of investigation is crucial for students to do before they apply for admission. I've watched many students start college, and those who had read the catalog were better prepared to settle down to learn. They enjoyed working hard, getting involved with their peers and made a valuable contribution to the campus community.

The increase of merit scholarships: a 2008 NACAC discussion paper reported that "In 1994, colleges and universities overall reported that 27 percent of their institutional aid funds were merit-based and 66 percent need-based. By 2007, the merit-based aid had increased to 43 percent."

As a result, Pell eligible and lower-income students are taking on more debt. By looking at the College Navigator from the National Center for Education Statistics (NCES), it's easy to notice that the average price is higher for the low-income families as a percent of their earnings. A family that earns from zero to $30,000 will pay $13,137 or 940% of their income, while a family that earns more than $110,001 pays $28,777 or roughly 30% of their income.

The ratio of the net price to total income is something that Mark Kantrowitz calls the College Affordability Index. If this ratio is greater than 25%, the college is unaffordable and the student will have to take on an unreasonable amount of debt to cover the college costs.

University of Massachusetts - Amherst			
Full-time beginning undergraduate students who paid the in-state or in-district tuition rate and were awarded Title IV aid by income.			
AVERAGE NET PRICE BY INCOME	**2016-2017**	**2017-2018**	**2018-2019**
\$0 – \$30,000	\$11,878	\$12,520	\$13,137
\$30,001 – \$48,000	\$12,508	\$13,829	\$14,474
\$48,001 – \$75,000	\$16,930	\$17,473	\$18,104
\$75,001 – \$110,000	\$23,131	\$23,176	\$24,051
\$110,001 and more	\$26,998	\$27,686	\$28,777

Granted, colleges and universities have specific goals to achieve. For example, a college or university may want to increase geographical diversity or expand its recruitment in other states to improve its name recognition nationally. It will likely give scholarships to students from those regions. A public university with a ho-hum profile might want to attract more top-notch students by publicizing their Honors program in-state and out-of-state. If they need more revenue, (and which college doesn't,) they might target visits to high schools in high-performing and well-to-do districts, where there are be more academically oriented students with wealthier parents.

To assess affordability, families should read the colleges' financial aid website pages carefully and read between the lines. There are hints that tell you whether the college will be affordable. Some colleges come right out with something like, "There's no denying it, a private college education like one at "Our Prestige College" is expensive." Such sentences should be a signal to the reader that the college is expensive and there's not much financial aid. If in doubt, call the financial aid office and ask how they award aid, whether it's on the basis of need or merit. Another example: the website or the admission counselor may say "students cannot make it here without parental support."

This means that after students take out their aggregate amounts of loans, parents must pay the remaining portion of costs. SEM does print out a sweeter package for those who need just a tad of aid, and issues a meager financial aid package to discourage those who can't pay. Unfortunately, some of those uninformed and financially needy students can get trapped in the SEM web and enroll nevertheless. Financial aid administrators can't very well say: Hey, our school is too expensive. Go to the college down the road from us where you will pay a lot less."

If colleges are looking to attract a diverse student body, you may wonder what they mean by "diversity." Do they mean African American or Native American or someone from Alaska? Harvard's Dean of Admissions, Bill Fitzsimmons, says he's so tired of the word "diversity" he'll be sick if he hears it again!" It's been clear however, that Harvard is looking for traditionally underrepresented minorities, people of color, native Americans, and, most of all, students who, despite living in tough circumstances, rose above them and still performed well in school. Harvard is one of the few schools that will consider race, ethnicity, and personal circumstances in admission. It's interesting to note that the 2023-34 FAFSA will contain these questions. I wonder if the U.S. Department of Education took the cue from Harvard!

For example, Ms. Elizabeth Murray was homeless in her high school years when her parents were living on the street due to drug abuse. She studied in libraries and slept outdoors on benches. While another Ivy League university rejected her application in 1998, Harvard accepted her. Ms. Murray went on to become an inspirational speaker and psychologist. Harvard uses a humanistic approach to admitting students, not a SEM plan based on mathematical calculations. SEM can pick up many academic, social and financial variables, and then produce financial aid awards that effectively leverage the aid, but it could never respond to a student's individual life experiences. When colleges use a humanistic model, they recruit students like Ms. Elizabeth Murray who made her Alma Mater proud.

Are there ways for families to avoid the trappings of SEM? Yes. It involves asking for transparency and appealing award offers that place too high a debt burden on the student and parents. It takes communicating with the college to understand what they really mean. It involves asking the financial aid administrators to explain how they assess families. Parents should refer to their budget and AFC to raise questions of affordability. It involves preparing the student for a competitive admission process as well. It's not the "well-rounded student" who gets in anymore. It used to be that the student who had taken a variety of classes and tried a variety of extracurricular activities was well-rounded.

But, students need to specialize earlier nowadays, and not all students can do that and benefit from it. It's like the tables have turned and colleges now strive to provide a "well-rounded" student body, made up of very different individuals. To that end they recruit students with unique abilities. Imagine the college population having the round shape of a pie. To fit into that pie, each student must have the triangular shape of a slice. Students who are more "angular" stand out more and are actually more desirable, at least at selective colleges that can pick and choose among applicants. For example, the student who plays the piano or viola at concerto level, or the competitive skier, or the student who conducted some unique research that got published, are angular students. I'm always surprised to meet these students at the highly selective colleges, from Bates, to Colby, Bowdoin among others. However, to be angular, a student would need to specialize at an early age, to the exclusion of other activities. Not everyone is cut out for that.

Need-Blind Admission: Enrollment practices vary from college to college. Some admission counselors will say their admission process is "need-blind." This is a most confusing term. What does this mean? It means nothing if the college doesn't meet the financial need of applicants. This leads to a practice called "Admit-Deny," where the student is admitted but the college doesn't provide enough financial aid for the student to afford to attend. Some colleges even choose to not fund the student. "Need blind" should mean that if the student gets in, the college will provide the funding. Instead, it means that students go through the process of admission but when it comes to the amount of need, they college will not fund it. It says: "you're admissible but if we admit you, we have no funding for you."

Even if a college is need blind, that puts low-income students at a disadvantage. Wealthier students can afford to pay for test prep classes and have the luxury of learning to play a musical instrument and engage in expensive sports and hobbies. It's not really a level playing field.

Students who need financial aid should not apply under the "early decision" program, because it is binding. If accepted, the student would be obligated to attend, even if the financial aid is not enough! Early decision prevents you from shopping around for a less expensive college with a lower net price. These students should instead apply for the non-binding early action and regular decision programs. If they need a lot of funding, they will fare best if they apply to colleges that meet as close to100% of need as possible. Students and parents must ask for clarification when they hear "need blind" or any term they don't understand. Before parents and students fill out forms, like the FAFSA, CSS Profile, or the colleges' internal financial aid applications, they need to decipher how the colleges will assesses their families under each methodology.

It's not unusual for SEM companies to sell their services by claiming that they can recruit "high-quality students." I took this to suggest that this SEM company thinks there are "low-quality students." I felt offended on behalf of students because all students are of good quality, regardless of their grades! When SEM starts sounding like students are a commodity, it can be dehumanizing and intimidating.

Parents of dependent undergraduate students must estimate their net costs *before* their student applies to colleges. Students must assess their chances of getting in realistically. I said it before, and it bears repeating it: students must apply to colleges where they rank at least above the middle 50% of the applicant pool. They will pay less and will be rock stars there.

While colleges continue to increase the amount of merit aid offered to students at the expense of need-based aid, it's unfair from a humanist point of perspective, even though it makes sense financially. Colleges cannot be just businesses. If colleges open their doors only to those who can pay, higher education will be like it was in the past, when only the wealthy went to college. This is a terrible waste of human potential. However, in these times when COAs at private colleges hover from $60,000 to $80,000, and college aid consists of loans, parents who don't qualify for need-based aid want to know which colleges will give their student a $20,000+ merit scholarship. Colleges will need to reflect back on their missions, goals, and values to decide whether their monies should be given out based on need or merit. It's no surprise that they are not likely to fund students at the bottom their applicant pool who do not help raise the school's profile. Leveraging financial aid, enticing students to enroll through scholarships are here to stay, despite economic conditions, the Covid-19 pandemic, and/or political and societal pressure.

Will online teaching lower costs? The Covid-19 pandemic resulted in colleges pivoting to online teaching and this change is likely to remain even after the pandemic, even when students live on campus. The virtual classroom is here to stay. It remains to be seen if the elite universities will offer online degrees along with the in-person degrees and if online admission might be easier to get into. It's disheartening when students are not accepted by one college even when they meet the admission requirements. They shouldn't take it personally, however. It may have little to do with them.

It may have everything to do with enrollment management goals, from increasing selectivity by raising the admission bar to admitting more students who live nearby in case they have to return home if Covid-19 spikes. In the fall of 2020, some well-known colleges on the I-95 corridor considered the student's home location in the admission process.

Students can gain excellent education at many lesser-known colleges that may be willing to discount their tuition. In-state public universities have regional campuses that often cost much less. And, let's not overlook the community colleges, which are the best bargains around. It's easy for students to become susceptible to the colleges' enrollment management practices. By researching the financial aid awarding policies of the colleges and remaining open to a variety of college options, students can find their college fit and affordability in one place.

References

Gaudiani, C. (2000). *Does Merit Aid a Toll Extract on Society?*

McGrath, M. (2014). *The Invisible Force Behind College Admissions*, Forbes.com

Muhlenberg College. (2010). *Preferential Packaging*

Hossler, D. & Christensen, C. (2009). *The Enrollment Management Review*

Hartung, E. (2009). *The Impact of Enrollment Management on NCAA Financial Aid Regulations at Division III Schools*

Schroeder, Alex (2019). *It's not necessarily helping affordability: Inside Recent College Price-Chopping*, WBUR

Noel-Levitz. (2009). *Connecting Enrollment and Fiscal Management*

Hanover Research (2019). *Strategies to drive matriculation*

McQuilkin, Hilary (2019). *What the strain of paying for college does to families*

NET PRICE CALCULATORS AND EMMA'S STORY

"Focus on net price, not the sticker price," is what colleges tell families. NPC stands for Net Price Calculator. NPCs are tools that can give you an approximate, personalized estimate of what it will cost to attend a particular institution. Now we'll dig deeper for a better understanding of how to use them. If this isn't your cup of tea, feel free to skip ahead!

Wouldn't it be nice if families could figure out how much a college would cost for them before their student applied for admission? What is the real cost for each individual student?

A little bit of history here is needed for context: the U.S. Department of Education (DoE), in an effort to improve transparency and fair access, mandated that each college should post a net price calculator to give an idea of what the costs would be at their particular college. This calculator was supposed to list the amount of federal aid each family could be eligible to receive. The DoE's intentions were to increase transparency, to help families determine affordability, and help them become better consumers. The DoE was quick to warn that estimates provided using the net price calculator did not represent a final determination, or actual award of financial assistance. The warning continued: "The price of attendance and financial aid availability may change. This estimate shall not be binding on the Secretary of Education, this institution of higher education or the state in which this institution of higher education is located."

Many colleges weren't satisfied with the federal NPC calculator because it didn't reflect the marketing and communication style of the college. Many, therefore, proceeded to devise "better" calculators that provided the amount of institutional aid and scholarships a student might receive. They proceeded to build their own or purchase one. The College Board's Net Price Calculator is the more popular in this industry. There are 200+ colleges that use it, and it's no coincidence that many require the CSS Profile form in addition to FAFSA. IECs can set up a "professional account" and families can register on the College Board NPC and save their demographic and financial information so they can check prices of other colleges without having to re-enter all their financial information again.

If all goes well, NPCs can be very useful in providing a personalized ball-park estimate of the actual cost of colleges. There are some hazards though. NPCs were not perfect before the pandemic and are even less than perfect during this pandemic, when colleges have changed the admission requirements and gone to a more holistic evaluation of applicants. Since ACT/SAT test sessions were cancelled, many students don't have standardized test scores, and colleges have pivoted to test-optional admission. Updating the Net Price Calculators isn't top of mind for colleges during a pandemic. As imperfect as Net Price Calculator may be, they're still valuable as a way to get an idea of costs before their student s apply. In this sense, NPCs are a step in the right direction.

Over the years colleges that award merit-aid have started awarding scholarships at the same time as they admit students or shortly thereafter. They are better at communicating that the net price is the cost you pay after discounts. For example, after parents file the FAFSA, they will receive federal aid. If the college has financial aid of its own, and the family has need, there may be more aid. Then enter your financial information and your student's. If the calculator requires grades/test scores it's trying to compute whether the student qualifies for some merit scholarship. The more accurate the information you enter, the more accurate the results.

Of all the different NPCs on the market, I find the NPC provided by the College Board to be more accurate. You will know if your college uses the College Board NPC if the college's financial aid pages take you to the College Board website. Parents can use the same login as their student used to register for SATs or AP exams. The financial information remains stored on the calculator so that you can check costs of other colleges without re-entering your information.

The general consensus with IECs is that the better NPCs will have more questions and families will be able to enter more academic and financial information. NPC questions typically start out as the ones you'll find on FAFSA, to establish the student status, gender, number of people that live in the home, number of dependent students in college at the same time, and so on. The financial questions require parents to enter the income and asset amounts. Parents should remember to enter the tax information from two years earlier, what colleges dubbed as "the prior-prior year." You'll know if the college uses Institutional Methodology (IM) to assess financial need if there's a question about your home equity. Be ready to answer: What is the value of your home (your principal place of residence)? How much is owed on it? Do you own other real estate or property? What is the value of non-retirement plans AND retirement accounts?

Colleges that use their Institutional Methodology are quick to say that retirement information doesn't impact the financial aid the student could get. However, I wonder then why do they ask? Parents will reveal the value of their 401(k), SEP, IRAs, ROTHs, and pensions. I learned in my statistics class that you don't collect data you're not going to use. We know that the College Board collects tons of personal and financial information when students take the SATs and parents file the CSS Profile. There's no way around it. The College Board sells the information to colleges that request the names of students with specific ranges of SAT scores. It enables colleges to reach out to the students they typically admit. The financial information of families is undoubtedly valuable to gauge the level of wealth of families typical for a college.

A "quicker" Net Price Calculator is the MyinTuition NPC. This gives a quick estimate useful for high-performing students who stand a good chance of getting into highly selective colleges. The claim to fame of this NPC is that it requires only 6 or 7 questions to spew out a net cost. Parents can complete it in three minutes. It's ideal for Pell-eligible students with a large amount of financial need. The MyinTuition NPC is used by 67 elite and Ivy League colleges that offer need-based financial aid only.

Case study: Benjamin wants to attend a private college that awards merit aid. The total COA (Cost of Attendance) is $60,000. What might be his Net Price? Let's say that Benjamin enters his grades, rank in class and test scores into the NPC. His parents enter their Adjusted Gross Income, number of people in the household, etc. and their EFC turns out to be $25,000. This leaves a balance of $35,000 ($60,000 - $25,000). Let's say that Benjamin ranks near the top of his senior class, (top 5%) and the NPC results show that he could get a merit scholarship for $15,000. This can be represented by this formulas:

Remaining Need = COA minus EFC minus scholarship

Estimated Net Price = COA minus scholarship

Once Benjamin receives the $15,000 scholarship, the estimated financial need is reduced to $20,000, after the family pays their EFC of $25,000. Remember that colleges will not fill your EFC with grants. Families that haven't saved for their EFC can get loans. You can see that families would be lucky to be able to pay only their EFC. Scholarships are seldom large enough to cover the EFC, although a few students occasionally do win some large scholarship competition. Typically, families pay more than their EFC because of the gap between financial need and financial aid. Let's say that the college meets only 10% of demonstrated financial need, which we've determined for Benjamin to be $20,000. Now 10% of the $20,000 is $2,000. The formula would look like this:

COA ($60,000) - EFC ($25,000) + Scholarship ($15,000) + need-based grant ($2,000) = Remaining need ($18,000)

The remaining need is 90% of $20,000. The unfilled need is $18,000. This is the gap.

The Net Price to pay for this college is: EFC ($25,000) + GAP ($18,000) = NET PRICE ($43,000).

If the family filed the FAFSA, the award letter will show a Direct Loan for Undergraduate Students for $5,500 in first year. This loan will finance part of the net price of $43,000, leaving $37,500. If parents can't pay their EFC or the gap, they can borrow it from the federal PLUS loan for parents.

If Benjamin applied to an elite college that awarded need-based only, then, assuming the college met 100% of demonstrated need, the net cost would be the parents' EFC plus the $5,500 student loan ($25,000 + $5,500) = Net Price of $30,500

If the family has computed its Affordable Family Contribution, (AFC) it will be easier to figure out if the $43,000 will be feasible. The family can expect that such cost will increase over the four years by 3% to 6% per year. It's a good question to ask the financial aid administrator.

Students are able to borrow more each year and I have the sneaky suspicion that college costs increase by this amount because they know that the loan for undergraduate students will cover the increase.

By looking at Benjamin's example, you can tell that he's looking at a private college or a prestigious out-of-state university. Typically, public universities don't charge $60,000 for in-state students, despite the continual cuts in federal and state funding. A college located just a few miles over the state line can cost twice as much as remaining on one's home turf. Some colleges set aside some funds for neighboring students. For example, Winthrop University in SC is so close to Charlotte NC that it receives many applications from North Carolinians, and it has special aid earmarked for those students.

Check the Net Price Calculators to see how you'd make out. Although they are not completely accurate, NPCs can give a general ball-park estimate. It's my hope that colleges will improve their NPSs and keep updating and refining them. In effect it's a public service that would benefit both families and colleges. Financial Aid Administrators (FAAs) take no comfort in working with families who can't afford their institution.

Do this:

1) Talk with Financial Aid Administrators after you use the NPC. No calculator can give you a precise idea of your costs as can a detailed review of your finances. While FAAs won't give you the actual net price unless you file the FAFSA and are admitted, a general conversation about your income and assets would help them establish if your NPC results are in the right ball park.

2) Regardless of what colleges want families to pay to have the student attend their institution, stick with your "Affordable Family Contribution." If you can't afford the college, consider other, more affordable colleges.

3) Visit the financial aid website of the colleges your student is interested in. Experiment with their Net Price Calculator. (Make sure you enter the same data in each, so you can compare apples with apples.) Then record the net costs the calculator prints out.

4) Check to see if the net price looks like the sticker price minus the usual $5,500 federal loan for first year undergraduate students, it means the college is tuition driven. Many colleges exist thanks to the federal financial aid that students can bring to it.

5) If there's any amount of Pell Grant, it means the student may have a chance of also getting Federal Work-Study, a form of self-help aid. This is something to ask the Financial Aid Administrators.

6) If the Net Price Calculator doesn't specify what's a loan or scholarship, do this: Call the admissions office, ask what level of merit scholarship your student can get with their GPA, test scores if any, and rank in class. Colleges establish scholarship grids that link the amounts to grades and test scores. Sometimes, even the student who answers the phone knows the scholarship criteria. They may have qualified for one themselves, or, they may be working in the admissions office to earn their work-study salary.

7) If you can't find the COA for the upcoming year, call the financial aid office and ask what it is or what they will expect it to be. It's incomprehensible that families must buy an expensive college education without knowing the price. While you're at it, ask the FAA if their Net Price Calculator is up-to-date.

8) After you establish rapport with the financial aid administrator, ask if your NPC results sound about right, given the adjusted gross income you entered. During the pandemic, college financial aid officers were even more responsive to parents' and students' questions.

Parents can involve their student in checking out these Net Price Calculators, to the extent that it is appropriate. I realize some parents worry that their children will become upset. Others don't feel comfortable sharing their financial information with their children.

I've noticed many students don't get affected one way or another by knowing what colleges cost, or by seeing their parents' tax return and amount of wages earned. It's a number to them, an amount they seem to forget once the numbers are entered into the right fields. Students are more interested in the output of the NPC and any scholarships they could get.

Granted some students are anxious, and in that case, those parents don't need to involve their student in the financial process. Occasionally, a student bursts into tears for fear that the parents will opt for a less expensive college, or no college at all! In my practice, I see that students who consider the costs of different universities start to think carefully about their choices.

Ultimately, choosing a college involves some level of compromise: the student likes the college in the mountains five states over, and the parents prefer the in-state flagship institution or a religiously affiliated college. Students who are in the know become invested in the choice of college and are less likely to squander the opportunity.

Students can be blinded by certain colleges they think are best. The size of scholarship is often an incentive to enroll. Parents love to boast that their student received a $20,000 scholarship. It certainly sounds more impressive than a $10,000 scholarship, but what was the sticker price? What is the net price after subtracting the scholarship? The more expensive the college the more discounting is possible.

Consider this example:

	College A	College B
Cost of Attendance	$69,000	$51,000
Merit Scholarship	$19,000	$10,000
Net Difference	$50,000	$41,000
4-Year Cost	$200,000	$164,000

Over four years, the savings would add up to $36,000 at the college with the smaller scholarship and lower Cost of Attendance. (This assumes, for the sake of the example, that costs will remain the same each year, which they don't. Historically, they increase from 3% to 6%.) It would be a mistake thinking that colleges with lower tuition costs are less valuable than the expensive ones.

In the final analysis, choosing a college that fits academically, socially, and financially involves some compromise. How well does the more expensive college fit the student, and in what ways? I found that certain lower-priced colleges are a better fit for students who need a less competitive learning environment, and want to enjoy a balance between academic work and social activities.

Keep in mind that students who barely meet the admission requirements would end up paying more. If the student has above average grades for "College B" they will likely pay much less, assuming these colleges award merit aid. The college benefits because a student with higher grades and test scores raises the institution's profile.

Meet Emma and a Net Price Calculator

Emma's experience with a Net Price Calculator (NPC) is not unique. As noted before, not all NPCs are accurate and up to date. Emma and her parents lived in Western Massachusetts and Emma was interested in a large metropolitan college in Boston, where else? So many high school students claim they're bored with living in suburbia. They have names for their towns like "Borington" instead of "Barrington."

I told her to complete the net price calculator of a private college that cost roughly $65,000, to get an idea of the net costs. She knew the price tag was way out of her reach and rejoiced when we saw a $20,000 scholarship for residents of that state. Maybe this private college would be affordable after all!

Then, just to be sure, I encouraged Emma to call the financial aid office. It turned out the scholarship was meant only for students applying from Boston's Title One schools. This meant the students would likely be Pell eligible. Emma didn't live in Boston and didn't attend a Title One school. The scholarship applied to students who were receiving means-tested federal benefits, such as free or reduced-price school lunch.

I went through the net price calculator myself and saw the same scholarship. So, I called the financial aid office and explained that the scholarship was coming up for everyone who used their NPC and it was misleading. This didn't seem to trouble the person who answered the phone and upon reflection I concluded it was not a financial aid administrator who answered. They do have work-study students who get employment in these offices. Still…

The scholarship got me thinking: a $20,000 scholarship is a lot of money for a Title One student, but not when the cost of the college costs $65,000! That scholarship would be just a drop in the bucket even if student was going to get the full Pell Grant and FSEOG grant. There's no way for low-income students with zero EFCs to pay for these colleges.

The scholarship was misleading and I ended up writing a note to the financial aid office, and never heard back. I'm enraged by enticements to lure for uninformed students and parents.

Consider this: these students will bring their federal aid to the school, like the Pell and FSEOG grants, and take on the subsidized loan for $3,500, the unsubsidized loan for $2,000, and Federal Work Study for large amounts. Once students have depleted their "self-help" aid, the cost would still be $30,000 and parents would be loaded with loans. No wonder the graduation rate was 60%.

This was the wrong school for my middle-class student and even worse for high need students from a Title One school who need 100% of help. If students from a Title One school applied there, they would quite simply end up with too much debt and possibly start a life of debt repayments like indentured servitude.

I began to reconsider the "tough love" method that some colleges that enact whereby the don't accept students who clearly can't afford their college. I know a number of colleges that do this. At first I thought it was cruel, but now I think they do the "humane" thing in rejecting those students who wouldn't be able to graduate and end up in debt after the first year.

Luckily for Emma, she didn't apply to this college and moved on to several others that proved to meet her "fit and affordability" test. She finally chose to attend UMass Boston. She paid everything with a bit of Pell Grant, work-study, a subsidized loan for $3,500, the $2,000 and unsubsidized loan. She also got the Abigail Adams Massachusetts scholarship. She graduated with just the undergraduate loans and her parents didn't have to take out loans. Emma double majored in business and economics. She found immediate employment at a financial firm in Boston and plans to repay her loans within a couple of years.

Lesson learned: If the NPC results seem really good or too good to be true, call the financial aid office to confirm your findings. Have the numbers you put into the NPC and the results at your fingertips when you call the college, and confirm your results from the net price calculator.

Ask to speak with a financial aid administrator and not just whoever answers the phone. They may not know whether the NPC is working properly or the website is updated, so you may be doing them a favor.

The final consideration us up to the student and parents. Is the college worth your financial investment? Are other colleges that fit your goals and values less expensive? Do you have specific learning disabilities that would be better supported at the more expensive college? Sometimes parents do need to spend more, and if it's for good reason it's money well spent. The goal is for students to choose a college that fits their learning needs so that they will be successful. In Emma's case, she moved away from the magnetic and blinding attraction of a college she initially thought she wanted, and ended up making a more academically and financially sound choice.

Resources

Laura W. Perna, Jeremy Wright-Kim, and Nathan Jiang, *QUESTIONING THE CALCULATIONS: Are Colleges Complying with Federal and Ethical Mandates for Providing Students with Estimated Costs?*, Penn AHEAD Research Brief, March 2019

DETERMINE YOUR ANNUAL NET COST: Download the live excel spreadsheet from www.eduave.com.

Financial Aid Award Letters

When you receive several award letters, you must compare them carefully. This is when you see what the actual costs will be. Put all your offers on the table and compare them, but make sure you compare apples with apples! Allocate the same amount to the cost of books and supplies for each college. Compare the price of the room and the number of meals in each plan. Adjust the cost of transportation depending on whether you will drive or fly to and from.

Ask why the costs may differ from college to college. Add up the amount of "free" aid such as scholarships and federal aid. Remember you qualify for the same amount of federal aid no matter where you attend school. Your federal aid is portable!

Free aid is like a gift that you don't have to pay back. On the other hand, work-study is a form of self-help because the student needs to work to earn an income, so it's not exactly "free aid." However, work-study is wonderful because a part-time job on campus removes having to commute to and from a job. It also helps with making friends and become involved in the community. Off-campus jobs will take longer to get to and from and the employers may not be as sensitive to your study schedule.

Loans are obligations and evaluate which portion is subsidized as opposed to unsubsidized. Evaluate your college costs line item by line item. Use the federal shopping sheet, also called a College Financing Plan, to analyze each college. This is a sheet that the U.S. Department of Education provides for colleges to use when they are awarding federal aid.

The beauty of this College Financing Plan is that there are two lines for the college to enter your EFC under the Federal Methodology and Institutional Methodology. If colleges enter those amounts of your expected family contribution, then you will know how they're being assessed. This would add transparency to this process.

The U.S. Department of Education "College Financing Plan" allows you to evaluate one college. If you want to compare several, you can use my live excel spreadsheet, available at www.eduave.com. It is similar to the College Financing Plan, but it lists several colleges, side-by-side.

You will see very clearly the sections with merit-gift-aid and the self-help aid. Is the amount need-based or merit-based, is it federal or institutional? Is the gift aid from the college renewable each year? What are the contingencies? Is the GPA required doable?

If you enter all of your awards into this form, you will understand your financial aid packages and will be able to compare the costs from each college.

Enter the loans under the "self-help" section of the excel spreadsheet. If you're granted work-study, also enter it under the self-help section, as this is an amount you will need to earn in order to pay down the costs. Some colleges can be lenders and give you loans from their institutions. Make a note if this is the case, and ask the financial aid administrator to clarify the terms. Some colleges end up canceling the loans if the graduates are not earning much.

NASFAA (National Association for Student Financial Aid Administrators) also publishes an excellent comparison worksheet, though it's not an interactive excel worksheet. Still, it offers an excellent format for recording if the aid is renewable and an excellent glossary of terms. Print this sheet, have your calculator in hand, enter your awards by hand, and add/subtract.

Remember, you don't have to send that commit deposit to a college until May 1st of senior year. It's an industry-standard approved by NACAC called the National Candidates Reply Date, also known as Decision Day. (Due to a settlement with the U.S. Department of Justice, Decision Day can no longer be enforced by NACAC, but many colleges will continue to expect students to make their decisions by May 1.)

Colleges invite you to deposit earlier and entice you to do so by saying that the best dorm rooms may be gone if you don't commit asap. However, I found this isn't always true, especially at colleges that aren't full.

It's best for students and families to wait until they have all their award offers on hand. Hopefully, you will have applied to a variety of colleges so that you will be able to compare different prices.

Some students and parents aren't entirely satisfied with their college selection. They may have applied just to one college, or to the wrong colleges.

No worries. There are still options. After May 1, some colleges that still have space available will submit their name to the National Association for College Admission

Counseling. and admit on a "rolling" basis. The College Openings Update (formerly Space Availability Survey) is released soon after the May 1 Decision Day.

Some colleges offer "rolling admission" which means they will accept your application even during the summer after you graduate from high school. These colleges are very likely going to discount their costs.

If you've completed your value sort exercises, examined your family budget, and established your Affordable Family Contribution, you will be able to assess which ones will yield the best education and career prospects for you.

Once you enter your financial aid awards into one of the above forms, the sheet could look like this:

Sonia's Award from Private College

See below Sonia's academics, Affordable Family Contribution and Colleges on her final list.

Sonia	GPA	SAT	ACT	EFC	AFC
CP track	2.9/5	1050	18	$20,000	$10,000

Cost of attendance

College Type	**Community College**	**In-State Public**	**Private College**
Choice: College List	RCBC	Rowan U	Rider
Tuition 2021-2022	$5,159	$14,000 -Fees: $5,328	$44,460
Room and Board	N/A	$17,961	$14,390
Books &Supplies	$1,200	$1,850	$1,500
Cost of Attendance	$6,359	$39,139	$60,350

Data obtained from The National Center for Education Statistics or college website.

Sonia's SAR (Student Aid Report) says her EFC is $20,094.

The Cost of Attendance at RCBC Community College cost less than their $10,000 AFC, and Sonia didn't want to go there. Mom considered that by paying $6,359 the family could start saving for the other children's college education. There was something that didn't square with her. Sonia really needed a small and nurturing environment given her learning and personal needs. They re-evaluated the two offers from the State U and Private College. COA at Rowan University: Tuition and Fees: $14,000. Room and Board: $14,854. Total = $28, 854. The only aid was the Direct subsidized loan for $3,500 and Direct unsubsidized for $2,000. The balance would be $23,354, including the loan.

The COA from the private college (Rider U) was: $58,325. Remember that Sonia's EFC was $20,094. When college costs are $10,000 more than a family's EFC, it's time to choose another college. In this case, the private college's aid was so generous that s Sonia's net price was similar to the in-state university cost. Once this family examined this award from Rider with a cost of $22,552, they realized this was a "preferential" package. This is where Sonia wanted to attend. Many small private colleges attract students like Sonia by discounting tuition as much as they possibly can. In Jeff Selingo's classification, this would be a "seller college" instead of a "buyer college" that is flush with applications. The seller college is trying to attract students and appreciates those who demonstrate an interest in their school, as Sonia did since the 9th grade. Sonia's full award letter is posted below:

This is Sonia's Real Award letter from the private college:

Dear Sonia,

We are pleased to offer this financial aid package to assist you and your family in planning for the 2020-21 academic year. All awards are based on the information you reported and are contingent upon making satisfactory academic progress and meeting all other eligibility requirements. Your award is based on your cost of attendance. If your housing or enrollment status changes, you must notify us and your award will be adjusted to reflect the appropriate cost of attendance. Other important terms and conditions appear on page 3.

Financial Aid Award	Amount (Year)	Fall	Spring
Campus Connection Grant	$3,000	$1,500	$1,500
Presidential Scholarship	$25,000	$12,500	$12,500
Federal Direct Subsidized Loan	$3,500	$1,750	$1,750
Federal Direct Unsub. Loan	$2,000	$1,000	$1,000
College Work-Study Program	$2,300	$1,150	$1,150

To ACCEPT your financial aid offer, please log into your College "NAME" of NJ portal at mycollege.edu and click on the "Applicant" or "Student" tab, then Accept my financial aid. Proceed to ACCEPT or DECLINE or REDUCE your loan offer(s). Yours Sincerely, Office of Financial Aid.

Tuition and fees	$44,460	Books, supplies	$1500
Room & Board	$14,390	**Total direct costs**	$60,350

Financial Planning Options

Cash, check, credit card payment, Monthly payment plans, Supplemental loan – Federal Direct PLUS loan, Remaining balance – alternative, a private loan

Complete the Stafford Loan Master Promissory Note and REQUIRED entrance counseling (if applicable) online at studentloan.gov after May 1. Loan origination fees are subject to change based on funding at the federal level.

Respond promptly to any information requests from outside organizations.

All awards are subject to change based on receipt of additional information, changes in enrollment or housing status, changes in academic standing, federal, state, or institutional requirements, availability of budgeted funds, or receipt of any additional scholarships or grants. The university may adjust or correct awards at any time.

Eligibility for a need-based loan is evaluated each year after you file your annual FAFSA.

You may be selected for verification at any time based on information provided on your FAFSA.

If you enroll in an accelerated program, you will not be eligible for institutional gift aid.

If you have been awarded aid that is NOT listed on this award letter, please contact our officers immediately so we can coordinate it with this award to assess your eligibility within the current fiscal year.

Eligibility for Campus Connection Grant is contingent upon living in campus housing.

If you examine Sonia's awards in my excel spreadsheet, you will notice that the Private College ends up costing the same as the in-state public university, which would be a high reach for Sonia. The Private College is a better fit for Sonia. Now that the grandparents are willing to help out with $10,000 each year, Sonia's parents are paying the AFC, their Affordable Family Contribution.

Use the federal shopping sheet to examine the amount of aid the federal government gives you: It should be the same amount at every college that accepted you.

Most colleges cannot fund the full demonstrated need of families, even after they offer sizeable merit scholarships, and state aid kicks in, as in Meredith's case below. The issue with this financial aid award is that the college included the PLUS loan for parents on the last line. The family wondered if his was a sort of aid that would be forgiven or a real loan. It can be confusing for uninitiated parents to figure it out.

Colleges use their own financial aid award forms that vary from college to college. It's not always clear what is federal, institutional and merit aid.

The U.S. Department of Education's College Financing Plan is very clear. There's a section where the college should enter the federal EFC and Institutional EFC. This would show families their expected family contribution and add transparency to the process. But, few colleges use this form.

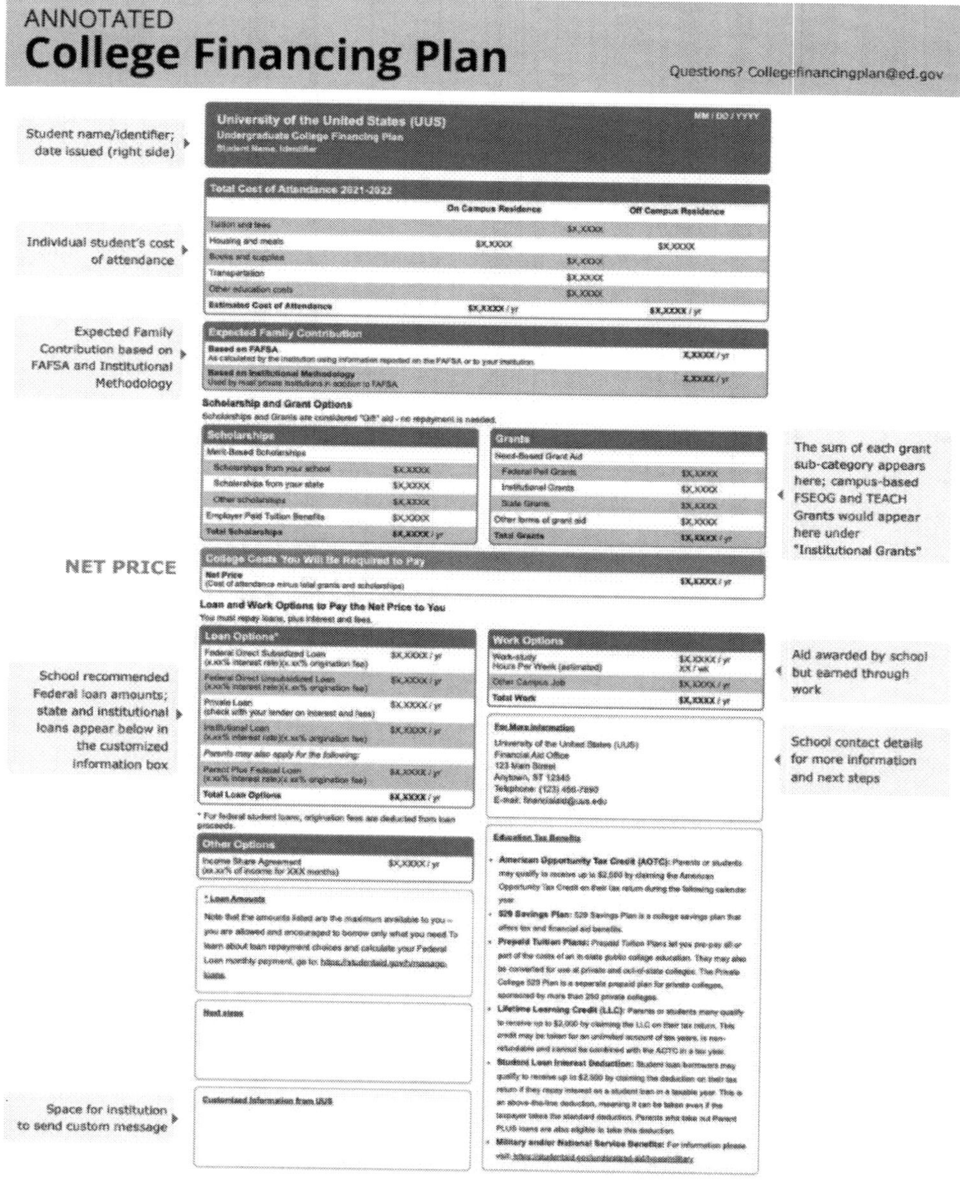

ANNOTATED

College Financing Plan

Questions? Collegefinancingplan@ed.gov

Student name/identifier; date issued (right side)

University of the United States (UUS)
Undergraduate College Financing Plan
Student Name, Identifier
MM / DD / YYYY

Individual student's cost of attendance

Total Cost of Attendance 2021-2022	On Campus Residence		Off Campus Residence
Tuition and fees		$X,XXXX	
Housing and meals	$X,XXXX		$X,XXXX
Books and supplies		$X,XXXX	
Transportation		$X,XXXX	
Other education costs		$X,XXXX	
Estimated Cost of Attendance	$X,XXXX / yr		$X,XXXX / yr

Expected Family Contribution based on FAFSA and Institutional Methodology

Expected Family Contribution	
Based on FAFSA As calculated by the institution using information reported on the FAFSA or to your institution.	X,XXXX / yr
Based on Institutional Methodology Used by most private institutions in addition to FAFSA.	X,XXXX / yr

Scholarship and Grant Options
Scholarships and Grants are considered "Gift" aid - no repayment is needed.

Scholarships	
Merit-Based Scholarships	
Scholarships from your school	$X,XXXX
Scholarships from your state	$X,XXXX
Other scholarships	$X,XXXX
Employer Paid Tuition Benefits	$X,XXXX
Total Scholarships	$X,XXXX / yr

Grants	
Need-Based Grant Aid	
Federal Pell Grants	$X,XXXX
Institutional Grants	$X,XXXX
State Grants	$X,XXXX
Other forms of grant aid	$X,XXXX
Total Grants	$X,XXXX / yr

The sum of each grant sub-category appears here; campus-based FSEOG and TEACH Grants would appear here under "Institutional Grants"

NET PRICE

College Costs You Will Be Required to Pay	
Net Price (Cost of attendance minus total grants and scholarships)	$X,XXXX / yr

Loan and Work Options to Pay the Net Price to You
You must repay loans, plus interest and fees.

School recommended Federal loan amounts; state and institutional loans appear below in the customized information box

Loan Options*	
Federal Direct Subsidized Loan	$X,XXXX / yr
Federal Direct Unsubsidized Loan	$X,XXXX / yr
Private Loan (check with your lender on interest and fees)	$X,XXXX / yr
Institutional Loan	$X,XXXX / yr
Parents may also apply for the following:	
Parent Plus Federal Loan	$X,XXXX / yr
Total Loan Options	$X,XXXX / yr

* For federal student loans, origination fees are deducted from loan proceeds.

Other Options	
Income Share Agreement (xx.xx% of income for XXX months)	$X,XXXX / yr

*** Loan Amounts**

Next steps

Customized Information from UUS

Space for institution to send custom message

Work Options	
Work-study Hours Per Week (estimated)	$X,XXXX / yr XX / wk
Other Campus Job	$X,XXXX / yr
Total Work	$X,XXXX / yr

Aid awarded by school but earned through work

For More Information
University of the United States (UUS)
Financial Aid Office
123 Main Street
Anytown, ST 12345
Telephone: (123) 456-7890
E-mail: financialaid@uus.edu

School contact details for more information and next steps

Education Tax Benefits

- **American Opportunity Tax Credit (AOTC):**
- **529 Savings Plan:**
- **Prepaid Tuition Plans:**
- **Lifetime Learning Credit (LLC):**
- **Student Loan Interest Deduction:**
- **Military and/or National Service Benefits:**

The Middle Class Squeeze

Take Meredith' situation: her EFC is $7,000. Her family just missed out of the federal Pell Grant, as her family's Adjusted Available Income was slightly over $65,000. However, even if Meredith qualified for a Pell Grant, the maximum amount for 2021-22 is $6,495 for full-time students. See Pell disbursement and payment schedule here in Dear Colleague Letter GEN-21-01. Her college cost is $61,326. A full Pell Grant would still be a drop in the bucket at colleges that cost over $60,000 a year.

After four years, Meredith would graduate with roughly $29,000 in loans for undergraduate, dependent students. Her parents would accrue roughly $80,000 of Parent PLUS loan debt. Meredith's first year cost will be $32,976.00 when we add the Parent PLUS loan for $19,550, Meredith's work study earnings and her loan for $5,500. This family would need to pay nearly four times their EFC to pay for first year. Her parents will have a hard time paying back the loans and will not be able to fund Meredith's younger brothers' college education. This isn't the right college for Meredith. It may be a match academically, but not financially.

What should Meredith do? What are this family's best options? If Meredith went to a community college, she would pay the entire cost of attendance because her EFC of $7,000 is higher than the usual tuition at public community colleges. It would be worth it if Meredith knew what she wanted to do. Let's say she was sure she wanted a degree in nursing or radiologic technology or assistant physical therapist. Degrees in the health sciences are in demand. But like many high-school graduates, Meredith isn't sure that she wants to work in the medical field. She could take liberal arts classes and then transfer to a four-year university. This would be a viable option. The second, more attractive option for Meredith is to start at a four-year institution.

Public universities offer a wide range of majors and are more affordable for in-state residents. Although public universities give out small scholarships if any, the Federal and State aid typically go farther because the costs are lower. Meredith's parents can afford the in-state public institution. Had they known that out-of-state universities charged their in-staters less, they wouldn't have applied.

Federal Loans

For Undergraduate Students and Their Parents

Few families have saved enough to pay for four years of college without incurring debt. Loans are integral part of paying for college and are here to stay.

"Loans" isn't the first word that comes out of admission representatives. They love to inform you of the programs, opportunities, and merits of their college, though not the costs, of which they're not sure. They may soften the shock of the cost of attendance by quoting the cost of tuition alone.

The costs of room, meals, general fees, transportation are variable and can add another $20,000.

Admissions representatives love to talk about scholarships. Everyone likes to get free money. Merit scholarships grab the attention of the public more than "discounts."

Admissions reps soften the blow by saying "there's financial aid." They don't say that it consists mainly of loans. That's the job of financial aid administrators, who know all too well that scholarships supplant need-based aid.

Colleges may discount their tuition by 10% or 15% via some merit scholarships for the student, but families can't bank on sending their kids to college without tens of thousands in reserve each year.

The colleges that meet 100% of demonstrated need are few and far in between and they typically reject 90% or more of applicants.

Families with high EFCs end up relying on their children getting merit scholarships to lower the sticker price. Middle-income parents need both merit and need-based aid, but it's hard to find both because merit scholarships have supplanted need-based aid. The latter is financial aid the college would have had to offer to meet demonstrated financial need.

Students whose families live below the poverty line will qualify for either a "simplified needs analysis" or "automatic zero EFC" under the federal methodology. These families qualify for some or all of the Pell Grant and Federal Work-Study. Still, they too must be willing to borrow if they want to go to college. This is when students may persuade their parents to borrow too much. I tell these students that it doesn't matter where they start college, and the community college offers an affordable alternative for the first two years. They could then transfer to a four-year college and graduate with two instead of four years of debt.

Federal Loans for Dependent Students

"High school seniors should receive help in how to think about a student loan and how to make sure that the education bought with the loan offers good prospects for repayment."

Richard Thaler, Nobel Prize-Winner in Economics.

Which loans are available for dependent undergraduate students?

Undergraduate students can borrow limited amounts of loans directly from the federal government. The U.S. Department of Education is your lender. It disburses the loans directly to the colleges.

Federal aid is the first source of funding that colleges to give out. Students must accept the federal aid available to them before colleges will consider handing out their institution's private aid.

- $5,500 in the first year
- $6,500 in the second year
- $7,500 in the third year
- $7,500 in the fourth year

Federal loans are also called William D. Ford "Direct" loans and "Stafford loans." You may see these listed on your award letter under any of those names.

Subsidized Direct Loan: If families demonstrate financial need, the government pays the interest on a portion of the Direct loan while the student is enrolled in school on at least a half-time basis. This is the *subsidized* portion of the Direct loan.

- $3,500 can be subsidized in the first year
- $4,500 can be subsidized in the second year
- $5,500 can be subsidized in the third year
- $5,500 can be subsidized in the fourth year

Any amounts the student doesn't get as a subsidized loan, they can borrow as an unsubsidized loan.

The additional $2,000 Direct Undergraduate loan is always unsubsidized. This list shows the maximum amount dependent students can borrow each year.

- $3,500 in the first year will be subsidized and $2,000 unsubsidized = $5,500.
- $4,500 in the second year will be subsidized and $2,000 unsubsidized. = $6,500.
- $5,500 in the third year will be subsidized and $2,000 unsubsidized. = $7,500.
- $5,500 in the fourth year will be subsidized and $2,000 unsubsidized. = $7,500.

As you can see, undergraduate students on can borrow up to $27,000 over four years. The balance is greater because of the interest accumulation. To borrow up to the aggregate limit, which is $31,000, requires borrowing for at least five years.

Dependent students whose parents are turned down for the Parent PLUS loan are allowed to borrow greater amounts, the same loan limits as independent students (e.g., $9,500, $10,500, $12,500 and $12,500). It's not always a good thing for the student because the debt burden increases. If the student will graduate in engineering or finance or computer science or nursing there's a better chance of finding gainful employment than if the student majors in a lower-paying field of study.

I advise my students to pay the interest each year on their unsubsidized loans, so that when they graduate, they will not owe more than the principal borrowed. **On the $2,000 unsubsidized loan, the yearly interest would be approximately $55.00, assuming an interest rate of 2.75%.**

The following table shows the annual and aggregate limits for independent and graduate students. Note that dependent students whose parents are unable to obtain Parent PLUS loans are eligible for the loan limits in the Independent Student column of the table.

Year	Dependent Students	Independent Students
First-Year Undergraduate Annual Loan Limit	$5,500 – No more than $3,500 of this amount may be in subsidized loans.	$9,500 – No more than $3,500 of this amount may be in subsidized loans.
Second-Year Undergraduate Annual Loan Limit	$6,500 – No more than $4,500 of this amount may be in subsidized loans.	$10,500 – No more than $4,500 of this amount may be in subsidized loans.
Third-Year and Beyond Undergraduate Annual Loan Limit	$7,500 – No more than $5,500 of this amount may be in subsidized loans.	$12,500 – No more than $5,500 of this amount may be in subsidized loans.
Graduate or Professional Student Annual Loan Limit	Not Applicable – All graduate and professional degree students are considered independent.	$20,500 – Unsubsidized only. Medical school students get a higher limit ($40,500).
Subsidized and Unsubsidized Aggregate Loan Limit	$31,000 – No more than $23,000 of this amount may be in subsidized loans.	$57,500 for undergraduates – No more than $23,000 of this amount may be in subsidized loans. $138,500 for graduate or professional students – No more than $65,500 of this amount may be in subsidized loans. The graduate aggregate limits include all federal loans received for undergraduate study.

Interest Rates for 2020-21

(from studentaid.gov)

	Undergraduate Borrowers	Graduate or Professional Borrowers	Parents and Graduate or Professional Students
Interest Rate	2.75%	4.30%	5.30%
Type of Loans	Direct Subsidized Loans and Direct Unsubsidized Loans	Direct Unsubsidized Loans	Direct PLUS Loans

The interest rates illustrated above from July 1, 2020 to June 30, 2021 are low considered to previous years' rates. The rates are pegged to the high yield on the last auction of Treasury Notes in May. Then the interest rates take effect from July 1 to June 30, and such rates are fixed for the life of the loan. In effect, every year new federal student loans have new interest rates.

Interest accrues daily as explained in the formula below:

From studentaid.gov: How is interest calculated? The formula below consists of multiplying your outstanding principal balance by the interest rate factor and multiplying that result by the number of days since you made your last payment.

Simple daily interest formula:
Interest Amount = Outstanding Principal Balance × Interest Rate Factor × Number of Days Since Last Payment

Additional notes: Interest continues to accrue during periods of non-payment, such as during deferment and forbearance. Even in default, the interest keeps accruing. **One exception**: as part of the Covid-19 relief effort, borrowers enjoyed a pause on student loan payments from March 2020 to December 2020. This was further extended by the Biden/Harris administration until September 30, 2021. In addition, during this 19-month relief period, the interest was waived.

This became the ideal time to rehabilitate defaulted loans without making any payments! I can only hope that the borrowers were contacted with this information and that this provision was clearly explained to them. To learn more about loan debt refer to The Institute for College Access & Success (TICAS).

For the most current interest rates and fees, visit https://studentaid.gov/understand-aid/types/loans/interest-rates

We can expect that many parents will take advantage of the low-interest rates on the Direct loan for dependent students when the terms are so favorable. It would be unwise for parents to borrow a PLUS loan at the rate of 5.3% and with 4% fees, no matter how good the rate is compared to previous years, when their student can borrow at the rate of 2.75% and roughly 1% fee. The glitch is that dependent students can borrow only limited amounts, and parents are left to borrow larger amounts at higher rates.

Don't Forget: Loans Have Fees

Young borrowers are often surprised by the loan fees. The fees are costs in addition to the interest rate. These are like points on a mortgage: the borrower pays to originate the loan. The lender, whether the government of a private bank, incurs expenses to disburse a loan to a college on behalf of a student. These fees can also include guarantee fees, to insure the loans against default.

Fees are subtracted from the amount disbursed to colleges. The loan fees that are a percentage of the total loan amount and deducted proportionately from each loan disbursement your school receives while you (the student) are enrolled in school. This means the schools receives slightly less than the amount you borrowed. Many colleges have started listing the loan fees on the award letters. I think this is a good idea so that the student will see that the school is receiving approximately one percent less than $5,500. It may incentivize the student to pay it.

Some borrowers opt to have the fees added to the loan balance, so that the amount disbursed is the amount borrowed. (Between the fees being added to the loan balance, and interest begin capitalized during the in-school and grace period, the loan balance at graduation can be about 20% greater than the amount disbursed.)

The fee for disbursing Parent PLUS loans is typically higher than the fee charged for federal student loans. The fee is 4.228% from October 1, 2020 through September 30, 2021. It's also deducted from the total loan amount disbursed. If parents need to borrow $10,000, the origination and disbursement fee will be $422.80. The college receives roughly $9,577, and parents are responsible for paying the entire amount of $10,000. If parents need exactly $10,000, they will need to borrow more, approximately $10,441 to net that amount.

An advantage of the Parent PLUS loan, like the federal student loans, is that the interest rate is fixed and the interest paid is tax deductible. Interest starts accumulating upon disbursement. While this may seem like a high-interest rate, those with average and below-average credit scores will find it challenging to get better terms in the private sector. The origination fee of 4.228% provides a life insurance policy. If the borrower were to die, the loan will be forgiven.

The chart below shows the loan fees for Direct Subsidized Loans, Direct Unsubsidized Loans, and Direct PLUS Loans first disbursed before October 1, 2021.

Loan Fees for Direct Subsidized Loans and Direct Unsubsidized Loans	Loan Fee
On or after 10/1/20 and before 10/1/21	**1.057%**
On or after 10/1/19 and before 10/1/20	1.059%

Loan Fees for Direct PLUS	Loan Fee
On or after 10/1/20 and before 10/1/21	**4.228%**
On or after 10/1/19 and before 10/1/20	4.236%

Advantages of Federal Loans

A benefit of the Direct Loan program for undergraduates is that it helps students establish credit. The student alone is the borrower.

A commercial lender or bank would not lend funds to a teenager without a cosigner. The federal government is absorbing the risk that students may not pay.

It is strange to hear that the majority of borrowers who default on their loans have a balance less than $5,000. I wonder why they give up when they're so close to the finish line. Were these students who left college without a degree? A $5,000 loan would be hard to pay if the borrower earns only minimum wages of $7.25 an hour.

In my practice, I do talk about student loans with my students. It opens their eyes to the investment they are about to make. They realize they have skin in the game. I take time to explain this debt must be repaid. This calculator shows what the average monthly cost will be over ten years.

Independent Students Can Borrow Larger Amounts

Independent students (see definition in Glossary) can borrow larger amounts than dependent students.

Who qualifies for independent status? Graduate and professional school students are considered independent. Other criteria: they're 24 years old or older, married with children they support, or have served in the military. They are orphans or wards of the court, homeless or at risk of being homeless.

Independent students can borrow a larger amount of loans:

- Up to $9,500 in their first undergraduate year, but no more than $3,500 can be in subsidized loans.
- In their second year, they can borrow up to $10,500, and no more than $4,500 may be in subsidized loans.
- In the third year and beyond, they can borrow up to $12,500 per year, and no more than $5,500 of this amount can be in subsidized loans.

If you refer to the loan limits for dependent students, you realize that these independent students are taking on more unsubsidized loans that are more costly.

Dependent students whose parents are turned down for the Parent PLUS loan are also eligible for the higher loan limits available to independent students.

The U.S. Department of Education offers a nifty calculator here: https://studentaid.gov/loan-simulator/

Parent PLUS Loans

How to cover yearly increases in college costs? No worries. Just take out a larger Parent PLUS loan. While dependent students can borrow only limited amounts, parents can borrow from the federal PLUS loan up to the full cost of attendance minus any other aid received. The same advice about paying the interest needs to be emphasized for Parent PLUS loan borrowers and graduate students who borrow the Grad PLUS loan.

Studies show that most parents and graduate students defer all interest payments until after graduation. Deferring interest payment is just a checkmark on the promissory note. It's one simple and easy question at the outset, but a difficult checkmark to change later. The devil is in the details. The deferral of all interest is the bane of borrowers' existence. It results in larger PLUS loan amounts because interest starts being charged on interest after the borrower graduates and the six-month grace period ends. Some parents are facing retirement while still repaying Parent PLUS loans!

When they sign the promissory note, parents need to pay careful attention and check the box "yes" for paying the interest as you go along. Finding the right private loan may result in savings, but again, borrowers need to do careful research, crunch the numbers, assess the risks, and read the fine print before checking the boxes on the promissory note. There's a reason why some parents aren't able to retire when they reach old age. If their children attended expensive universities, they are paying off student loans.

Grad PLUS Loans

Graduate students can also borrow from the Federal Direct PLUS loan program. These are the same loans as the Parent PLUS loans, but they are called Grad PLUS loans because they are borrowed by graduate students.

Students heading to professional schools, such as medical school, veterinary school, and law school, end up borrowing very large amounts.

Graduate and professional school students can start repayment immediately or they can opt to postpone repayment of both loan and interest until six months after graduation. If they are in school full-time it will be hard to start repaying the interest while in school.

Those students accepted into fields that will bring a high return on their investment, such as medical, veterinary, dental, or elite law schools, will likely be able to pay back their debt.

It's when they borrow large amounts to pay for a Master's degree in graphic design, photography, or music management that they may find it hard to get jobs or well-paying jobs upon graduation. I'm a huge believer in trying to get assistantships, fellowships, teaching positions or resident advisor positions to help pay for graduate school.

The chart shows that students graduate with approximately $30,000 of loans (including interest) while parents typically borrow close to $40,000 on average to make up for what they haven't been able to save. Chart by Mark Kantrowitz and the New York Times study. https://www.nytimes.com/2018/07/11/your-money/student-loan-debt-parents.html

Most of the students I work with have parents who have planned for college expenses and can tap into various resources to pay for college. Typically, they have 529 plans, savings, checking accounts, a line of home or business equity. They easily qualify for federal PLUS loans for parents. Typically, parents borrow larger amounts to pay for the third and fourth years of college.

Definitions of Loan Terminology

Dependent students in each of their undergraduate years can borrow limited amounts from the William D. Ford Federal Direct Loan program: $5,500 in the first year, $6,500 in the second year, $7,500 in the third and fourth year. These limits prevent dependent students from overborrowing. Given the high cost of four-year colleges, these loan amounts are not enough for the highest-cost colleges. Parents must be willing and able to borrow the remaining charges.

Financial aid is a misnomer. They should be called "student loans" because student and parent borrowers repay them with the added interest rate and fees. However, federal loans offer better lending terms, more income-driven repayment options, undergraduate students can borrow some amounts on their own without cosigners, and are typically less expensive than commercial loans. For example, during the Covid-19 pandemic, the U.S. Department of Education suspended the collection of monthly payments. Such helpful measures during a national emergency wouldn't be implemented by commercial banks. The private lenders offered special Covid-19 forbearances, where they suspended the repayment obligation for a few months, but continued to charge interest on the loans.

Capitalization of student loan interest: Compound interest is charged based on the full balance of the loan, including both principal and interest (i.e., charging interest on interest). This occurs when the interest is capitalized (added to the loan balance). Interest capitalization makes the loan more costly. Some lenders capitalize interest only once, when the loan status changes. Other lenders capitalize interest more frequently, such as monthly.

College is possible for those who graduate from high school and want to earn a college degree. However, depending on the choice of college, families can either end up in debt, or easily afford some institutions.

The PLUS loan for parents is part of the federal government efforts to lend funds to parents to help them pay for college. Parents can borrow up to the full cost of education minus any other aid. The PLUS loan is often the vehicle with which parents pay their EFC and gap. Perhaps as a result of enrollment management strategies, colleges have leverage financial aid and cover the gap by offering parents the PLUS loan. "College is possible if parents are willing to borrow" was the mantra I heard from financial aid administrators. While PLUS loans offer a better deal than private loans, the amount of borrowing does make a difference in the length of repayment and cash flow hindrance.

Private Loans

Loans are the more common way to fill the gap between the EFC and the cost of college. When federal loans are not enough, private loans may fill the gap. This table shows the differences between federal and private loans.

Federal education loans	Private or commercial education loans
Loan interest and fees are deductible on federal income tax returns. Loans for Undergraduate students include the subsidized and unsubsidized Direct Loan. Students can take these out on their own. They don't need a cosigner. Interest rates are fixed. The PLUS loan for parents has a lighter credit check than for private loans. Parents with good to average credit can still qualify for the PLUS loan and this may be cheaper for them than a private loan. The borrower of a PLUS loan must not have an adverse credit history, such as a bankruptcy discharge, foreclosure, repossession, tax lien, wage garnishment or default determination within the last five years. Borrowers must also not have a serious delinquency (90 or more days) on $2,085 or more in debt within the last two years. If you default on a federal loan, you will not be eligible for another. Once parents have used their savings and a portion of current income, colleges evaluate parents for PLUS loans eligibility. Cannot be discharged in bankruptcy (except under extreme circumstances).	Loan interest and fees are deductible on federal income tax returns. Undergraduate students cannot take out private loans by themselves. Private loans have more restrictive credit standards and require at least one cosigner with good credit. Some newer loans offer a cosigner release after several years of on-time payments by the student. Interest rates are fixed or variable. With private loans, a better the parent's credit score yields a better interest rate. Here's an example that shows how variable interest rates linked to credit rating: Excellent credit: 3.609% (790-850) Strong credit: 6.09% (650-780) Good credit: 10.99% (take the PLUS instead) People with ongoing employment may be able to get lower rates. Some loans check students' grades as well. Very difficult to discharge in bankruptcy.

If a borrower is in default, the federal government can garnish your wages, take away your tax refund and offset Social Security benefit payments to repay your loan. Standard repayment (10-years), graduated, extended repayment and income-driven repayment plans are available . Federal loan consolidation is available. Parents can choose to defer paying interest and principal until six months after graduation. Federal loans offer autopay discounts of a 0.25% interest rate reduction.	No origination fees are charged but private loans may have only one repayment plan. Private loans may require repayment immediately upon disbursement. Banks cannot garnish wages without a court order. It's in part why private lenders require cosigners, so they can go after two or more individuals to get repayment. Private loans can reduce your interest rate by 0.25% or 0.50% if you make payments through automatic bank transfers.
If the borrower becomes permanently disabled or dies, PLUS loan will be cancelled.	If a borrower becomes disabled loans don't get cancelled. If the borrower dies the amount borrowed is charged against the estate. About half of private loans offer death and disability discharges similar to the ones available on federal loans.
Federal loans offer income-driven repayment plans and Public Service Loan Forgiveness (PSLF).	Private lenders generally do not offer income-driven repayment plans or loan forgiveness programs.

Private lenders may be able to offer competitive rates with the PLUS loan depending on market fluctuations and the borrower's credit scores. The PLUS loan interest rate is fixed. Theoretically, if families have excellent credit scores (790-850), they might be able to get a private loan at a lower interest rate with no points or fees. But such loans may not have the death and disability benefits of a Parent PLUS loan. If the borrower of a Parent PLUS loan dies, the loan is forgiven.

PLUS loan borrowers, whether parents or graduate students, can defer payment while the student is enrolled in school on at least a half-time basis. This can be useful to a point. If borrowers let all interest and origination fees capitalize until after the student graduates, then it can be quite a shock to start repayments. Parents and graduate students must gauge the risks and forecast whether they will earn enough to pay back this debt.

How do private loans compare with federal loans? A typical private loan is either cosigned by the parent or borrowed by the parent. The best interest rates go to the strongest credit and you can choose fixed or variable rates, and can stretch out the repayment period. The interest rates on federal loan are set annually on July 1 and are fixed for the life of the loan. Every borrower gets the same interest rate, regardless of credit scores and credit history. The interest rates on private loans may change more frequently (e.g., monthly or quarterly) and depend on the borrower's credit profile. In some years the Parent PLUS loan may be more or less advantageous to you, based on your credit rating and what's available in the marketplace. Parents should shop around carefully for the loans with the best interest rates and terms.

Just like everything else in life, one size doesn't fit all. Families need to become well informed about loans. It's my hope that readers will spend time sizing up their amount of risk tolerance when selecting loans and sizing up whether they will be able to meet the terms of the loan.

Whether parents borrow from private lenders or the federal government, I would strongly advise using the repayment simulators. These will show how much the loan will cost if interest is deferred until after graduation and after the six months grace period versus whether the interest is paid all along. There are many loans out there and families need to figure out their risk tolerance, the likelihood of being able to pay back within a specific time frame and fulfil the terms of the loan as written.

Lending is a profitable business and a college education typically leads to profitability over the lifespan of a person. It's why parents and students are willing to borrow to compete a degree or even to get a foot in the door of a university. It's still the ticket to higher earnings – but only if you can get into a program that gives you the training you prefer. It's useless to get a degree you're not interested in or good at.

Fast forward to the new lending landscape: even colleges have gotten into the business of lending. For example, Davidson College doesn't participate in the federal student aid program, except for the federal Pell Grant. When it comes time to offer loans to pay for college, Davidson College offers its own institutional loans. According to the Associate Dean of financial aid, Mr. David Gelinas, those loans have a much lower interest rate and easier repayment terms. It also shelters the college from federal oversight on the success rate of graduates repaying their federal loans.

During the Covid-19 pandemic, the House passed a two trillion dollars stimulus bill, the CARES Act, on March 27, 2020. This bill included a provision for federal student loan borrowers: they could stop payments on their loans for six months, through September 30, 2020, during which time there would be no further accumulation of interest, penalties or fees on the remaining balances. Federal loan servicers were supposed to reach out to borrowers and inform them that interest was set at 0% for the following six months.

These beneficial changes went into effect from March 13, 2020 until September 30, 2020. They applied to defaulted and non-defaulted Direct loans made directly by the government. It did not apply to those "older" loans made under the FFEL program where the lender was a commercial entity, nor did it include Federal Perkins loans owned by colleges. For example, if loans were made by a Sallie Mae lender or MEFA or RISLA or PHEAA, not to single them out because every State Higher Education Authority couldn't keep their hands out of the "education loans" cookie jar. Those "older" loans need to be discharged because most borrowers have more than paid the principal. They took the loans that the colleges offered under FFELP not knowing that they could choose the government's Direct Loans which cost less and offer more flexible repayment terms. This CARES Act relief program came out of the blue with broad-brush benefits for newer borrowers who may have done just fine without it, and those who borrowed from private lenders got nothing.

The payment pause and interest waiver was later extended through December 31, 2020, then January 30, 2021 and most recently through September 30, 2021.

While so much is said about the 1.6 trillion dollars of student loan debt, it's actually a source of revenue for the government. Of the 45 million borrowers, less than 10% are 90 days or more delinquent in their payments. The short-term 3-year cohort default rate is 9.7%. Most defaults occur within the first five years after the borrower enters repayment.

Under FFELP, in the 80's, 90's and early 2000's, students and parents accepted whichever Stafford and PLUS loans that the colleges recommended. These were more costly loans, guaranteed by the government but handled by private lenders. Many of these "older" borrowers have paid the principal amount twice over. I feel sorry for them because those loans are sold to collection agencies for pennies on the dollar. Then collectors harass and threaten the borrowers and add fees upon fees. They inflict undeserved pain and anxiety on borrowers who may have already paid the principal several times over if it weren't for the penalties, compound interest and fees.

Studies show that the majority of borrowers default when they have a small balance left to pay. This is what happened to Mr. Snyder, who declared bankruptcy and assumed all his debts were discharged. Yet, a collection agency came knocking at his door twenty years later, demanding twice the amount he'd borrowed. The lender, originator, servicer and finally third-party collection agencies all make money off these borrowers. Servicing companies, banks and other lenders should not be allowed to sell defaulted education loans to collection agencies. They hunt down the borrowers like criminals. When banks and other commercial lenders write off nonperforming loans they receive a tax deduction.

It should end there for both the bank and the borrower. But it doesn't. The banks then can sell the bad-debts to collection companies. It should be illegal because it's inhuman. The money that borrowers are paying in fees and interest are excessive. Older loans should be discharged.

This CARES Act spread a lot of goodies to newer borrowers as if at random. Some were managing just fine but took advantage of not having to pay for six months, and having it look like they did make payments, which established better credit. But those "older" borrowers who took student loans from private companies got nothing. With those funds they could re-build their life and the money would find their way into the economy.

Promissory note: Before you sign a loan promissory note, ready all the fine print. Typically, federal loans are better than private loans. They are more flexible and provide several repayment methods based on the borrower's income. Private companies encourage both parents to sign the promissory note or find additional co-signors who can be your back up. In other words, can your sister, aunt, grandparent also sign the promissory note?

They say this way they can lower the interest rate, usually by an infinitesimal amount. I learned that there's more involved with a loan than the interest rate. If the borrower misses a payment, or, God forbid, should die, the cosigners may be responsible for repaying the debt. For example, my student's dad passed away when she was in her third year of college. Because he alone had signed the promissory note, the loan was cancelled. Had his wife also signed the note, the loans would now be hers.

Parents need to be careful with those promissory notes and keep all paperwork on file. Since 2004, student loan debt for those 60 years of age and older has grown faster than any other age group. Collectively, individuals ages 50 on up owe 22% of the current $1.6 trillion of federal loan debt. They are also much more likely to be in default on their debt than younger borrowers. These people took loans to pay for their own education and the education of their children and grandchildren.

Going to college is a highly charged, emotional decision. Most parents recognize that it's their duty to support their children and want to contribute to their college education. Students typically recognize that it's their duty to contribute to their cost of education, and often earn some money during summer jobs or babysitting. We all know that students can't possibly pay for college out of their earnings. The landscape of education loans may be unchartered territory for families. Students and parents may be led astray by wishful thinking and false assumptions. By becoming informed consumers, families can gain the freedom they need to make better choices over their finances and the current system of higher education.

References

The Institute for College Access and Success (TICAS)

- Student Debt
- Private Loan Info
- Trends in Affordability

Federal Grants

Pell Grant Awarded to undergraduate students who have exceptional financial need and who have not earned a bachelor's, graduate, or professional degree; in some cases, students enrolled in a postbaccalaureate teacher certification program may receive a Federal Pell Grant.

- A student who meets certain requirements might be eligible for a larger Pell Grant if his or her parent died as result of military service in Iraq or Afghanistan or in the line of duty as a public safety officer
- Pell Grant lifetime eligibility is limited to 12 semesters or the equivalent. The annual award for students with zero ability to pay is up to $6,495 for the 2021–22 award year.

FSEOG Grant Federal Supplemental Educational Opportunity Grant) Awarded to undergraduate students who have exceptional financial need and who have not earned a bachelor's or graduate degree

- Federal Pell Grant recipients receive priority
- Not all schools participate in this program
- Funds depend on availability at the school; check for the school's deadline.

TEACH Grant: Teacher Education Assistance for College and Higher Education: For undergraduate, postbaccalaureate, or graduate students who are enrolled in programs designed to prepare them to teach in a high-need field at the elementary or secondary school level

- The TEACH Grant provides up to $4,000 a year
- The recipient must agree to serve for a minimum of four years (within eight years of completing or ceasing enrollment in the program for which the student received the grant funds) as a full-time teacher in a high-need field in a school or educational service agency that serves low-income students
- The recipient must attend a participating school and meet certain academic achievement requirements
- Failure to complete the teaching service commitment will result in the grant being converted to a Direct Unsubsidized Loan that must be repaid, with interest accruing retroactively from the date of disbursement.

Iraq and Afghanistan Service Grant For students whose parent or guardian was a member of the U.S. armed forces and died as a result of performing military service in Iraq or Afghanistan after the events of 9/11

- Must be ineligible for a Pell Grant due to having less financial need than is required to receive Federal Pell Grant funds
- Must have been younger than 24 years old or enrolled at least part-time at a college or career school at the time of the parent's or guardian's death.

- The grant amount is the same as the Federal Pell Grant

Occasionally a student may have to pay back part or all of a grant if, for example, he or she withdraws from school early or doesn't fulfill the requirements of the TEACH Grant service obligation.

529 College Savings Plans

I've met financial planners and CPAs at conferences, Rotary meetings, and parties, who ask me how 529 college savings plans affect financial aid. By now, you know there's no easy, yes-no, black or white answers in financial aid. There are lots of "It depends" answers. There are factors, conditions, (and headaches) that come into play. Who owns the 529 plan? Is it the student, or a parent, grandparent, or another individual such as an uncle? Does the student qualify for free aid such as grants based on demonstrated need? Is such aid federal or institutional?

You'll remember that student assets increase the EFC by a larger percentage than parent assets. If the student is the owner of an UTMA/UGMA account, the asset increases the EFC by 20% of the asset value under the Federal Methodology and 25% under the Institutional Methodology.

The treatment of 529 plans is different.

- If a 529 plan is owned by a dependent student's parent, the EFC will increase by up to 5.64% of the asset value. Distributions for a parent-owned 529 plan have no impact.
- If a 529 plan is owned by a dependent student (e.g., a custodial 529 plan), it is reported as a parent asset on the FAFSA, increasing the EFC by up to 5.64% of the asset value. Distributions from a student-owned 529 plan have no impact.
- If a 529 plan is owned by anybody else, such as a grandparent, it is not reported as an asset on the FAFSA, but distributions count as untaxed income to the student on a future FAFSA, increasing the EFC by up to 50% of the distribution amount.

Thus, a grandparent-owned 529 plan can have a big impact on the EFC. In that case, it would be better for grandparents to transfer the 529 Plan to the parents or rollover assets from the 529 plan to a parent-owned 529 plan so that the increase to the EFC would be less.

If the transfer or rollover occurs after the FAFSA is filed, it won't be reported as an asset on the FAFSA, and the distribution will not be reported as untaxed income on a future FAFSA.

One caveat: Some states consider an outbound rollover to an out-of-state 529 plan to be a non-qualified distribution, causing taxes on the earnings portion of the rollover. This can be avoided by setting up a parent-owned 529 plan in the same state as the grandparent-owned 529 plan.

If the student receives need-based aid, including work-study or a scholarship, the timing of the 529 plan distributions from grandparent-owned 529 plans can make a difference. Since the FAFSA is based on prior-prior year income, distributions starting on January 1 of the sophomore year in college will not be reported on a subsequent year's FAFSA, if the student graduates within four years. So, one workaround for grandparent-owned 529 plans is to delay taking a distribution until then. But, what if the student doesn't graduate in four years? What if the student attends a college that requires the CSS Profile?

Another option is to wait until the student graduates, and then use a qualified distribution from the 529 plan to repay student loans. There is a $10,000 lifetime limit per borrower.

I worked with a student who qualified for the free and reduced lunch program. When the maternal grandmother died, the student's mother receives a small inheritance, including $25,000 in a 529 plan. I felt sympathy for this mom and her son, who had special needs besides. I would want her to make the most out of that 529 plan. So, I referred her to my colleague Paula Bishop, a CPA in Seattle, WA. She knows how to stretch a budget to yield the most. She knows all the tax implications and how particular colleges will evaluate the 529 Plans, Coverdell and tuition payment plans, UGMA, and more. I know she will make grandma's 529 funds go further.

If students receive no need-based aid, it makes no difference when the 529 funds are disbursed to the college. The owner may be more interested in the tax credits and needs to know what to do.

The 529 plan will send the account owner an IRS Form 1099-Q to report distributions from the 529 plan. The family may also receive an IRS Form 1098-T from the college to report payments received for qualified tuition and related expenses. This can help when trying to determine eligibility for the tuition tax credits.

Tax Credits and Other Tax Breaks

The Consolidated Appropriations Act, 2021, adjusted the income phaseouts for the Lifetime Learning Tax Credit (LLTC), so it now has the same income phaseouts as the American Opportunity Tax Credit (AOTC).

Both provide a tax credit based on amounts paid for tuition and textbooks.

- The AOTC provides 100% of the first $2,000 in qualified expenses and 25% of the second $2,000, for a total tax credit of up to $2,500. It is partially refundable (up to $1,000) and is claimed per student. It is limited to four years.
- The LLTC provides 20% of the first $10,000 in qualified expenses, for a total tax credit of up to $2,000. It is claimed per taxpayer. It is available for an unlimited number of years.

You cannot double-dip, so you can't claim both tax credits for the same student.

Both tax credits phase out at $80,000 to $90,000 in modified adjusted gross income (single filers) and twice that for married filing jointly. Taxpayers who file separate returns are not eligible.

The Consolidated Appropriations Act, 2021, has also permanently repealed the Tuition and Fees Deduction. So, the cost of tuition and fees is no longer deductible on federal income tax returns.

The tax-free status for employer-paid student loan repayment assistance programs, or LRAPs, has been extended through the end of 2025. IRC 127 lets employers help their employees pay for college and repay their student loans, for up to $5,250 per year.

Scholarships are tax-free if used to pay for tuition and textbooks. Amounts used to pay for room and board, transportation and other living expenses are taxable.

The Student Loan Interest Deduction lets you deduct up to $2,500 in interest paid on federal and private student loans each year. This deduction is claimed as an above-the-line exclusion from income, so you can claim it even if you don't itemize.

Student loan forgiveness is tax-free through the end of 2025.

Financial Aid Appeals

Before you file for an appeal for more financial aid, you must review your award letters. Be sure to enter all awards onto my live excel spreadsheet at www.eduave.com/Resourcelibrary so that you clearly note the amounts that each college has provided.

When you calculate the amount of indirect costs, allocate the same amount for books and supplies, transportation, and miscellaneous personal expenses, so you're comparing apples with apples. This means that if you allocate $50 for living expenses at one college, you should do the same for the other. Enter the direct costs such as the tuition, room and board, fees and loan fee expenses. Then, enter the amount of federal aid, state aid, and the aid the college awarded you. The excel spreadsheet allows you to see which amounts are self-help aid as opposed to grants. The amount of federal aid should be roughly the same.

The U.S. Department of Education provides the College Financing Plan that colleges can use to provide clarity about their financial aid awards. I believe you could mention this sheet if you should talk with a financial aid administrator.

For example, you could say that you've entered the award from their college on the form and have questions. The vital question is the amount of contribution under the Federal Methodology and Institutional Methodology that they've assigned to you.

The gap between your EFC and the COA is prohibitive. Some colleges will say "we can only fill 25% of demonstrated need."

You should also review the college's appeal form on their website, to examine the type of information they're asking.

If one college awards significantly more or less aid, it may be useful to ask why. For example, one college awarded more FSEOG grant or larger Pell Grant and Federal Work Study.

According to Mark Kantrowitz, if parents find that the difference between colleges is more than $5,000, over four years the difference will be $20,000, and you can find colleges that will charge you less.

However, parents need to be careful when they engage in "negotiations" with financial aid administrators. They may be offended if you use that term. It's better to ask for help understanding the financial aid award letter before asking for more funds.

Financial aid administrators can apply professional judgment to change the FAFSA data elements and/or cost of attendance and thereby create more financial need for you. They have to carefully document the changes, so they will need documentation of your special circumstances.

Financial aid administrators are more likely to make an adjustment to the FAFSA or cost of attendance when you present them with documentation of special circumstances that affect your ability to pay.

For example, remember that the FAFSA is based on two-year-old income information. If your income has changed a lot since then or you lost your job, the college financial aid administrator may approve your appeal. Provide the financial aid administrator with a copy of a recent pay slip or proof of recent receipt of unemployment benefits.

If you have any unusual expenses, tell them about that as well. It might be that you're paying private K-12 tuition for the student's sibling. Or, maybe you have a special needs child or elderly parent who needs expensive accommodations or nursing care.

Private funding from the college itself is more difficult to figure out. It's better if students themselves call the financial aid director whose signature is at the very bottom of the financial aid award letter.

After all, the student is the beneficiary and the college wants to make sure this student is committed to attending their school, and not just shopping around. Which is what you're doing. I encourage it. But only if you're truly committed to attend and remain there all four years if the school should increase the award.

Mark Kantrowitz has written a 279-page book, *How to Appeal for More College Financial Aid.* There's a free one-page tip sheet on the book's web site, kantrowitz.com/books/appeal, that summarizes the key steps in appealing for more financial aid.

I know it's hard for students to move away from the college they feel is "the right fit." But if your net costs turn out to be unreasonable, undoable, costly beyond your imagination, and the financial aid administrator cannot change your award, you must persuade your student to move to another college.

It's better to compromise than to graduate with large loans for both the student and the parents.

Which sort of situations and changes can be appealed?

If the Coronavirus pandemic caused you financial hardship, you'll find that financial aid administrators to be more than sympathetic. They are used to helping families facing unexpected natural disasters, from floods to droughts to forest fires.

The federal methodology considers the family income from the prior-prior years. A family's financial situation could have changed since then.

If you had unexpected bills, a car accident, or a medical emergency that resulted in costs that were not covered by your insurance, these can be brought to the administrator's attention. They will be especially sympathetic to costs that are due to factors beyond your control.

If you used the college's Net Price Calculator and the net cost on the award letter is much higher.

I've had divorced parents file an appeal when the student wanted to attend an out-of-state university located where one parent was a resident. The student was awarded in-state tuition without much trouble.

More than likely, administrators themselves will say you need to file an appeal and may give you the link to the form on their website. Be sure to review this tip sheet for situations that typically are very appealable. College Board Tip Sheet for Appeals and the situations are listed at the bottom of this chapter "Appeals."

Even if your situation doesn't fit within the appeal cases listed by the College Board, a conversation with your financial aid administrator will give you a better understanding of how your resources were assessed. You'll be able to explain why your out-of-pocket costs are out of line. Remember, you need to know your EFC under the Federal Methodology, if the college uses the FAFSA form only, and Institutional Methodology if the college uses the CSS Profile. As mentioned, the easiest way to get an approximate EFC is to run your numbers through the College Board's EFC calculator.

Sometimes there could be mistakes made in the processing of the application. If the net cost is going to strap your family financially you may want to explain it. For example, do you have other children who also need to get a college education? Did your circumstances change between the time you filed the CSS Profile and now? A Profile school collects three years of tax information, but FAFSA-only schools have the tax returns from the prior-prior year which is a snapshot that is two years old. If your current situation has changed since then, you have reason to appeal.

Don't be afraid to appeal. Do so *after* you see the financial aid award letter with the aid that the college is willing to give. Involve your student and let the student carry this bucket of water. Plan the talking points and prepare to prove them.

Note that nothing is preventing a financial aid administrator from adjusting your financial assistance package as long as your reasons are legitimate and you provide evidence.

Use your EFC as a starting point of what you're already contributing from your finances. Use your family budget sheet. Explain what has changed in your situation. Be sure you confirm with the financial aid administrator the amount of your Expected Family Contribution (EFC) under the Federal Methodology (FAFSA) and Institutional Methodology if the school uses the CSS Profile.

If dependent undergraduate students take out the $5,500 Direct Loan and work-study, they are doing all they can to help pay for college. They can't borrow more than that.

The financial aid administrator may suggest ways the student can work on campus, especially if he/she doesn't qualify for Federal Work-Study jobs. FWS jobs are partially funded by the federal government and the college, for students who demonstrate financial need. If students are not eligible, they need to look for non-FWS jobs. It's more expensive for the college to offer non-federal work-study jobs. For the student it's better if they can find work on campus because they won't have to spend time commuting. On-campus employers are more flexible with scheduling when students need the time to prepare for tests and final exams.

When you review your financial aid offer, you must deduct the FWS amount, because this form of "self-help aid" is not guaranteed, and students typically don't deposit these earnings into their bursar's account to pay their tuition. That's nothing but gas and pocket money! I know there are conscientious students who use it wisely, but many spend it instead of using it to pay for tuition.

We've talked about the "gap," which is the difference between your federal and/or institutional expected family contribution and the amount in addition to your EFC that you must pay.

If the net cost remains high, a student will need to apply to a college that has lower admission requirements. Lower-ranked private colleges accept students with barely average grades and test scores, and will work with them as if they were diamonds in the rough. I love those colleges that pick students up from where they are, and turn them into lovers of knowledge.

Appeals will not work if a student is borderline for a college and barely scrapes in. The parents will have to pay extra and bribe the college to take that student! Just kidding here.

I've referred to the "gap" as the cost that isn't covered by the college. The size of the gap speaks volumes about whether it's affordable for the family or not. Consider these two different ways of calculating the net price.

- **COA minus your FM EFC minus grant aid & scholarships = net cost. (In this idyllic scenario, you would pay your <u>federal</u> EFC only.)**
- **COA minus your IM EFC minus grant aid, scholarships = net cost. (In this idyllic scenario, the family would pay only the <u>institutional</u> EFC.)**

When your net cost is much more than your EFC, and when your EFC is much more than your AFC (Affordable Family Contribution) then parents need to consider other colleges for their student. I am going to make a generalization here: many expensive colleges aren't worth much more than the less expensive ones. I should like to start a movement in favor of parents paying only their AFC Affordable Family Contribution. Unfortunately, families pay much more than their AFC. The EFCs are often high, higher if the colleges gap. Many colleges are unable to meet 100% of need, and their academic merit scholarships are not sufficient to cover the bulk of the costs. When there's a gap between the EFC and COA, you need to consider the cost-value relationship:

If the EFC plus any other aid is not equal to the COA, there's a Gap.

You will remember that all students who file the FAFSA will receive a financial aid award letter with the typical amounts of federal loans available to undergraduate students.

If the Direct loan is subsidized, the college considers it to be "financial aid". The unsubsidized loan and Parent PLUS loans are not financial aid because eligibility is not based on demonstrated financial need.

This is a bit ridiculous, since all loans must be repaid with interest and fees. They may help you pay the college bills, but they do not cut college costs. They don't save you money. Subsidized loans may be a little less expensive, but they are still loans.

Colleges are not supposed to list the amount of unsubsidized loans and Parent PLUS loans on the student's award letters because of this distinction between need-based loans and non-need-based loans, but they do.

These loans are like any other bank loan, except that the government is offering it, and the terms typically are better than those offered by banks. The high origination fee provides a life insurance policy. If the borrower should die, this loan is forgiven. Other loans may require more than one signer, and are not forgiven. Yet, certain private loans may provide parents with what they want. In the end, it comes down to risk tolerance and the family's financial calculations.

In the above calculations, I've provided a live excel sheet and the U.S. Department of Education College Financing Sheet. You now know how to calculate your net cost without loans. If you include the $5,500 Direct loan for first-year undergraduate students, then your net cost will be lower by $5,500, but this loan is an obligation, whether or not it's classified as "financial aid." Banks will not allow teens to borrow money without a cosigner. The federal government is absorbing the risk here.

Consider that every college has a **scholarship "grid"** based on the student's academic performance. (While most colleges award merit scholarships at the admission level, the more elite colleges don't give merit scholarships. For example, Amherst, Williams, Harvard, Yale, Princeton among others provide aid based on demonstrated financial need. Families must file the CSS Profile and submit all additional forms that colleges require).

You may want to appeal if two colleges that have similar admission requirements and similar costs give you a different amount of institutional grant, especially if the colleges rank at the same level of selectivity. The amount of Federal Pell Grant should be the same no matter where you apply for college. Ask yourself why there's a difference. Is it the amount of scholarship? That is discretionary to the college. If there's a significant difference you may want to call and ask. Did one college have information about your extenuating circumstance and not the other?

Appeals fail when families have no documentation, the appeal is written poorly or in a negative tone, and is just not compelling enough! There's a way to negotiate for better financial aid awards and that starts by asking respectfully, offering proof that what you're saying is the truth, and if nothing else works, grovel! There's something about "groveling" that works in some cases! LOL!

Don't ask for a specific amount of money. Instead, provide evidence of the special circumstances that affect your ability to pay. The change in the college's financial aid offer will be based on the financial impact of the special circumstances

Q: Can you bargain with colleges? A: Not usually. If the college is selective, it can pick and choose whomever they want. That being said, if your child got into MIT and received more funding at Harvey Mudd College, then you could raise the issue. MIT fills 100% of demonstrated need, as does Harvey Mudd. Maybe your student applied after a deadline passed? Colleges will likely review the awards if you're talking about differences between colleges that are in the same league. If they are very selective, however, they won't listen to a parent who says, "My kid got $17,000 at a second- or third-tiered university in my state." It's not a fair comparison.

Check the average cost of the colleges on the College Navigator tool provided by the National Center for Education Statistics (NCES). How does your award letter compare with the "average" net price listed on College Navigator?

More than a third of American workers lost their jobs during the 2020 Covid-19 pandemic. Others caught the virus and incurred medical and unexpected expenses in order to isolate themselves. Some families had to purchase a computer so that their kids could continue to learn online. Those who waited to appeal an award may have lost money. Parents should file appeals as soon as the award is received. I advise my families to let the college make the offer and then go back to negotiate. There's no sense upping the ante before the family knows what the college is already willing to give. Parents worry that colleges may have more grant funds at the beginning of the year, rather than at the end. It's likely that if they want you, they will find some funds to help you out.

These appeals need to be resubmitted each year. Some colleges publish their appeal forms on their websites. Otherwise, you will need to write a letter. Mark Kantrowitz, an authority in the field of financial aid, says it's better to submit the form or state your case in bullet form. Documentation is essential, so attach copies of anything that can support your claim. This documentation could be a copy of your unemployment benefits, medical bills, divorce decree, and settlement. You could also appeal if your prior-prior year income doesn't represent an accurate picture because your current year income is much lower, or you lost your job.

When colleges give out more federal aid, they have to document it for the U.S. Department of Education, which audits almost a third of financial aid files. Even if colleges give you their institutional aid, they need documentation.

It's good to send an appeal by return-receipt mail or via an email and request a delivery and read receipt. If you don't hear in a week, call the financial aid office to make sure 1) they received your message, and 2) ask if they need any additional information you need to provide.

Mark Kantrowitz points out that it's a mistake to propose the amount of money you need. If the college accepts your appeal, it might have granted you more than that if you hadn't provided them with a number.

I think it's terrific if the financial aid appeal results in grants but not if it results in loans!

Professional Judgment (PJ)

What is PJ? By now you learned many abbreviations, such as COA, EFC, AGI, SAR, FAFSA, CSS Profile and more. The next abbreviation is PJ, which stands for Professional Judgment.

Every Financial Aid Administrator (FAA) has the prerogative to change the way that federal financial aid is awarded to the student if the formulas don't fit the student's financial circumstances. They can do this in two ways:

- FAAs can change the data points on the FAFSA in order to take into consideration a unique situation that may not be covered in the usual way.
- FAAs can change the cost of attendance to reflect special circumstances, such as unusual expenses, high dependent care costs and disability-related expenses.

Some FAAs are reticent to make changes because everything in financial aid is highly formulaic and policy regulated.

Federal rules are strict and detailed in what FAAs can and cannot do. For every question in financial aid the answer is "it depends" or "there's an exception to that."

Some of the more common changes include:

- The FAA can change a student's classification from "dependent" to "independent."
- The FAA can deny or reduce the amount of Federal Direct loans available to the student.
- The FAA can increase some elements of the COA (Cost of Attendance). Increasing the expenses will increase the amount of financial need and thereby increase eligibility for need-based financial aid.
- FAAs can assist students whose parents refuse to file the FAFSA. Unwillingness to pay doesn't excuse parents from contributing. An exception would be if physical or mental harm would be the result if the student to request the aid from parents. This would need to be proven with police reports and such concrete documentation.

We've seen that independent students can borrow larger Direct loans. FAAs can exercise Professional Judgment and do a "Dependency Override." This means that the FAA can give a "dependent student" the status of "independent," which means the student can obtain larger Direct loans.

Some FAAs worry about the amount of debt some students take on, especially if they are young, have no parental support, and may leave school without a degree. However, according to Annemarie Weisman from the U.S. Department of Education, FAAs should consider that loans could help the student graduate or sit for a certification. Ms. Weisman continued "It's not the amount of loan that makes a difference in who defaults." I found this to be counterintuitive. I guess the graduate students who complete medical or veterinary or dental school with hundreds of dollars of loans can earn it all back. Looking at my dentist bills, I'd say they can!

As IECs, school counselors and parents, we need to be aware that FAAs have this power. Typically, it's the director of financial aid who is more likely to have the power make these decisions. Apparently, some institutions decide not to exercise PJ at all, and I'm thinking of the hapless students who don't get more aid due to the refusal to exercise PJ on the part of the administrators. It's not an easy job, I understand. However, some students need additional funds just to sit for a certification that would then open them up for better employment.

Some students may have majored in a foreign language and need additional funding to study abroad. This could be a once in a lifetime opportunity to become fluent in another language.

Families need to provide appropriate documentation to help the FAA adjust the data elements in the FAFSA. For example, if the student's cost of transportation, books and supplies, meals are higher than what the college allowed in the student budget, the student should save receipts to support the case: credit card and bank statements, tax documents, court documents, insurance payments, police reports, birth certificates, and death certificates.

Under the Institutional Methodology expressed in the CSS Profile, professional judgment involves a lot more review. Colleges that have internal, non-federal funds to give out, do so only after examining families' resources, and turning over every single leaf. Take a look at the College Board "PJ Tips" below, and you will see examples of professional judgment and types of documentation FAAs would require.

Tip Sheet for Parents to Check Out Before Appealing

https://professionals.collegeboard.org/higher-ed/financial-aid/im/tips

Financial Aid Administrators may get offended if families try to negotiate with them as if they were purchasing a car or some such item.

They are limited in what they can do with dispensing federal aid because it's highly regulated by federal policies. However, they can bring your case to a committee and exercise "Professional Judgment" to alter your amount of federal and also, institutional aid.

The examples below will give parents an idea of the items and documentation they need to provide. I think the cases are more complex because parents who can afford expensive colleges are likely to earn more and own more assets.

Examples of Tip Sheets provided by the College Board to Financial Aid Administrators.

These can be used to examine appeals and exercise Professional Judgment:

- COVID 19 Resources for Financial Aid Professionals
- Using an Alternate Year Income
- Consumer Debt
- Distribution of Retirement Funds
- Elder Care
- Exceptional Expenses
- Fluctuating Parent Income
- Imputing Asset Values
- Income and Assets Not Proportional (Low Income/High Assets)
- Medical Expenses
- Natural Disaster Tips sheet
- One Time Taxable Income
- Parents' Educational Debt
- Parents' Educational Expenses
- Additional Professional Judgment Tip Sheets
- Co-owned Assets
- Combat Pay
- Family Size
- Foreign Income
- Income Losses from Business
- Noncustodial Parent
- Rental Income and Losses
- Sabbatical Leaves
- Siblings' College Costs
- Siblings in Graduate or Professional School
- Stepparents

Other Topics

Federal Aid Can't Keep Up with Cost Increases

We can't expect federal and state governments to keep funding the continual increases of college costs. Tuition, fees, room, meals, loan fees, books and supplies, transportation and other charges that have risen far above any index.

According to an article in Yahoo! Finance, today's average college tuition is 31 times more costly than it was in 1969. From 1969 to 2019, the average annual cost of a four-year public university has soared 3,009 percent, increasing more than any other sector of the economy, including medical costs.

The federal government knew way back in the sixties that it couldn't help families pay for college without the help of the states. Every U.S. state offers aid directly to colleges, and indirectly to students, via scholarships or need-based aid, often funded by state lotteries. Public colleges receive state appropriations to keep their tuition costs low for in-state residents.

During the 1980s under the Reagan administration, the government sought help from the banks. Under the benign name of "Family Federal Loan Education Program" banks made federal loans using their own funds but with a federal guarantee against default. They were guaranteed to get paid by the full faith of the federal government. The federal government also guaranteed that the lenders would get a market rate of return, with the federal government paying the difference between the interest rates paid by borrowers and market interest rates.

Banks charged the consumers origination fees up to 3% each and a 1% guarantee fee. These loans had variable interest rates that could change throughout the loan term. Then lenders sold the loans on the secondary markets and the borrowers had to figure out where to send their payments. The default rate was high.

The U.S. Department of Education intervened and began to assess the default rate of colleges, and threaten to stop lending if the school's default rate kept increasing. In 2010 with the passing of the Health Care and Education Reconciliation Act (HCERA), commercial lenders exited the federal student loan marketplace. All new federal loans were made by the Direct Loan program starting on July 1, 2010. It was a blow to banks, but as of 2020, there is a new growth of private lenders that try to compete with the terms of the federal loans.

If borrowers have a very high credit rating, from 750 to 850, they may be able to obtain a private loan with an interest rate that is competitive with the interest rates on Federal Parent PLUS loans.

Federal loans don't depend on the borrower's credit score or debt-to-income ratios. As long as borrowers haven't had a bankruptcy discharge, foreclosure, repossession, tax lien, wage garnishment or default determination in the last five years, or a serious delinquency of 90 or more days on more than $2,085 in debt in the last two years, they can get a PLUS loan to pay for college.

The Federal Direct Stafford loan does not depend on the borrower's credit history at all.

Each year's new loans have a new interest rate, resetting each July 1. That interest rate is fixed for the life of the loan.

Once they graduate, borrowers can use a federal consolidation loan to combine two or more federal student loans. Private student loans cannot be included in a federal consolidation loan. However, borrowers can include both federal and private loans in a private refinance. But, if they do so, the better benefits of federal loans will go away. For example, during the coronavirus pandemic, federal loans but not private loans were eligible for a payment pause and interest waiver, with no interest accruing on the loans.

Federal loans provide flexible repayment terms for borrowers than commercial, private and alternative loans. Federal loans offer a standard 10-year repayment plan, two graduated repayment plans, two extended repayment plans, four income-driven repayment plans and a few alternative repayment plans. The standard, ten-year repayment plan of 120 payments is still the shortest, lest expensive repayment plan.

Borrowers in an income-driven repayment plan must re-certify their income and family size each year, so that the loan payments can be adjusted based on their income and the poverty line.

Federal loans also offer deferment and forbearance provisions (see glossary for explanation.) These loans also include a life insurance policy so that if the borrower dies the loan is forgiven.

Many young families are crushed under loan repayments for years. Ironically, the pandemic made it possible to work from home, and many parents defrayed child-care costs because they worked at their computer while babysitting their small children.

Colleges complain that their state cut funding, and to compensate, cut faculty jobs. The University of Vermont cut 27 programs from the Departments of Arts and Sciences in December of 2020. More layoffs are expected especially in the liberal arts teaching faculty. (Burlington Free Press).

As sources of state funding decrease, colleges are especially dependent on tuition revenues. Loans are the major source of revenues for colleges. Once the lender disburses the funds, the colleges get the funding, and the borrower will deal with the lender and servicer for a decade or two or three.

The families I serve in my practice are more than willing to pay. In fact, they overpay to make sure their children get a high-quality college education.

A Pell-eligible student is accepted to New York University and the parents are willing to take out ten times the amount they earn each year, because they have hung their hat on the hope that their student will recoup it.

When a family applies for a mortgage, the debt-to-income ratio is carefully assessed by the lender, so they can buy the entire house. College lasts four years, and as long as parents qualify for one year of funding, the student can enter the classrooms. Imagine buying one fourth of a house, with no plan for paying for the remaining three years!

As IECs, we work on a pro-bono basis with Pell-eligible students. Our middle-class families also make huge sacrifices. IECA consultants create college lists with one or two "affordable" colleges. We can lead a horse to water but sometimes, the very people who need to count their pennies are the ones who get blinded by the "name" schools.

It's essential that IECs, school counselors and college advisors consider affordability when they work with families. The twenty-first century is the time to push for affordable higher education.

No one is asking for a free ride. Just a fair cost that makes higher education more accessible to traditionally under-represented students, from Blacks to Hispanics to low-income families.

If we learned anything through the coronavirus pandemic, it's that online teaching is possible, less expensive, acceptable and workable for many students and many fields of study.

This is the decade to push for less costly and better access to higher education.

Lowering College Costs Via Tax Savings

Education Tax Benefits (Information from the U.S. Department of Education)

The **American Opportunity Tax Credit (AOTC)** gives tax-filers a $2,500 tax credit, each year, for a total of $10,000 over four years. It's meant to put money directly into families' pockets rather than disbursing it to colleges.

529 Savings Plans offer tax savings and financial aid benefits. Earnings accumulate on a tax-deferred basis and distributions are tax-free if used to pay for qualified college costs. 529 plans are also treated more favorably by financial aid formulas. Qualified distributions from grandparent-owned 529 plans will no longer be reported on the FAFSA.

Prepaid Tuition Plans let you pre-pay all or part of the costs of an in-state public college education. They may also be converted for use at private and out-of-state colleges. The Private College 529 Plan is a separate prepaid plan for private colleges, sponsored by more than 250 private colleges.

Lifetime Learning Tax Credit (LLTC) Parents or students may qualify to receive up to $2,000 by claiming the LLTC on their tax return. This credit may be taken for an unlimited account of tax years, is non-refundable and cannot be combined with the AOTC in a tax year. If you qualify for both the AOTC and LLTC, choose the AOTC, as it is worth more.

Student Loan Interest Deduction: Student loan borrowers may deduct up to $2,500 on their federal income tax return each year based on the interest they paid on federal and private student loans. This is an above-the-line deduction, meaning it can be taken even if the taxpayer takes the standard deduction. Parents who take out Parent PLUS loans are also eligible to take this deduction.

Military and /or National Service Benefits: For information, please visit https://studentaid.gov/understand-aid/types/military

For-Profit Colleges

I hope it's clear from my harping on that low-income students simply cannot attend colleges that still cost $20,000 to $60,000 a year after federal and institutional aid is applied.

When parents of Pell-eligible students borrow a Parent PLUS loan, it is typically ruinous. There are many colleges out there that provide training and education, and I don't mean the for-profit colleges that over-charge for entry-level training that leads to minimum-wage jobs.

For first-generation, low-income, minority students and adult students who don't have time to study for two years at a community college, the for-profit companies seem to offer an alternative: short programs for quick degrees. For-profit colleges have extremely aggressive and slick admission representatives who do a great job of reeling in unaware prospects.

At the time of this writing there's a well-known for-profit university that is advertising on major TV channels as offering millions of dollars in scholarships. "Come and see which scholarship you qualify for!" An added benefit of this school is that it promises to help with finding employment not just after graduation but anytime after.

These are no bargains. Do check out these for-profit colleges on collegescorecard.ed.gov You will likely find that the graduation rate is less than 50%, the salary is equivalent to entry level wages, and the financial aid is just federal grants and loans for most students.

Look for ways to save on college costs for the first two years by utilizing the community colleges. Get your Associate's degree, then transfer to a four-year university.

Also, if you live near a college, take advantage of the proximity and the fact that you could save by living at home. For example, my student Maria lives near a university - not the state flagship with the famous football team - but a campus all the same. By living at home and paying for her tuition with her Pell Grant and state grant, neither her parents nor she will need to take out loans.

Students who are Pell-eligible can't afford to apply to for-profit and other colleges that are 100% dependent on tuition revenues. Many less-funded colleges keep their doors open thanks for the federal aid that students bring to in.

Sometimes, even when a college is the best fit, if the price is too high it's not going to last. Always apply to your state institution and community college. For example, when I met Devon at his AME Church, he told me he started college at a Historically Black College (HBCU). I was glad for him because HBCUs provide a great quality education. Their students learn to advocate for themselves and succeed in college and in life. HBCUs honor students' background and experiences, as well as instill confidence in themselves and their futures.

However, it was disappointing for me to find that Devon was unable to continue because he was saddled by sizeable debt right after their first year. I was in disbelief when he told me he'd maxed out of his undergraduate loans, his mom and aunt had cosigned a PLUS loan and wouldn't be able to make the payments.

Student loans are not dischargeable in bankruptcy. They follow the borrower throughout their life. If you default on a federal loan, your income tax refunds and wages can be offset and garnished.

I fear that there's not enough financial aid guidance for under-represented students and low-income students when it's time to select a college that is affordable.

These students hear the refrain "go to college" and are eager to do so, but don't receive enough information to make fit and affordable choices.

These students are the last people who should get mired in loan debt. Higher education should be a benefit to all those qualified to be admitted. Yet these low-income students often do not complete a degree and end up saddled with loans due to the sheer lack of academic guidance and financial planning.

These students need personalized guidance. If they can complete a degree and find employment, these low-income students are shown to lift their entire family out of poverty.

Upper-income students will find affordability in their in-state institutions. If they decide to attend private colleges or out-of-state universities they will pay more, but the additional costs are not likely to burden them to the extent that it does students who live at poverty level.

Lottery-funded state scholarships: In southern states like Florida, Georgia and South Carolina, state aid based on academic merit, such as grade point average, rank in class and test scores. The scholarships are funded by the sale of lottery tickets.

Low-income people account for the majority of lottery sales, while sales are highest in the poorest areas. See https://www.ncbi.nlm.nih.gov/pmc/articles/PMC4103646/

In effect, these poorer households are paying for state scholarships for wealthier students. Wealthy families could afford to pay for in-state public tuition even without state scholarships.

Lottery-funded scholarships should be awarded based on household income alone.

Get to Know Your Loan Servicer!

After the loans are disbursed to the college, students and parents will deal with the student loan servicers.

Federal loan servicers are private companies that have contracts with the government. The largest ones are Great Lakes, Nelnet, AES/FedLoan, and Navient (formerly Sallie Mae).

Each of these servicers has a long history with the U.S. Department of Education. Some have done a fair job of educating student borrowers about the income-based repayment choices available to them. Others improperly posted payments. Currently, in 2020, these servicers collect nearly 90% of all federal student loan payments.

How do student loan borrowers get into trouble?

Borrowers need to bear in mind that if they have any unpaid fees, back interest, and penalties, the next payment covers those first. For example, if there are five dollars of interest left outstanding from the previous month, that's paid first, and your current payment will be short by five dollars. If not rectified immediately, more penalties and fees accrue.

You get further behind if the next payments don't cover the previously accrued interest, last fees and penalties. Some students send in slightly more money than their regular bill just to make sure the back interest is paid.

They discovered that the additional amounts were not posted to pay back interest and others were posted as an early payment of the next month's installment. The Navient website publishes this warning but in small print: "Interest is charged as soon as disbursements begin. Interest continues to be charged during any grace or separation periods, such as summer break, during deferment or forbearance. Interest continues to accrue until the loan is paid in full. Any unpaid interest is added to the principal."

NSLDS: National Student Loan Data System

Few students and parents know where to check up the balance of their loan. NSLDS is a U.S. Department of Education database that records federal student loans and other federal aid. It contains data from schools, guaranty agencies, the William D. Ford Federal Direct Loan (Direct Loan) program, and other U.S. Department of Education programs. To their credit, the DoE (U.S. Department of Education) merged the NSLDS website with the studentaid.gov website. Borrowers can access records of their loan payments with their FSA ID on the same studentaid.gov website. This will make it easier for borrowers to resolve issues. Students and parents should still check how their payments are applied to interest and principal.

Federal Income-Driven Repayment Plans

In order to help borrowers repay their loans, the U.S. Department of Education has created several income-driven repayment plans. These flexible repayment plans can be a huge help to borrowers who are not able to make immediate repayment.

For example, say that you graduate or leave college and can't find a job until eight months later. The grace period is only six months long. If you apply to get into an income-driven repayment plan, say Pay-As-You-Earn Repayment (PAYE), your payments will be zero until you find a job. It's critical, however, to remember that you must recertify every year. It's not enough to file once. You need to file every single year. The same goes if you are working for a non-profit organization and are seeking Public Service Loan Forgiveness.

The four income-driven repayment plans are:

- **Income-Contingent Repayment (ICR).** The monthly payment is 20% of the amount by which adjusted gross income exceeds 100% of the poverty line, with a 25-year repayment term.
- **Income-Based Repayment (IBR).** The monthly payment is 15% of the amount by which adjusted gross income exceeds 150% of the poverty line, with a 25-year repayment term.
- **Pay-As-You-Earn Repayment (PAYE).** The monthly payment is 10% of the amount by which adjusted gross income exceeds 150% of the poverty line, with a 20-year repayment term.
- **Revised Pay-As-You-Earn Repayment (REPAYE).** The monthly payment is 10% of the amount by which adjusted gross income exceeds 150% of the poverty line, with either a 20-year or a 25-year repayment term. Borrowers who have only undergraduate loans get a 20-year repayment term.

Keep in mind that federal student loans are not dischargeable, even in bankruptcy. For example, if you declare bankruptcy, most of your debt, including mortgage, personal loans, credit card balances, and medical bills, will go away. With bankruptcy, your credit will be ruined for years, but you will not owe money to anyone. You will not get banks to lend you anything for a long time, but you will no longer be responsible for any consumer debt or mortgage. Not so for federal student loans. You will owe that debt until every last cent is paid off. If you default on your federal student loans, the government can garnish up to 15% of your wages and Social Security checks and offset your federal income tax refunds.

Private loans do not have income-driven repayment plans. It's why people have to pay bank loans first before they pay the federal loans. Federal loans are much better in comparison because of the flexibility of repayment and possible income-driven repayment plans that help borrowers avoid default.

Think about this for a minute. Many young people in their late 20s and 30s are putting off buying a car, an apartment, or getting married because they need to pay their student loans. "Buying anything is off the table for me, [and] I'm not getting into a relationship with someone who has student loans," said Stacey, who worked for a marketing company. She admits that she "shopped poorly" by going to a high-cost college. In the end, she had to move back home (in another state) and return to live with her parents so that she put her rent money towards paying her debt. This could be avoided if more colleges said to students, "You can't afford to come here." Colleges are very good at assessing the financial strength of families. It's a short-term disappointment versus a lifetime of debt.

Anyone who thinks they can get away from paying student loans by hiding or absconding has another thing coming. I was at a meeting of RI financial aid administrators when the presenter, a federal investigator, explained that his job was to chase down "disappearing borrowers." He did so even for amounts of undergraduate loans I considered negligible. This investigator would find out the borrower's new address, check out the type of car he drove, and wait for a time when he could be found at home. The amount of loan the student owed was less than $1,000.

It's noteworthy that undergraduate students can borrow without a credit check: They are the sole borrower, and there's a fixed interest rate, with slight fees that cover origination and disbursement. Typically, this "Direct Loan" is the cheapest available.

Federal loans have many discharge and cancellation options: If there is misconduct on the part of the school, or the school closes, or the borrower becomes disabled or dies, the loan can be discharged. Very few private loans offer these insurances.

When repayment starts, loans are automatically placed in the 10-year, 120-payments schedule. This is a quick way to repay loans, and there's no penalty for prepayment. When students graduate or leave college, if they can't find work, as new borrowers they have a variety of repayment choices. These include four income-driven repayment plans (ICR, IBR, PAYE and REPAYE), extended repayment, and graduated repayment. It's complex to have so many repayment plans, but at least the payer has choices if life events happen. And life happens. I will cover PSLF (Public Service Loan Forgiveness) in another chapter. Deferments and forbearances are useful for students who have a liquidity issue, are unemployed or are experiencing economic hardship. Forbearance may be mandated if the student is serving in a residency or serving in AmeriCorps or in the military. Interest can be deferred until after the six-month grace period.

The catch here is that there are limits to the amounts that students can borrow on their own when they are undergraduates. Also, only a part of the loan can be subsidized, meaning that if the student demonstrates need, the interest is paid by the government while the student is enrolled in school.

Don't Combine Federal Loans with Private Loans!

If you decide to consolidate your loans, consolidate federal loans with the federal government, and private loans with private banks. Don't comingle them.

Be careful not to consolidate your federal loans with your private loans. This is called a private refinance. It is a private loan. Private loans don't offer deferment, forbearance, income-driven repayment plans, and even payment-pauses during extreme circumstances like during the Covid-19 pandemic.

Over four years of college, students receive four loans with four <u>different</u> though <u>fixed interest rates</u>. After they graduate, they can consolidate the loans so they can make just one payment. But, consider whether one of the loans has a much higher interest rate than the others. If so, you do not want to consolidate that loan. Instead, you can make extra payments on that loan to pay it off quicker. That will save you money by reducing your average interest rate.

If you refinance your federal loans with a private bank and do not consolidate them in a Federal Direct Consolidation Loan, the wonderful federal repayment benefits will go away. No private lender offers income-driven repayment plans, as many deferment and forbearance options, cancellation of loans if you become disabled or die, or Public Service Loan Forgiveness. Borrowers need to carefully assess the costs, risks, and tradeoffs of private vs. federal loans.

The Bonanza! In 2020, as a result of Covid-19, the federal government passed the CARES Act which included the cessation of payments on all federal student loans until September 30, 2020, which was later extended through September 30, 2021. If you had a federal loan owned by the U.S. Department of Education, the interest rate for the loan was brought down to 0% as a result of the CARES Act. Servicers were told to not charge interest to the loans during this federally authorized payment pause. If borrowers kept making payments, the servicers were supposed to apply them only to the principal balance of the loans.

This was the perfect time for borrowers in default to redeem their loans. Consider that if borrowers made nine, consecutive, on-time payments their loans were rehabilitated. Since the payment pause lasted more than nine months, if the borrowers contacted the U.S. Department of Education they could have rehabilitated their defaulted loans without making a payment! Every borrower should have benefited from the payment pause by giving them time to get back on their feet and get ready to start making payments. I hope the servicers contacted every borrower who was in default!

If you do want to refinance your federal loans into a private loan,

check the rate on each of the loans you took out over the four years of college. Don't refinance them if they have lower interest rates. I wonder if we will ever see gain the 2.75% rate for loans disbursed between July 1, 2020 to June 30, 2021. If the interest rate on these loans is lower than the refinance rate, students should keep the original loan.

Consider the $1.64 Trillion Student Loan Debt

In January of 2020, Moody Investors Services reported that the $1.6 trillion student loan debt is due to borrowers barely making a dent into repaying their loans. The federal income-driven repayment plans can be negatively amortized, where the loan payments are less than the new interest that accrues, causing the loan balance to increase. Students graduating from for-profit colleges typically have the hardest time paying down their loans. This issue is a talking point with politicians. Bernie Sanders, the Senator from Vermont, was the only one who advocated for canceling all student loan debt. Joe Biden proposed forgiving $10,000 of debt. Senators Elizabeth Warren and Chuck Schumer want to cancel up to $50,000. Senator Bernie Sanders would cancel all student loans. I don't believe all loans will be forgiven.

Federal education loans are a significant source of revenue for the federal government and the collection agencies. Imagine how many federal loan servicers and slew of employees would suddenly become unemployed if there were no student loan payments to collect each month. If the U.S. Department of Education stopped lending to students and parents, the federal government would lose a steady stream of revenue. The vast majority of the 45 million borrowers that collectively owe $1.64 trillion are making payments. Less than 12% of loans are defaulted. The majority of borrowers are sending their money to the loan servicers each month. There are nine loan servicers that get a cut out of each and every monthly payment they collect on behalf of the government.

The employees are responsible for educating borrowers so that they may avoid default. However, they haven't been too clear about deferment and forbearance (see Glossary), or the many income-driven repayment plans that are in fact difficult to explain. This type of advice requires that the employees at the call centers be professionally trained so that they can help borrowers figure out which of the income-driven repayment plans would be best for the borrower.

Public Service Loan Forgiveness (PSLF)

Oh, I can have my loans forgiven if I work for some "do-good" organization?

Don't count on it!

Many students have heard of loan forgiveness and are banking on this. As of fall 2020, hundreds of thousands of students applied and less than four thousand were approved.

Some citizens don't like the idea of loan forgiveness. Many articles in newspapers such as the WSJ take the position "public service loan forgiveness" is unfair to taxpayers to forgive students of their obligation to repay their loans!

This couldn't be farther from the truth. The government makes money on loans by charging fees, interest, penalties and interest-upon-interest. The public needs to be disabused of the notion that the government and therefore, the taxpayer is losing money on federal loans!

PSLF kicks in after the student borrower makes 120 on-time payments, under the standard plan or a qualifying income-driven repayment plan. Borrowers must work for a non-profit employer that is so classified by the federal government. If at the end of this period there's still a balance left to pay, the amount forgiven will result in a taxable event.

Imagine paying thousands of dollars with interest, origination fees, interest on penalties, interest upon interest, over two or more decades and then, when the person is penniless, if there's any balance left, it is forgiven, it counts as income to the borrower who has to pay tax on it!

Getting back to the number of applicants and the few people that got PSLF, part of the problem is that few employers were "approved" as non-profit companies as defined by the U.S. Department of Education. Borrowers must make sure their employer qualifies as a not-for-profit entity and send their employer's EIN to the U.S. Department of Education. This is like asking a person for their Social Security Number. Imagine how many employers will be glad to give an employee their company's EIN number!

Many borrowers worked enough years for what they believed was a non-profit but didn't qualify for PSLF because their employer was not on the approved list of the U.S. Department of Education. For example, hours spent in religious instruction, worship services, or proselytizing do not count. Working for a government contractor doesn't count. Borrowers must work full-time, which means at least 30 hours per week. It's ok if borrowers have two part-time jobs as long as the hours add to full-time status. Students must recertify for this program <u>each year</u>, and must make sure they're filling out each field correctly, such as their Employer Identification Number. Some employers refused to give this number to the employee and it actually caused some attrition.

Students must keep track of payments made to other servicers (not just FedLoan) and be aware that Consolidating Direct Loans will erase any qualifying payments previously made. The clock will start anew! Borrowers shouldn't wait to submit their employment certification forms until after they have made 10 years of qualifying payments. They should submit the forms as soon as they enter either the standard, ten-year repayment plan or an income-driven repayment plan. They should submit the employment certification form whenever they switch jobs and at least once a year.

As you can see, it's not that simple to obtain PSLF and get any balance forgiven.

Of the borrowers who were rejected for PSLF after applying, 59% did not have the correct number of qualifying payments (120), 26% were missing information on the application (e.g., the employer's EIN) and 11% had no eligible loans.

So, if you are reading this and do plan to count on PSLF, make sure you know the rules.

PSLF may work for those who remain in low-paying jobs and have to be in an income-driven repayment plan, work for a true non-profit, can handle the minute details and recertify every year, and don't miss any payments. These employers typically are hospitals, public schools, or research institution like the Mayo clinic or some such foundation. I met with a student who was in a low-paying job and had a chance to get a better paying one. She was wondering if she should stay but when we ran the numbers, it wasn't worth it. The new job was going to enable her to pay off the principal balance faster. Waiting for PSLF can be like waiting for Godot. Take the better paying job!

The Impact of Debt Burden

My sympathies are with the borrowers.

Yes, the amount of student debt in 2020 is $1.64 trillion and rising but borrowers are making the payments. Only 11% of student loans are 90 days or more delinquent or in default Borrowers are not taking advantage of taxpayers' money. The government is making money on these loans. The vast majority of borrowers are still in repayment. They send their monthly payments to semi-government corporations that have a positive relationship with the U.S. Department of Education.

The major loan servicers are Sallie Mae, Nelnet Inc., PHEAA, MOHELA, FedLoan, and others. These servicers earn a percentage amount for each monthly payment they collect.

This is a highly lucrative industry. By this I mean that when the government spends taxpayer money on health care, it's gone. When the government lends to students, it collects more money because of the added interest and fees. Anyone connected with the life of each student loan is making money on the back of the borrower.

The Congressional Budget Office analysis shows that reducing federal lending to students and parents would cause a shortfall of federal revenues. The government is making money off desperate parents who need to give their kids a college education.

Undergraduate student borrowers are inexperienced when they take out loans. I've come across parents who sheltered them from the worry of loans and haven't even talked with them about this debt. As a result, many students remain less informed and repayment comes as a shock.

For example, I was eating lunch at an Applebee's restaurant when the waitress told me she'd recently graduated from nursing school. She said she was waiting for her job to start. She didn't know how much she owed because her father had signed for all her loans. Every one of them. She smiled and said her dad didn't want her to worry. This left me perplexed: this well-meaning father didn't want his daughter to worry but the loans were in her name. If anything happened, the daughter would be responsible.

Meet Erika

Erika's story is not unique. I was shopping at a women's retail store when I met Erika, who helped me find tops and bottoms. (You can tell I like to shop and eat out.) She had just left the University of Miami (FL) with a Master's Degree in Psychology.

As I tried on clothes and she helped me find the right sizes, she said her name was Erika and we continued to chat. She clarified that she didn't have her degree officially, because she hadn't been able to pay a bill. The university was holding her diploma.

In addition, she owed over $80,000 in student loans for the two graduate years she spent there. I nearly choked. I asked her if she got commission at this retail store and she shook her head. She was paid minimum wages. I asked her if she'd tried to find more lucrative work and she shook her head again. She revealed that she lived with her mother so she wouldn't have to pay rent. She let it slip that she couldn't make her loan payments.

I felt sorry for her. I was spending quite a bit of money on quite a few items of clothing, which was starting to look excessive, and I felt I needed to give her a tip, since she was so helpful. I felt obliged to also give her some advice, and to this day I hope she took it. I told her there were several private boarding and day schools in the region that might just need a young person with a Master's Degree in Psychology, to work as a dorm parent, teacher or administrator. I gave her some tips about how to present herself when applying for these jobs and put her in touch with the director of a school I knew personally.

I called the store to follow up with her a few months later, hoping that the store manager would say that she was not working there anymore. It would mean that she'd found a better job. Unfortunately, she wasn't working on that day but she still worked there.

Erika's loan balance is not uncommon. As of September 30, 2020, 45% of the outstanding federal education loan debt was held by the 10% of borrowers owing $80,000 or more, according to data from the U.S. Department of Education's FSA Data Center.

Meet A Waitress

I seem to continually meet recent graduates who are working for minimum wages. The loan payments start six months after they graduate or leave school. It doesn't seem to be sufficient time for them to find good paying jobs. One wonders how hard the universities work to find leads for employment for their grads. Once the loans come due, the servicers are on the phone asap, and do a good job of telling them to work, to take anything as long as it's work. (I wish this mandate came earlier in life.) Students are automatically placed in the "standard" repayment plan, which is for 10 years, 120 payments. Students need to know that the problems start with the first payment: they have to pay for both the interest and principal, to avoid interest accrual and further loan growth.

I wonder how effective the exit counseling that students must go through when they leave college. That counseling session could be amped up and offered again, six months after the student leaves, because they need to know that to do if they can't make the entire monthly payment. There are income-driven repayment plans, such as PAYE (Pay As You Earn), and too many others. There are too many income-driven repayment plans for newer borrowers, and not enough for old borrowers stuck with older plans. Students can easily get confused when the servicers don't explain which repayment plans would fit the borrower. These plans are complicated and require several hours of careful reading to deciphering them. The details can confuse the borrower who doesn't understand them. This is real math, and students need to play with loan repayment calculators to compare which income-based plan works best for specific borrowers. Then, they must requalify for these plans each year.

I may have said it already and I cannot say it often enough: student loans are not dischargeable in bankruptcy, even if the student left college before earning a degree, even if the college didn't teach anything marketable, even if students didn't learn anything useful.

Some college graduates work at Lowes or Home Depot, or clean houses, or work retail like Erika does. One of my well-to-do students graduated and couldn't find work. She ended up selling ice-cream from a cart downtown. Perhaps that's what she needed to experience because she went after higher paying jobs and found work with an online company.

Getting back to loans, they're like taxes. They follow the borrowers till death does the parting. Graduate students carry an even larger debt because parents don't pick up the tab. According to the U.S. Department of Education, 2% of borrowers carry more than $200,000 of debt.

Good Reads

It's essential that graduate students attend graduate schools that are worth the cost. A good read is John Grisham's book *The Rooster Bar*. It's premised on a scam by a proprietary law school that accepts students with low LSAT scores and encourages them to continue to take out loans even though they have little chance of passing the bar.

It's important that graduate students choose fields where they can recoup the costs, such as medical, dental, veterinary or an established law school! In today's economy, a graduate degree can yield higher salaries throughout life.

Good money management starts at the undergraduate level and can pave the way to becoming responsible borrowers in graduate school and in life. Loans, whether federal or private, need to be weighed against the prospects of obtaining work after graduation. I'm all about getting as much education as possible for the least possible expense.

Another good novel about student loans is John Sandman's *Debt Collectors in Love.*

Avoid Default at All Costs

Your loans are yours, to hold, to keep, for better or worse, and to pay them back with the added interest and fees.

If I could pass on a message to students and parents who owe student loans, I'd say: "Do what you have to do to repay the loans before they go into default."

Anecdotally, a lawyer told me that she advised her client, a young nurse who'd recently graduated from college, to go back to live with her parents. She'd sold her car and was walking to work each day, and yet after she'd paid her rent and food, she could make only interest payments on her loans. After looking at her income and living expenses, her debt would continue to grow if she remained in Charleston, SC, where her wages were low and her expenses high. To begin to make a dent into paying the principal balance and avoid default, the lawyer advised her to live with her parents for a few years, until she could pay down the principal balance.

If borrowers can't make the monthly payments, after 270-360 days on federal loans, the loan is placed in "default" status. The government can garnish wages and Social Security checks and seize income tax refunds to repay a defaulted loan. Borrowers must also pay collection charges of as much as a fifth of each payment before the rest is applied first to interest and last to principal. This slows progress in repaying the debt and is designed to keep the borrower stuck in repayment for decades.

The government, banks, and servicers themselves can write off these loans. Banks can even get a tax cut. Then, these defaulted loans are sold to collection agencies for pennies on the dollar. At that point, it's a free for all for collectors. They chase after the borrowers and make their life miserable. They tack on additional fees, penalties, even bogus charges.

Why the government doesn't simply cancel those debts, especially after the borrowers have more than paid the principal balance is beyond me. These borrowers would be able to buy a car or put a down payment on a house if they didn't have to make those student loan payments. Those monthly payments would find their way into the economy.

Pay Your Federal Loans!

While grants and scholarships are gifts, loans, whether federal or private, are obligations that students and parents will pay back over time.

After you earn your Bachelor's degree you will be able to work and earn more money than with a high school diploma. While you're a student, it's wise to live on the cheap. It's better to live like a student when you are one than when you're an older person.

Do research your college options carefully not just for academic fit but also for financial fit. Which college will yield a greater benefit to you? Which field of study is in demand and matches up with your interest and abilities? Consider the academic and social fit while making affordability an absolute part of the fit.

Federal loan limits for undergraduate dependent students are $5,500 in first year, $6,500 in second year, and $7,500 in third and fourth year. If you don't borrow more than this, you should be ok repaying your loans, if you graduate. If you drop out of college, all bets are off.

Students file the FAFSA, which has a Data Retrieval Tool to download each family's tax return directly from the IRS, and thus a family's expected family contribution (EFC) gets computed. Typically, there are gaps between the expected family contribution and the cost of attendance. Colleges are not obligated to fill that gap, or meet families to the point where they would pay only their EFC. Some families have high EFCs and can't believe they're expected to pay that much each year. Yet, the EFC is only a minimum.

Most families end up paying much more than their EFC. You'll remember that the FAFSA and CSS Profile are designed to assess families' income and assets in an equitable manner. Families with similar wherewithal to pay are expected to contribute a similar amount (horizontal equity). Families with uniquely different situations are treated in uniquely different ways (vertical equity). Most families pay even more than what FAFSA says they can pay out of their own resources because most colleges don't meet 100% of need. So, there's a gap between the family's EFC and what the college is willing to give.

When Parents Are Turned Down for the PLUS Loan

Some parents are turned down for the PLUS loan if:

1. They are in arrears paying their taxes and have had a tax lien placed on their property.
2. They have student loan defaults.
3. They recently declared bankruptcy.
4. They have a recent foreclosure or repossession.

If a parent is not eligible to receive the federal PLUS loan, a dependent student becomes eligible for the same higher unsubsidized federal student loan limits as independent students. (You'll recall that graduate students already have independent status and can borrow larger amounts on their own.)

While undergraduate students can borrow limited amounts from the federal government, the balance of costs rests squarely on parents' shoulders. Since college typically lasts four years or more, it's a considerable expense. Many parents haven't figured out how to pay for all four years. It doesn't help that colleges post estimates of tuition costs for only one year at a time, and don't quote future years' tuition, room and board, and fees, which go up by 3% to 5% each year unless the college (like the University of Dayton in Ohio) guarantees that costs will remain the same.

Where would we be if we bought a car or a house knowing only what the cost for one year? I've come across many families who can't wait for their kids to finish. If they have younger children, they pay lots of attention to their in-state colleges, often limiting the choices available to younger siblings.

Finding the right loan for families who don't qualify for the Parent PLUS loan may be as complex as finding the right college. In my practice, I explain to my students and parents how federal loans work. When it comes to private loans, many parents need to figure it out by themselves. However, if you don't evaluate loans ahead of time, the colleges will offer federal loans first, and then a list of private lenders with whom they do business. The larger student loan companies are Sallie Mae, Navient, and Nelnet, but there's a slew of other companies as well. Your band or credit union may offer better terms. Shop carefully!

Some parents can take out an equity line of credit on their home or business or borrow from their retirement plans. Bottom line, it's your choice to decide from whom you borrow. It's you who will make those 120 payments (assuming you choose a 10-year repayment plan). Some lenders will gladly extend that repayment period to 20 and 30 years which will add more interest expense to the loan. As long as you haven't signed the promissory note, you have a choice.

I view federal student aid as the students' funds. Students can choose to spend their federal funds at any college. For example, if students are eligible for $6,000 worth of Pell Grant, they can spend the amount at a public or private college of their choice. Their Pell Grant will likely cover tuition at a community college but not at a flagship or private institution. In effect, the student does the college a favor by enrolling there and giving their "coupon" to the college. When students begin to think of federal aid as their one opportunity to get an education at any college out there, they may begin to think carefully where to spend that precious resource. Hence, when colleges say they have no more aid for the student, the question to ask is "do you mean federal aid or something else?"

Deferring interest payment is just a checkmark on the promissory note. The U.S. Department of Education reports that the majority of borrowers, whether undergraduate, parents or graduate students, defer all interest payment until graduation, deferring interest payment is just a checkmark on the promissory note.

It's one question asked at the outset, a difficult checkmark to change. The deferral of all interest is the bane of borrowers' existence. It results in larger loan amounts because interest accumulates on interest. Some parents are facing retirement while still paying Parent PLUS loans.

When they sign the promissory note, parents need to pay careful attention and check the box "yes" for paying the interest as you go along, so it doesn't capitalize on top of the loan. Finding the right private loan can mean savings, but again, borrowers need to do careful research, crunch the numbers, assess their risk tolerance, and read the fine print before checking the boxes on the promissory note.

Some Differences between the PLUS loan for parents and private loans.

According to America for Progress, there is an estimated $119 billion in private loans for college in repayment. Others report higher estimates.

Income-driven repayment plans created after 2010 apply to "new'' federal student loan borrowers. (Not enough is being done to help "old" borrowers who took loans under the FFEL Program.)

This federal website at studentaid.gov explains the various income-driven repayment plans and tools to use listed below:

- Loan calculators
- Budget calculator
- Bank balancing tool
- Income-based repayment calculator
- Savings calculator
- Student loan debt/salary wizard
- Student loan repayment calculator
- Loan consolidation calculator

ERISA: It's Possible to Pay with Pension Funds (In Some Rare Occasions)!

Borrowing from a pension plan under ERISA can be quite advantageous.

A few parents and grandparents will have a pension or retirement plan. There's a lesser-known clause under ERISA (Employee Retirement Income Security Act of 1974), whereby married couples can use part of their retirement funds to pay for college. It's called In Marriage QDRO®. This puts a new twist onto the mantra "don't ever take money out of your retirement to pay for college!"

This exception was brought to my attention by Attorney Stephanie Prestridge in Baton Rouge, Louisiana. She explained how this can be done. I didn't understand it at first, but when she told me her personal story I got it. It moved me to tears.

Attorney Prestrige is a mom with small children. She said she will be paying Sallie Mae until she's 90 years old. She attended a small private college and, afterward, Loyola Law School in New Orleans. Tuition was handled by both scholarships and loans; despite the scholarships the loans required to cover all of tuition and expenses was significant. According to Stephanie, if she pays only the minimum payments, she will be paying Sallie Mae until she's almost 90 years old.

However, had her family been able to use QDRO® to cover education expenses, Stephanie would have been able to make payments to her mother, who would be able to retire in comfort.

Instead, her mother is still working and Stephanie is still working, paying hefty premiums to Sallie Mae each month.

Many families I work with are paying for their children to attend colleges that cost around $70,000 a year or $280,000 over four years.

If they have an ERISA retirement, the 10% withdrawal penalty is waived for qualified necessities. This could be helpful for some families who have a pension. Under ERISA rules, they can withdraw funds without penalty and lend them to their children who can then pay them back with interest.

Admittedly, this is not the right choice for every family. There must be a level of trust between the parent and child regarding repayment expectations. Under the right circumstances however, this is a wonderful tool for addressing education expenses for addressing education expenses without involvement of a traditional lending institution or the imposition of significant interest costs.

HCERA, "Obamacare"

With the passage of the Health Care and Education Reconciliation Act of 2010, also called "Obama Care," the FFEL (Family Federal Education Loan) program ended. Commercial lenders were banned from making education loans through the federal government. Many commercial banks and private lenders started offering private loans. Today's banks may be offering better interest rates and lower fees than the PLUS loan for parents.

Private lenders cannot begin to compete with the loans that the government makes available to undergraduate students, however.

Federal loans carry contingencies if borrowers get into trouble repaying the loans. These are deferment, forbearance, and income-driven repayment plans. The income-driven repayment plans lower payments based on the borrower's income. Those who work in non-profit organizations may qualify for Public Service Loan Forgiveness. There are no such terms with private loans.

Consolidated Appropriations Act of 2021

The FAFSA Simplification Act was included in the Consolidated Appropriations Act of 2021, taking up 167 pages of the 5,593-page bill. The changes will be effective starting on July 1, 2023 for the 2023-2024 academic year. This will give the U.S.

Department of Education time to implement the changes. For more information, the reader may choose to refer to the original bill: Consolidated Appropriations Act, 2021, pages 5139-5307

I also recommend reading Jeff Levy's explanation of the changes because he explains them very well. Go to Jeff Levy's website or read Mark Kantrowitz' excellent article in Forbes.com. https://www.forbes.com/sites/markkantrowitz/2020/12/02/senate-passes-student-loan-scam-legislation/

Some takeaways from this chapter

1. Federal "Direct" loans for undergraduate students typically offer low rates, grace periods, deferment and forbearance, and income-driven repayment terms. No private, commercial loans offer these benefits.
2. Parent PLUS loans are the go-to loan for most families. Parents with average to below-average credit scores will not be able to find cheaper loans than the Federal PLUS.
3. Parents with excellent credit scores may find cheaper loans in the private sectors but must be careful to check the terms of these loans.
4. Federal loans are the first line of defense against college costs. https://studentaid.gov/understand-aid/types/loans/subsidized-unsubsidized
5. Many colleges would have nothing to offer in an award letter if there were no federal loans for students.
6. Some say if federal loans went away, colleges would have to provide their own financing, and maybe college costs would go down.
7. Without Title IV funding, many colleges would go out of business.

References

History of older loans issued under the FFELP Federal Family Loan Program https://www.finaid.org/loans/dl-vs-ffel.phtml

What About Tackling the Causes of Student Debt?, New York Times, November 19, 2020

Student loan forgiveness may come with a tax bomb. How lawmakers might fix it. CNBC, November 24, 2020.

Go Ahead, Forgive Student Debt: Debt forgiveness is not the best form of stimulus available. But Joe Biden shouldn't waver. The Atlantic, November 21, 2020.

Student Loan Deferment Down Slightly, Experian Research, October 15, 2019.

State Aid Sampler

Don't forget to check how much aid a student would be eligible to receive from your state of residence. Also, note that in many states, if the student attends college out-of-state, this aid doesn't travel. In many states, once students file the FAFSA the state awards need-based or merit-based aid. However, do check the deadlines for applying for state aid in your state of residence. The list is available on the FAFSA website at https://studentaid.gov/sites/default/files/2021-22-fafsa.pdf

Disclaimer: State financial aid can change yearly due to budget adjustments. For the most up-to-date and accurate information, go online to the state government's website for higher education.

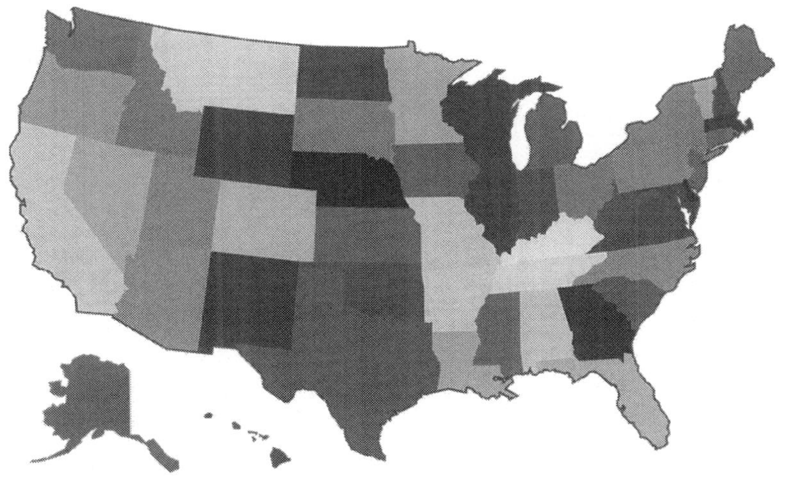

***

Alaska

The Alaska Performance Scholarship provides three levels of awards for students attending Alaska colleges, universities, or vocational/technical programs based upon GPA and SAT or ACT scores. The Alaska Education Grant provides need-based financial aid to residents eligible for Title IV aid. Alaska Native Americans have funds available through Native corporations, such as the Bering Straits Native Corporation. Alaska Commission on Postsecondary Education in Juneau has a number of loans available for residents. For the most up-to-date and accurate information on Alaska aid, go to https://acpe.alaska.gov/FINANCIAL-AID.

***

California

For the most up-to-date and accurate information on California state financial aid, go to the California Student Aid Commission at https://www.csac.ca.gov/financial-aid-programs.

Cal Grant Programs require students to complete the FAFSA or California Dream Act Application (CADAA), meeting eligibility and financial requirements, and have at least a minimum GPA. Cal Grants can be used at any University of California, California State University, or California community college, as well as qualifying independent and career colleges or technical schools in the state.

According to CSAC, "There are three kinds of Cal Grants — A, B and C — but you don't have to figure out which one to apply for. Your eligibility will be based on your FAFSA or CADAA responses, your verified Cal Grant GPA, the type of California colleges you list on your FAFSA and whether you're a recent high school graduate."

The Chafee Grant provides scholarships for foster youth. The Middle Class Scholarship (MCS) is available to students whose families earn up to $177,000 a year; these can be applied to UC and USC schools. There's a scholarship for National Guard, State Military Reserves, and Naval Militia members to improve competencies, and another for dependents of California law enforcement officers killed or completely disabled on duty.

In addition to the California Student Aid Commission website's details on various grant programs, CSAC has created a portal called WebGrants 4 Students (mygrantinfo.csac.ca.gov) with the goal of providing students "the resources, information, and tools needed to assist . . . with the college financial aid process."

The deadline is usually March 2.

***

Delaware

For the most up-to-date and accurate information on Delaware aid, go to the Delaware Department of Education's website at https://www.doe.k12.de.us/Page/1893. Delaware residents have 12 possible areas of financial assistance, from scholarships to loans.

The B. Bradford Barnes Scholarship provides full tuition, fees, room and board, and books at the University of Delaware, renewable yearly, to Delaware students who graduate high school with a GPA of 3.0 and an SAT score of 1290. The Charles Hebner Scholarship provides the same full coverage of expenses at UD and Delaware State.

The student must have a 3.0 and at least 1000 on the SAT; he or she must major in humanities or social sciences, with preference given to political science majors. For children of deceased veterans or police officers, the state will pay for tuition and fees if certain conditions are met. The Herman Holloway Scholarship will pay full tuition and more at Delaware State if the student has a 3.0 and 1000 on the SAT.

Delaware has incentives for teachers and nurses. The Christa McAuliffe Teacher Incentive Program provides up to $5,000 per year for full-time students enrolled at a Delaware college in an undergraduate program in teacher certification, with preference given to applicants planning to teach in a critical need area, such as world languages or math. For the teacher incentive program, students must have a 3.0 and 1010 on the SAT. The nursing incentive program also awards $5,000 a year to nursing students who graduate high school with at least a 2.5 GPA.

There are smaller scholarships for cross country athletes, for those who will major in environmental engineering or sciences, for children of parents in the Wilmington Maritime Society. The Diamond State Scholarship awards $1,250 a year, and the Scholarship Incentive Program (ScIP) awards $1,000 a year. Finally, the Delaware Teacher Corps provides loans for undergraduate or graduate teacher education.

***

Florida

For up-to-date information, go to https://www.floridastudentfinancialaidsg.org/

General requirements for student eligibility for state financial aid awards and tuition assistance grants:

- Student must achieve the academic requirements of and acceptance at a state university or Florida College System.
- Student must reside in the state of Florida for at least one year preceding the award of aid.
- For renewal, a student must earn a minimum 2.0 with 12 credit hours per term.
- Undergraduate students are eligible to receive financial aid for a maximum of 8 semesters or 12 quarters.

Students with a documented disability are eligible to be considered for aid while attending part-time.

Florida Bright Futures Scholarship Program

The Florida Bright Futures Scholarship program is a lottery-funded scholarship to reward Florida high school graduates who merit recognition of high academic achievement and who enroll in a degree, certificate, or applied technology program at an eligible Florida public or private postsecondary educational institution. It comprises four awards: the Florida Academic Scholarship (FAS), the Florida Medallion Scholarship (FMS), the Florida Gold Seal CAPE Scholarship (GSC), and the Florida Gold Seal Vocational (GSV) Scholarship. Students submit a single application for all awards. The student must be a Florida resident, graduate from a Florida high school, and be accepted by and enrolled in an eligible Florida public or private postsecondary educational institution.

At the beginning of the school year, Florida school districts must give each junior and senior a Florida Bright Futures Evaluation Report and Key. The report must also identify all requirements not met per award, including the GPA, as well as identify the awards for which the student has met the academic requirements. That includes all courses they took, and identifies all requirements not met. work attempted, number of credits, and the student's GPA. So Florida students learn what it takes to get this state scholarship. To determine the GPA, additional weight is given to AP, IB, dual enrollment, and some other classes. The Bright Futures calculation of GPA may differ from the school district's calculation.

Eligibility requirements may change with each legislative session. The Florida State Board of Education will publicize the exam score required for a student to be eligible for the Florida Academic Scholarship and the Florida Medallion Scholarship. It is based upon a national percentile (89th percentile for FAS, 75th for FMS) and therefore subject to vary from year to year.

Florida Gold Seal CAPE and Gold Seal Vocational Scholarships

Gold Seal CAPE (GSC) and Gold Seal Vocational (GSV) scholarships may only be used at postsecondary institutions that offer an applied technology diploma, technical degree education program (associate in applied science or associate in science), or a career certificate program. For more about these vocational scholarships, see the Florida Department of Education.

Florida Public Student Assistance Grant

- Available to degree-seeking students who enroll in at least 6 semester hours
- Grant awarded annually for the amount of demonstrated unmet need for the cost of education; may not exceed an amount equal to the average prior academic year cost of tuition, fees, and other registration fees for 30 credit hours at state universities.
- Must apply for the federal Pell Grant
- Priority in distribution shall be given to students with the lowest total family resources.
- Funds are distributed directly to eligible institutions.

Access to Better Learning and Education Grant

- Apply through financial aid offices of eligible private Florida colleges and universities
- Must be a Florida resident who does not owe money to any state or federal program
- Must not have a bachelor's degree already
- Enroll at least 12 credit hours per term in eligible Florida college/university toward baccalaureate

- Meet Florida's general eligibility requirements for state aid
- Not be enrolled in religious degree program

***

Georgia

For the most up-to-date information on Georgia aid, go to https://gsfc.georgia.gov.

Georgia students who meet the requirements to qualify for the HOPE scholarship may use the funds for any in-state public school; some private schools may also qualify for a portion of the funds. There are two levels of the HOPE scholarship: a 3.0 will cover part of in-state tuition, and a 3.7 GPA covers full in-state tuition.

In addition to the GPA requirements, students must submit either the FAFSA or the Georgia Student Finance Application, meet certain rigor requirements, and maintain a 3.0 (3.3 for full tuition).

The HOPE scholarship has changed the landscape of the public universities in Georgia. Many of the most promising students choose to attend UGA or Georgia Tech for their undergraduate work because it is an amazing cost reducer. In turn, Georgia schools have become increasingly difficult for in-state students to gain admission.

***

Maryland

For the most up-to-date and accurate information on Maryland aid, go to https://mhec.md.gov or call (800) 974-0203.

The Maryland Higher Education Commission (MHEC) offers scholarships and grants to Maryland residents. No assistance is automatically applied; you must apply through MHEC.

The Community College Promise Scholarship provides tuition assistance at community college for any student eligible for in-state tuition; it also will provide financial aid to those in qualified apprenticeship, licensure, and certification programs. To be considered, you must submit the FAFSA or the Maryland State Financial Aid Application (MSFAA), have a high school GPA of 2.3 or higher, have a family income of no more than $100,000 for single-parent household or $150,000 for two-parent household, and complete at least 12 credits a semester in good standing. The annual award goes up to $5,000, or actual tuition after all non-loan aid is applied, whichever is less, and covers tuition only. Awards will be prioritized by need. Recipients must work in the state of Maryland for one year after earning a certificate or associate's degree.

For community college students who earn an associate's degree, Maryland offers the 2 + 2 Transfer Scholarship to encourage transfer students from Maryland community colleges to attend a four-year institution within the state. A Maryland College Aid Processing System (MDCAPS) account is necessary for this program. Your family EFC must be $10,000 or less as reported on the FAFSA, and the award is for $1,000; however, students enrolling in science, math, engineering, teaching, or nursing may receive $2,000 per year.

For those who filled out the FAFSA but did not get federal grants, Maryland has the Educational Assistance Grant; those with the lowest EFC are awarded first. Maryland also offers grants and scholarships for part-time and graduate students.

The Teaching Fellows of Maryland Scholarship encourages students who don't yet have teaching certification to major in education or to change careers and move into education. Students must promise to serve in a Maryland school that has at least 50% of students on free or reduced-price meals for as many years as the state covered tuition. If you meet the eligibility requirements, the state will pay 100% of tuition, fees, and room and board. You must have or establish an MDCAPS account to apply.

Legislative scholarships can be obtained by contacting your Maryland delegate or state senator. Unique populations may receive aid; these populations are primarily military. Tuition waivers are available for foster care recipients, homeless students, Maryland National Guard, and students with disabilities.

If you are a Maryland resident, start with https://mhec.state.md.us and see if you might qualify for any of the state's programs.

***

Massachusetts

For the most up-to-date information on Massachusetts aid, go to https://www.mass.edu/osfa/programs/programs.asp.

Massachusetts offers grants, scholarships and tuition waivers, each with its own set of guidelines and rules. They all require the filing of FAFSA, Massachusetts state residency, no default on loans, compliance with Selective Services, not having a bachelor's degree, and making satisfactory progress in school. Unless otherwise noted, the money applies to public, private, for-profit, and not-for-profit institutions.

Massachusetts provides grants to foster children, students with low EFCs, some nursing students, part-time students, students who lost a parent or spouse killed in the line of public service, and paraprofessionals who want to become certified teachers. Scholarships are available for rural students, at-risk students, early childhood educators, students in the top 25% of their class, entrepreneurs, and many more categories of students. There are also a large number of tuition waiver programs, including those for aspiring teachers, valedictorians, and high technology scholars. This state provides numerous avenues to financial aid. Be sure to go to the

Massachusetts Department of Education, Office of Student Financial Aid to see if you might fit into a category that receives assistance.

***

New Jersey

For the most up-to-date information on New Jersey aid, go to https://www.hesaa.org The New Jersey Higher Education Student Assistance Authority (HESAA) oversees the NJ grants for higher education. There are no opportunities to use the grants out of state, but some do allow monies to be used at private schools and trade schools. To be eligible for New Jersey grants and scholarships, a student must meet general federal aid eligibility requirements and several additional requirements, such as being a New Jersey resident for at least 12 months immediately prior to enrollment.

The state offers the New Jersey Community College Opportunity Grant and the Tuition Aid Grant (TAG). TAG may cover up to the cost of tuition, depending upon financial need and cost of tuition, and can be used at public and private institutions. The Educational Opportunity Fund (EOF) is designed for economically and educationally disadvantaged students.

The Governor's Urban Scholarship program is a merit scholarship available to students in the top 5% of their class, with at least a 3.0 GPA. These monies are available only to students in certain urban areas of the state. Surviving dependents of the 9/11 attacks may qualify for the New Jersey World Trade Center Scholarship. NJSTARS, or New Jersey Student Tuition Assistance Reward Scholarship, is available to those who graduate in the top 15% of their class and will cover up to 18 credits a semester at the student's county college.

In addition to the aid listed here, New Jersey provides tuition assistance to many other categories of students, including females and minorities. For more information, see https://www.hesaa.org.

***

North Carolina

For the most up-to-date and accurate information on North Carolina aid, go to https://www.cfnc.org North Carolina state formed the College Foundation of North Carolina to administer all scholarships, grants, and loans in the state. See: https://www.cfnc.org/static/pdf/paying/pubs/pdf/FANC.pdf Appropriated Grants are for North Carolina residents enrolled in good standing as full- or part-time undergraduate, graduate, or first professional degree candidates in constituent institutions of the University of North Carolina. Awards vary. Apply for need-based financial aid at the institution and eligible students will automatically be considered for grants.

North Carolina Need-Based Scholarships (NBS) are need-based scholarships for North Carolina students who qualify for the Federal Pell Grant attending private North Carolina institutions of higher education. When completing the FAFSA, applicant must list at least one qualifying private North Carolina institution and consideration is automatic. See CFNC.org/NBS.

North Carolina Community College Grants are for North Carolinians enrolled in at least six credit hours per semester in a curriculum program and making satisfactory academic progress. Eligibility is based on the same criteria as the Pell Grant, but students who are not eligible for the Pell may be considered based upon their EFC. See CFNC.org/NCCCG.

North Carolina Education Lottery Scholarship (ELS): North Carolina students enrolled in at least six credit hours in a degree, certificate, or diploma program at UNC campuses or NC community colleges. Students who qualify for the Pell Grant or whose EFC is $5,000 or lower may be considered for the ELS. For more information, see CFNC.org/ELS.

North Carolina Teaching Fellows Program, a forgivable loan to be used for tuition, fees, and books at identified institutions, is available now for students in a program that leads to teacher licensure. For the 2019-20 year, students may receive $4,125 per semester. See ncteachingfellows.com for details.

The UNC Campus Scholarship Program is designed to promote diversity on the 16 North Carolina public university campuses. A portion of the program is reserved for Native American students.

***

South Carolina State Aid

The state provides three levels of merit scholarships, all based on academic achievement. Students must meet two out of three criteria.

1. HOPE: $2500/year award just needs a SC Uniform GPA of a 3.00+
2. LIFE: $5000/year (replaces HOPE) must have a 3.00+ GPA and one of the following:
   a. Rank in the Top 30% of their HS Class
   b. Have 1100 + SAT or 24+ ACT
3. Palmetto Fellows: (replaces LIFE)
   a. Must rank in Top 6% of HS Class and have a 1200+ SAT or 27+ ACT
   b. Have a 4.00+ SC Uniform GPA and a 1400+ SAT or 32+ ACT

The Palmetto Fellows Scholarship is $6700 in the first year, but changes to $7,500 in Sophomore, Junior and Senior years. There's also a Science Enhancement Scholarship that adds $2500 to both LIFE and Palmetto Fellows from Sophomore to

Senior years if students are enrolled in certain Science majors. SC scholarships are funded by the SC lottery. Residents who purchase the lottery tickets are often poor, while the students who get high test-scores and often rich. In this way, the lottery funds the merit scholarships of wealthier students who could probably pay for in-state tuition anyway. During the Covid-19 Pandemic, the public universities accepted students without standardized scores, and it remains to be seen how the SC legislation will adapt to these changes. If less emphasis was placed on standardized tests, more low-income students would qualify for the scholarships.

Applications for state aid have varying deadlines. Many states award aid based on your filing the FAFSA. Others require a separate application. Check the deadlines.

Glossary

This chapter provides definitions of terms mentioned in this book. Some of the definitions listed below come from StudentAid.gov.

Ability-to-Benefit (ATB): To receive Title IV funding, a student must have earned a high school diploma or equivalent, such as a GED. If they have neither, they can take an approved ability-to-benefit (ATB) test. Another way to demonstrate your ability to benefit is to complete six credit hours or the equivalent coursework toward a degree or certificate program offered by the institution.

Accuplacer: Community college students can meet reading and writing proficiency by taking these tests, especially if they didn't take any other standardized tests such as the ACT or SAT or have low GPAs and scores.

Adjusted Gross Income (AGI): This income figure comes from your federal tax return and then reported on the FAFSA or the CSS Profile. On your tax return, the AGI is your total gross income minus federal adjustments and deductions. For example, contributions to a retirement plan or pension are deductions on tax returns. On the FAFSA they are added back to the AAI (Adjusted Available Income) because retirement contributions are "earned income" nevertheless.

Adviser: In this book, "adviser" refers to several professionals who help students with the college admissions process. The professional may be called an Independent Educational Consultant (IEC), Could be a member of IECA or HECA, or could be or a school counselor at a high school.

Affordable Family Contribution (AFC): The AFC is a name that Claire uses to indicate an amount that families can pay after they examine their budget, savings, and ability to borrow federal loans. The AFC is the amount you can reasonably afford to pay from your resources.

Bear in mind that your AFC is your ideal amount to pay. The closer the colleges come to your AFC the more affordable your costs and likelihood that your student will have enough funding to graduate.

Aggregate loan limits: The total amount you can borrow over the life of the loan. Federal student loans may have annual and aggregate limits on the amount you can borrow.

Award Letter: After students get accepted, colleges send out an email message or printed letter that lists the amount of federal, state and institutional aid that the college awards the student. The first financial aid awarded consists of federal loans and, if the student demonstrates financial need, federal grants. Many institutions award only federal aid. Others award scholarships if the student ranks near the top of their applicant pool. Elite universities typically don't award merit scholarships but meet a higher level of demonstrated financial need.

To compare your award letters, use College Financing Plan, previously known as the shopping sheet.

To compare multiple award letters, use Claire's Excel spreadsheet, which you can download from www.eduave.com.

STUDENT NAME:		
Superscores: SAT: CR M V ACT:	GPA:	Personal rating:
Choice of Major/Minor fields of study		
Colleges that accepted student:		
Est. Family Contribution (From FM Formula)		
Est. Family Contribution(from IM Formula)		
* Workable Family Contribution		
COST OF ATTENDANCE	NAME OF COLLEGE	NAME OF COLLEGE
(+) Tuition & Fees		
(+) Room & Board		
(+) Est. Books & Supplies		
(+) Est. Personal Expenses		
= Total Cost of Attendance	$0	$0
(-) Estimated Family Contribution FM or IM		
= Financial Need At This College	$0	$0
Financial Aid Breakdown:		
(+) Merit Scholarships		
(+) Need Based Grant	$0	$0
(+) Estimated State Grant	$0	$0
(+) Federal Pell Grant	$0	$0
(+) Federal SEOG Grant	$0	$0
(=) Total Gift Aid (A)	$0	$0

Capitalization: Loans, whether federal or private, have a variety of interest rates. In 2020-21, the interest rate on the Direct loan for Undergraduate students was only 2.75%. Interest on loans is added to the principal amount borrowed if it is not paid as it accrues. This is called interest capitalization. Students and parent(s) will repay the entire amount with interest. It's the same method: buy now, pay later. The whole amount equals the actual amount borrowed plus the interest that accrues over time.

Career Exploration: www.onetonline.org is your tool for career exploration and job analysis! O*NET OnLine has detailed descriptions of the world of work for use by job seekers, workforce development and HR professionals, students, researchers, and more! Keyword or O*NET-SOC Code: Browse groups of similar occupations to explore careers.

Certified Educational Planner (CEP): To be a certified educational planner, consultants and counselors must pass a board-certified assessment, hold a Master's degree, visit and evaluate a prescribed number of educational institutions, and be evaluated every five years on the basis of:

1. Earned continuing education credits
2. Participation in continual professional development
3. Ongoing in-depth visits to enhance knowledge of colleges, schools and educational programs.

A CEP is an experienced professional who is committed to providing the highest quality of service to students and families. www.aicep.org. Claire Law earned her CEP designation in 1999.

Charts: https://www.bigjeducationalconsulting.com/resources These charts show domestic undergraduate students and the colleges where they received need-based aid or merit aid. Updated as of August 2020 by Jeff Levy and Jenny Kent, this chart helps with building a college list. If you know that your family's EFC is higher than the COA this chart shows the merit scholarships, which is likely all that you will qualify for. You will also see which colleges award aid and what percentage of demonstrated need each college covers.

College: I capitalize the letter "C" to indicate I'm referring to the name of a specific college. Lower-case "c" refers to colleges, universities and community colleges in general.

College Navigator: College Navigator is a tool created by the National Center for Education Statistics at the U.S. Department of Education that provides information about the cost, financial aid, net price, admissions rates and graduation rates at colleges and universities. Visit https://nces.ed.gov/collegenavigator/

College Scorecard: The College Scorecard is the best resource for parents, students, and IECs who want to make decisions based on facts about the colleges that interest them. It contains even more data than the College Navigator, including average debt at graduation and income after graduation, by academic major at each college. https://collegescorecard.ed.gov/ College Scorecard collects data elements from both the colleges directly and the National Student Loan Data System (NSLDS).

Cost of Attendance (COA): The cost of attendance is the total amount (not including grants and scholarships) that it will cost you to go school during one academic school year.

COA is made up of direct and indirect costs. Direct costs are tuition, housing and meals. Indirect costs are books, and supplies, transportation, allowances for rental of a personal computer, personal expenses, dependent care, and reasonable costs for study-abroad programs.

Concordance Tables ACT/SAT: Concordance tables show the mapping between SAT and ACT test scores, showing which SAT score likely correlates to an ACT score. https://www.act.org/content/dam/act/unsecured/documents/ACT-SAT-Concordance-Tables.pdf

Consolidation Appropriations Act, 2021: Passed on December 27, 2020, the Consolidated Appropriations Act, 2021, included simplification of the FAFSA on pages 5139-5307.

CSS Profile: The CSS Profile is a form that about 200 private and elite colleges require in addition to the FAFSA form in order to more accurately assess a family's financial strength and ability to contribute to paying for college. It's used by many elite universities before they award institutional scholarships or need-based financial aid. This money comes not from the federal government but from the school itself. https://cssprofile.collegeboard.org/

Data Retrieval Tool (DRT): The IRS Data Retrieval Tool, or DRT, is a FAFSA option that allows you to transfer your prior-prior year taxes directly from the IRS and uses that data to populate the correct fields on the FAFSA form. Not everyone can use the DRT, but if you can, then your financial information is verified and you will not be selected for verification. If you don't use the DRT to provide your tax information to the college, you will need to get an official tax return transcript from the IRS. Visit www.IRS.gov and click on "Order a Transcript" or call 800-908-9946.

Default: Default is failure to repay a loan as outlined in the agreed promissory note. Most federal student loan default occurs when a payment isn't made in more than 270 days. It can result in legal consequences and a loss of eligibility for additional federal student aid. If you are reading this book, you will avoid this situation. When you are approved for a loan, you sign a promissory note. Read the fine print on the prom note. You are warned that if you do not pay it back, according to the terms specified, you will be in default. This means that the lender or servicer will notify the national credit bureaus, the IRS will withhold your tax refund, and even garnish your wages to pay the loans. Yes, the IRS can ask your employer to withhold part of your salary. It's very, very, very difficult to clean up a default. Don't borrow more than the wages you expect to earn upon graduation. (If you borrow the amounts allowed for dependent undergraduate students, and you graduate in four years, you will owe slightly less than $30,000. Most college graduates are successful in paying back this amount.) To clean up your defaulted loan: https://studentaid.gov/manage-loans/default/get-out

Default remediation: During the Covid-19 pandemic, the U.S. Department of Education ceased all activities on trying to collect defaulted federal loans. The payment pause registered as a payment made. To rehabilitate a defaulted loan, borrowers need to make nine, on-time payments. In addition, the interest was set to 0% to provide relief during the payment pause. Those borrowers who were in default never had a better chance to rehabilitate their federal loans and personal credit.

Deferment: This is a very useful program to know: If you run into trouble and can't pay your federal (not private) student loans and need a short reprieve, you can apply for a deferment, which means you can postpone paying your loans. During a deferment, the interest keeps accruing on unsubsidized loans, but not subsidized loans. Any accrued but unpaid interest will be capitalized on top of the principal borrowed at the end of the deferment period. This is a last-ditch measure to avoid delinquency and default. You don't want to get into this situation!

Dependency Status: A student is either dependent or independent. Dependent students must report their and their parents' information on FAFSA. Independent students report only their own financial information and their spouse if married. Dependent students are younger than 24 years of age, are not in graduate school, have not served in the U.S. Armed Forces, are not married, do not have children. Dependent students depend on their parents for financial support.

Direct Loans: Federal loans are called "Direct" because they originate directly by the U.S. Department of Education, and not banks or commercial lenders. Prior to 2010, there were many private lenders authorized to make federal loans through the Federal Family Education Loan (FFEL) program. The Health Care and Education Reconciliation Act of 2010 ended the FFEL program. All new federal education loans starting on July 1, 2010 have been made through the Direct Loan program, where the funding comes from the U.S. Department of Education and is paid directly to the colleges. Consequently. federal loans are now less expensive, more flexible and offer many repayment plans.

Direct Subsidized Loan: A subsidized Direct Loan is a federal loan where the U.S. Department of Education pays the interest on the loan while you're in school at least half-time and for the first six months after you leave school, (called a "grace period"), and during periods of deferment (a postponement of loan payments). Direct subsidized loans are awarded to students who demonstrate financial need. These are also known as subsidized Stafford loans.

Direct Unsubsidized Loan: Eligibility for unsubsidized loans does not depend on financial need. The borrower is responsible for paying the interest on an unsubsidized loan during all periods. If you choose not to pay the interest while you are in school, and during grace periods and deferment or forbearance periods, your interest will accrue (accumulate) and be capitalized (that is, your interest will be added to the principal amount of your loan). These are also known as unsubsidized Stafford loans.

Divorced Parents: Typically, the FAFSA asks for financial information for only the parent with whom the student lives the majority of the time. Typically, it's the parent who provides food and housing. If the student lives exactly 50/50 with mom and dad (a rare occurrence), then the FAFSA considers the parent who is providing greater financial support.

Institutions that require the CSS Profile form consider both biological parents' income. If the biological parents have remarried, the college may have set up the CSS Profile formula to consider the income of the new spouses as well. This can vary from college to college.

If both biological parents live together, even though they never married, both parents' financial information is required on the FAFSA and CSS profile.

Sometimes, parents are divorced but live in the same household. In this case, both parents' financial information will be assessed on both the FAFSA and CSS Profile. Some parents try to list a different address for each; however, the income tax returns from previous years would list the address. Other documentation, such as proof of a signed lease and monthly payments, would provide sufficient verification.

Education Tax Benefits: The education tax benefits include the American Opportunity Tax Credit, (AOTC), 529 Savings Plans, Prepaid Tuition Plans, Lifetime Learning Tax Credit (LLTC), Student Loan Interest Deduction, and other tax breaks.

EFA (Estimated Family Assistance) consists scholarships, grants, loans and other financial aid aside from federal, state and institutional aid. The federal financial aid formula subtracts EFA from financial need to determine the remaining financial need.

EFC: See also Expected Family Contribution. This is a misnomer because families typically pay more than their EFC, which is supposed to be a "reasonable amount" based on the family's resources. However, families pay much more than their federal EFC because colleges don't fill 100% of their financial need. You can use the EFC to figure out the size of the gap, which can reveal how much the college is really interested in the student. Many parents were thinking that the EFC was their net cost, and this may be the reason why U.S. Department of Education is changing the name from EFC to Student Aid Index, or SAI. This new system will make it harder to detect what would be a "reasonable" amount for the family to contribute according to the federal methodology. My hope is that the Student Aid Report will show the index on the SAR. If families follow my rubric and determine what is their Affordable Family Contribution or AFC, then regardless of the name or amount the colleges charge, the family will look for colleges that are more in line with what they can afford, and thus will be in control of their spending.

Eligible Citizens: You must be one of the following to receive federal student aid:

- U.S. citizen
- U.S. national (includes natives of American Samoa, the Republic of Palau or Swain's Island)
- U.S. permanent resident who has an I-151, I-551, or I-551C Permanent Resident Card

International students in the U.S. on an F1, F2, J1, J1, M1 or M2 visa are not eligible for federal student aid.

Enrollment Management Firms: Noel-Levitz, Maguire Associates, Ruffalo-Cody, Destiny Solutions, Strategic Enrollment Management; SEMworks, IntelliCampus, AACRAO

Expected Family Contribution (EFC): Your EFC is an index number that college financial aid staff use to determine how much federal financial aid you would be eligible to receive. It is based on the information you reported on your FAFSA form. This is not the amount you will pay for college. It is not the amount you will receive in aid from the federal government.

The Expected Family Contribution is also called Student Aid Index which results from filing the FAFSA. The federal formulas provide an amount that families should be able to afford based on their income and assets.

The EFC is calculated according to a formula established by Congress. Your family's taxed and untaxed income, assets, and benefits (such as unemployment or Social Security) all could be considered in the formula. Also considered are your family size. The EFC Formula Guide is updated each year and shows exactly how the federal EFC is calculated.

Private colleges and a few public institutions use an institutional contribution which results from families filing the CSS Profile.

The federal EFC can be higher or lower than the Institutional or institutional EFC.

FAFSA Mobile App: Students can file the FAFSA using the myStudentAid mobile app on a smartphone. Students can create an account, view and update it, complete the FAFSA, and access a personalized dashboard that summarizes their aid, highlights upcoming loan payments, and provides content and checklists. It gives the name of their loan servicer and remaining balances of Direct Loan and Pell Grant eligibility. If graduates are working for a non-profit company, this app keeps track of the payments toward the public service loan forgiveness in a summary of payments.

Federal Student Loans: Federal student loans include loans through the Direct Loan program, such as the subsidized and unsubsidized Federal Direct Stafford Loan, the Federal Direct Parent PLUS Loan, the Federal Direct Grad PLUS Loan and the Federal Direct Consolidation Loan. Additional information is available at

Federal Supplemental Educational Opportunity Grant (FSEOG): The FSEOG is awarded to the neediest of Pell-eligible students. The FSEOG is available up to $4,000 per year. The FSEOG is a form of campus-based aid, where the federal government allocates a fixed sum of money to each college and the college financial aid administrator has the discretion to determine which students receive the awards.

Federal Work-Study: Federal Work-Study is a federal student aid program that provides part-time jobs while the student is enrolled in school to help pay their education expenses. The student must seek out and apply for work-study jobs at the college. The student will be paid directly for the hours worked and are not automatically credited to pay for institutional tuition and fees. The student would need to go to the bursar's office and deposit the check into his account. The amount you earn for federal work-study cannot exceed the amount allotted in your financial aid award letter. The availability of work study varies by school. Work-study jobs are not guaranteed until the student actually finds a job and earns the funds. Federal Work-Study earnings are taxed like other income, but are exempt from FICA taxes (Social Security and Medicare taxes) if the student works less than 20 hours a week. However, the income you will earn will not be counted against you when calculating your Expected Family Contribution on the FAFSA.

Financial Aid Administrator (FAA): A financial aid administrator is a college employee who is responsible for determining a student's eligibility for financial aid, preparing financial aid award letters, and explaining to students and parents the awards they received. An FAA can also make professional judgment changes to the data elements on the student's FAFSA when supported by documented special circumstances. Be sure to understand your financial situation, such as your budget, your expenses, and most of all, be sure you understand your award letter before you make an appeal and ask for professional judgment.

Financial Literacy: The U.S. Department of Education and U.S. Treasury Department are committed to providing financial literacy support services and resources to student borrowers. can contribute to student success. They also support colleges and share in their coordinated approach to financial literacy to help students make smart financial decisions that contribute to academic and financial success.

Financial Need: The difference between the Cost of Attendance (COA) at a school and your Expected Family Contribution (EFC). While COA varies from school to school, your EFC does not change based on the school you attend.

Forbearance: Borrowers who cannot make their monthly payments due to illness or hardship may be able to defer their payments for a limited and specific period of time. Like a deferment, a forbearance can be up to three years. Some forbearances are much shorter. The interest continues to accrue during a forbearance. Forbearance should be seen as a last-ditch measure to avoid default.

Free Application for Federal Student Aid (FAFSA):Available on October 1 of the student's senior year of high school and each subsequent year, the FAFSA must be filled out in order for the student to be considered for federal student financial aid. When the FAFSA refers to "you," it's referring to the student. If you get stuck filling out the FAFSA, call the FAFSA hotline at 1-800-433-3243.

Gap: A gap is the amount of unmet financial need. This means that the college is not meeting the full demonstrated financial need. Rather, the amount financial aid is less than the amount of financial need. Colleges with larger endowments can meet full need and therefore are able to attract the best students. Colleges that struggle to fill classes even when they discount tuition through merit scholarships often are unable to meet the full demonstrated financial need.

Grad PLUS: Graduate students can borrow unsubsidized Direct Loans as well as the Grad PLUS loan. The Grad PLUS loan does not have an aggregate loan limit and the annual limit is up to the cost of attendance, minus other aid received. Graduate students need to gauge their future earnings before borrowing too much to complete a graduate program. Finding assistantships and fellowships is a much better way to earn a graduate degree. Some employers pay for their employees to earn a graduate degree.

Grants and Scholarships: Grants and scholarships are gift aid, a type of student aid funds that do not have to be repaid. Federal grants are need-based. Examples include the Pell Grant and the FSEOG. Scholarships are usually merit-based. Scholarships are awarded based on the student's academic, athletic, or other merits. You may have to repay part or all of a grant if, for example, you withdraw from school before finishing the semester. (Read Bella's case study.) If you use a grant or scholarship to cover your living expenses, the amount of your scholarship may be counted as taxable income on your tax return.

IECA: IECA is the Independent Educational Consultant Association. Professional members are required to pledge adherence to Principles of Good Practice when admitted to membership and annually with membership renewal. The highest designation is the Certified Educational Planner.

Income Share Agreement (ISA): An Income Share Agreement (ISA) is a contract between a student and their institution of higher education or other financial entity. The student receives money from the lender to pay for their education. In exchange, they agree to pay the lender a percentage of their income after graduation for a set number of years.

Independent student status: Graduate students, veterans who served and were not dishonorably discharged, married students, students who responsible for more than half of the support for their children, a youth who is homeless or at risk of being homeless, any student who is an orphan or a ward of the court and students who are 24 years of age or older are all considered to be independent students. If a student is an independent student, their parents' financial information will not be reported on the FAFSA, and they can borrow larger amounts from the federal loan programs.

Institutional EFC: The Expected Family Contribution (EFC) is a measure of the family's ability to pay for college. A college may have a different EFC than the federal EFC for awarding its own grant funding. Although colleges vary in how they use the institutional methodology, designed by the College Board, the biggest difference is that it considers home equity, business equity, the value of any vehicles, and other types of assets. If divorced, the noncustodial parent's income and assets are assessed as well.

IRS Data Retrieval Tool (IRS DRT): The IRS Data Retrieval Tool transfers income and tax information from the IRS to the FAFSA. Data elements that are transferred to the FAFSA are not selected for verification. This can save the family time and effort. Transferred information is masked to protect the privacy and security of the information.

Loans: Loans are borrowed money that must be repaid with interest and fees. Loans from the federal government typically have a lower interest rate than loans form private lenders. Federal loans, listed from most advantageous to least advantageous are: Direct Subsidized loans, Direct Unsubsidized loans, Parent PLUS loans and Grad PLUS loans. You'll find more information at StudentAid.gov Going to college is synonymous with taking out loans. Students who file FAFSA are automatically offered Direct Loans by the college's financial aid office. Parents and students need to know what types of loans are available to undergraduate and graduate students and parents. Plan ahead for the amount of money you can afford to borrow. Families must consider the difference between federal and private loans, the consequences of default, and how to best manage the debt.

Loan Limits: A loan limit is a cap on the amount of debt you can borrow. There may be annual loan limits and aggregate loan limits. Dependent undergraduate students can borrow up to $5,500 in the first year of college, $6,500 in the second year, $7,500 in the third and fourth years. Independent undergraduate students can borrow up to $9,500 in the first year of college, $10,500 in the second year, and $12,500 in the third and fourth years.

Loan Servicers: The U.S. Department of Education will assign the collection of your monthly loan payments to a federally-approved company called a loan servicer. Servicers are your point of contact to make sure your payments are recorded and allocated correctly. For example, assume your monthly payment is $700 and one day you send in an additional $150 toward the principal. You need to check with the loan servicer to make sure this happens correctly, and the amount is not sitting in escrow, but it's applied to your principal balance.

National Student Loan Data System (NSLDS): NSLDS is a database that contains information about all federal student loans, including the origination, disbursement, loan servicer, interest and payments. In short, it has the complete history of your student loans. The outstanding principal balance listed on NSLDS may be as much as 120 days behind. You can contact your loan servicer for more up-to-date balance information. This government website tracks the history of each student's loans, the amounts owed, the name of the loan servicer, interest, and fees that were paid. Students can use their FSA ID or social security number to access this site so they can be completely aware of how their loan payments are performing, their balances, and penalties applied. NSLDS is accessible through the StudentAid.gov website.

NCES: NCES is the National Center for Education Statistics at the U.S. Department of Education. They publish several tools, such as the College Navigator, that families can use when crafting a college list. The College Navigator includes information about average costs, retention from the first to the second year, and graduation rates.

Net Price: The net price is the actual cost that a student and his or her family need to pay in a given year to cover education expenses for the student to attend a particular institution. Net price is determined by taking the institution's cost of attendance and subtracting any grants and scholarships awarded to the student.

Net Price Calculator (NPC) A Net Price Calculator is a tool that provides prospective students with a personalized estimate of the net price of attending a selected college. The NPC is located on each college's website and can be found by clicking on the financial aid page. Student contact information should not be required to complete the NPC, but the financial information entered should be as accurate as possible. NPCs that ask a larger number of questions tend to be more accurate.

Origination Fee: An origination fee is an upfront fee charged by a lender for processing a new loan application. It is compensation for putting the loan in place. Origination fees are quoted as a percentage of the total loan amount.

Parent PLUS Loan: A Parent PLUS Loan is a federal loan available to parents of dependent undergraduate students. The PLUS loan amount can cover the full cost of education minus any other aid awarded to the student. As a result of enrollment management strategies, colleges have been able to leverage financial aid and cover the gap in funding with the PLUS loan. "College is possible if parents are willing to borrow" was the mantra I heard from financial aid administrators. While PLUS loans offer a better deal than private loans, the amount of borrowing does make a difference in the length of repayment and cash flow hindrance.

PLUS Loan: The PLUS loan, previously known as the Parent Loan for Undergraduate Students, is a federal loan made to graduate school students (Grad PLUS) and parents of undergraduate students (Parent PLUS). It is an unsubsidized loan. The loan limit is up to the total cost of attendance minus other aid received. Borrowers must not have an adverse credit history to qualify for the PLUS loan. An adverse credit history includes bankruptcy discharge, foreclosure, repossession, tax lien, wage garnishment or default determination within the last five years or a serious delinquency of 90 or more days within the last two years. Eligibility does not depend on credit scores or debt-to-income ratios.

Preferential Packaging: With preferential packaging, the college awards the same amount of aid to a student, but gives a better mix of grants vs. loans to students they want to recruit. This sweeter financial aid package that will contain more "gifts" or "free money" than loans, reducing the net price. The 'gap' will be smaller too.

Principal: The principal is the amount of money borrowed. Interest and loan fees add to the cost of borrowing. Interest is charged based on the principal balance of the loan, plus any capitalized interest.

Private lenders: Banks, credit unions, and other private lenders offer private student loans and private parent loans, as well as private refinance. They are no longer able to lend federal education loans, as they did under the FFEL program. Private, commercial loans are less flexible than federal loans and require a credit check — the lower the credit rating, the higher the interest rate and costs. A cosigner is often needed.

Professional Judgment (PJ): Financial Aid Administrators have the authority to make case-by-case adjustments to the data elements on the FAFSA and the components of the cost of attendance based on special circumstances. These discretionary decisions are commonly known as professional judgment (PJ). Special circumstances include changes from the prior-prior year, such as job loss and pay cuts, as well as financial circumstances that differentiate the family from the typical family. Families need to provide documentation, such as layoff notices and bank statements to justify the special circumstances. The financial aid administrator can then verify your individual situation and make adjustments to the Cost of Attendance and the data elements that produced your Expected Family Contribution.

Promissory Note: A promissory note is a legal document that students and parents sign when applying for loans, where they agree to repay the debt. The promissory note specifies the terms and conditions of the loan, including interest rates, repayment plans, late fees and penalties for not repaying the loan.

Satisfactory Academic Progress (SAP): Students receiving federal financial aid must make progress toward their degree. If they fail classes, they will not be given additional financial aid. Satisfactory Academic Progress requires the student must maintain at least a 2.0 GPA on a 4.0 scale and be making progress consistent with graduation within 150% of the normal time-frame.

Scholarship Displacement: When a student wins a private scholarship, some colleges will reduce their institution's grant to the student. Families should keep an eye on where exactly the outside scholarship goes. Scholarship displacement occurs because of college policies and not because of federal law.

Scholarships from colleges can be merit-based aid, awarded based on grades, test scores, or individual talents and contributions. Are they renewable? Often, colleges use these scholarships to discount tuition costs and attract students. Scholarships are at the opposite end of federal aid. The subsidized portion of any federal aid goes to students with demonstrated financial need. If the family doesn't show any financial need, then federal unsubsidized loans are available. These are better than commercial loans because students can borrow some money without a cosigner, whereas a bank would not lend funds to a teen with no credit and no cosigner. However, when the cost of college is high, parents end up paying the balance with Parent PLUS loans.

Scholarships from outside the college are funded by private scholarship-granting organizations, such as foundations, philanthropists, community foundations and companies. Families need to know that colleges can use outside scholarships to reduce the college's financial aid rather than reduce the family contribution. This is called scholarship displacement. Outside scholarships are helpful if the college reduces the gap and the loan portion of the package. It's a shame when scholarships that a student may have worked hard to secure from an association or business are then used to lower the institutional aid. Parents need to be vigilant and appeal such a decision.

Self-Help Aid: Self-help refers to student loans and student employment. Some colleges require that financial need be met with a specific amount of self-help, known as a self-help level, before the college will award institutional grants.

Selective Service Registration: Male students age 18-25 must register with Selective Service. Starting in 2023-24, Selective Service registration will no longer be required for male students to receive federal student aid. However, male students will still be required to register with Selective Service.

State Aid Deadlines: See https://studentaid.gov/apply-for-aid/fafsa/fafsa-deadlines for the state deadlines for filing the FAFSA to qualify for state grants.

Strategic Enrollment Management (SEM): Strategic enrollment management uses statistical analysis to help colleges recruit students. SEM provides education analytics and data, so colleges and universities become more efficient in allocating resources to optimize student recruitment and tuition revenue.

Student Aid Index: Starting with the 2023-2024 FAFSA, the Expected Family Contribution (EFC) will be renamed the Student Aid Index (SAI).

Student Aid Report (SAR): After students file their FAFSA, they will receive a Student Aid Report by email or postal mail from the U.S. Department of Education. The Student Aid Report contains the information you entered on your FAFSA. The SAR also includes your Expected Family Contribution, or EFC, in tiny numbers on the top of the first page. It's the number used to determine your eligibility for federal student aid. Students need to pay attention to this email sent to your email address, the one you listed on FAFSA. You'll recall that undergraduate students defined as "dependent" enter their parents' information on the FAFSA. A sample SAR can be found on the eduave.com website showing an example of a first-time undergraduate student who qualifies for the Pell Grant because the EFC is $2,251.

Tax Information: The FAFSA is based on income and tax information from the prior-prior year, sometimes called the second preceding tax year. For example, the 2021–22 FAFSA form requires 2019 tax information. While completing your FAFSA, do use the IRS Data Retrieval Tool to transfer your tax information into the FAFSA fields. This is the fastest, most accurate way to input your tax return, and then the information will be considered "verified" because it came directly from the IRS. It will reduce your paperwork as well as that of the colleges.

TEACH Grant Program: The TEACH Grant provides grants of up to $4,000 a year to students who are competing or planning to complete course work needed to begin a career in teaching. TEACH Grant recipients must work as a teacher in a national need area for four of the eight years after graduation. If you do not satisfy the requirements of your service obligation, your TEACH Grants will be converted to Direct Unsubsidized Loans, with interest accruing retroactively from the date the grants were disbursed.

Verification: About a third of all submitted FAFSAs are verified. (The U.S. Department of Education has stated a goal of reducing the verification percentage to 18% by using machine learning algorithms to select which FAFSAs should be verified.) If families use the IRS DRT, they are less likely to be verified. Low-income families are verified at a much higher rate, perhaps because the verification process is intended to reduce incorrect awarding of Federal Pell Grants recipients. If your file is selected for verification, it means the college needs to review additional documents, such as records of income and assets. If you did not use the DRT, you may be required to provide a copy of your Tax Return Transcript by filing IRS Form 4506-T, by calling 800-908-9946 or using the online tool at https://www.irs.gov/individuals/get-transcript. Make sure to request the "IRS Tax Return Transcript" and NOT the "IRS Tax Account Transcript."

Resources

Awards Comparison Sheet – Claire's live excel form for comparing offers of financial aid. Download from www.eduave.com/libraryresources

Claire's Household Budget on Excel Spreadsheet - go to www.eduave.com/libraryresources to download a copy.

College Board Trends in College Pricing – available at https://research.collegeboard.org/trends/college-pricing

College Data provides a useful college search tool with detailed information about each college.
https://www.collegedata.com/cs/search/college/college_search_tmpl.jhtml

College Navigator from the National Center for Education Statistics provides cost and financial aid information about each college, as well as the net price and retention/graduation rates. https://nces.ed.gov/collegenavigator/

College Scorecard provides debt and income information for specific academic majors at each college. https://collegescorecard.ed.gov/

Colleges that meet 100% of need and EFC calculator https://myintuition.org/

Debt Calculator: https://bigfuture.collegeboard.org/pay-for-college/tools-calculators includes the EFC calculator as well as such calculators for student loans, student loan repayment, student loan repayment comparison, parent debt calculator, etc.

Department of Education Student Loans and Loan Repayments: https://financialaidtoolkit.ed.gov/

IM – What is it? https://www.reed.edu/financialaid/pdfs/CSS_IMwhatisit.pdf

IFAP Information for Financial Aid Professionals https://ifap.ed.gov/

FAFSA (paper version) https://studentaid.gov/sites/default/files/2021-22-fafsa.pdf (file online at www.fafsa.gov) Use this form to 1) see the questions and 2) note the state aid deadlines on the right side of the first page. Do not mail this form. Use as rough copy only. File the FAFSA using the web or app versions instead.

FAFSA online is available at FAFSA.gov, which redirects to https://studentaid.gov/h/apply-for-aid/fafsa

FAFSA Formula Guide 2021-22 https://ifap.ed.gov/efc-formula-guide/2122EFCFormulaGuide

Financial Health of Colleges: https://tuitiontracker.org/fitness/

"Find the Perfect College For You" https://www.amazon.com/dp/B01M188JY0/ref=rdr_kindle_ext_tmb an evaluation of MBTI® personality type in college By R. Marie and C. Claire Law

IECA Ten Important Ways IECA Members Are Different https://www.iecaonline.com/wp-content/uploads/2019/09/IECA-10-Important-Ways-Flyer-2019.pdf

IECA How to find the right college https://www.iecaonline.com/wp-content/uploads/2017/09/IECA_College-Brochure-Web.pdf

Merit and Need-based aid: Jennie Kent & Jeff Levy's charts: https://www.bigjeducationalconsulting.com/resources

Student Loan Debt in the US https://www.thebalance.com/student-loan-debt-statistics-4173224

https://www.savingforcollege.com/article/student-loan-statistics

Check Your Knowledge

A student's dependency status affects the amount of financial aid they can receive. Most high school students are financially dependent upon their parents. If the student can answer "YES" to one of the questions below, are they dependent or independent?

1. Is the student 24 years of age or older?
2. Is the student an emancipated minor?
3. When the student was 13 years old or older, were both of the student's parents deceased, or, was the student in foster care, or, was the student a dependent or ward of the court?
4. Did the student receive an official determination that the student is an unaccompanied youth who is homeless or at risk of being homeless?
5. Is the student a veteran of the U.S. Armed Forces for other than training purposes, or is the student currently serving on active duty?
6. Is the student be working on a degree beyond a bachelor's degree, such as a graduate or professional school degree (e.g., Master's degree, Ph.D., M.D., LLB, JD, MBA, MSW)?
7. Does the student support dependents, other than a spouse, AND provide more than half of their financial support?

Correct Answer: This student qualifies for "independent" status if he can answer YES to any one of the questions above.

What should students do with the Student Aid Report or "SAR"?

1. Students should review the SAR carefully to make sure it's correct and complete, as well as to make sure all the schools that are supposed to receive the SAR are listed.
2. If they need to make corrections on the SAR, students can go online at fafsa.ed.gov and select "make corrections to a Processed FAFSA."
3. Students can also make changes by calling the Federal Student Aid Information Center at 1-800-4FED-AID (1-800-433-3243). Students must have their Data Release Number (DRN) available – listed on the first page of the SAR, above the EFC.
4. All of the above

Correct Answer: #4

What is the gap?

1. The gap is an amount of funds that families need to provide in addition to their EFC.
2. The gap is the difference between a family's demonstrated financial need and the financial aid.
3. If the gap is the size of the Gulf of Mexico, it means the college isn't meeting the financial need of the family, much less the Affordable Family Contribution (AFC).
4. All of the above

Correct Answer: #4

What is Title IV funding?

1. Title IV funding consists of federal student financial aid, established by the "HEA" (Higher Education Act of 1965). HEA is the primary authorizing legislation for post-secondary programs. Amendments must be approved by Congress before Title IV programs can change. Examples of Title IV funding are the Direct subsidized and unsubsidized loans for undergraduate students.
2. Title IV funding consists of legislation that says that schools must give equal consideration to male and female applicants during the process of admission, financial aid and athletic recruitment.
3. Title IV funding consists of the major sources of federal aid for needy students, and only very poor students can obtain it.
4. Title IV funding consists of federal and private financial aid programs.

Correct Answer: #1

What are examples of Title IV programs?

1. The Subsidized and Unsubsidized Direct loan for undergraduate students (also called "Stafford loan" or "William D. Ford Loan") and the Federal Direct PLUS loan (Parent Loan for Undergraduate Students)
2. Federal Pell Grant, FSEOG (Federal Supplemental Educational Opportunity Grant)
3. The TEACH Grant, ACG and SMART grants.
4. FWS (Federal Work Study)
5. All of the above

Correct Answer: #5

How would you describe the EFC (Expected Family Contribution) also called the SAI (Student Aid Index)?

Parents and students are expected to make a "reasonable" contribution from their own resources first, before any federal or institutional aid is awarded. By submitting your FAFSA, the Central Processing Service at the U.S. Department of Education (DoE) calculates an amount that families are expected to contribute from their own resources.

1. Your EFC is an amount of funds you can contribute on your own.
2. Even if you don't qualify for need-based federal student aid, you will qualify for unsubsidized federal loans.
3. College financial aid administrators use your EFC (Expected Family Contribution) or SAI (Student Aid Index) to determine how much federal aid you will be eligible to receive.
4. The financial aid administrator will certify you for the amount of loans you decide to accept or the loan limits, whichever is less.
5. All of the above.

Correct Answer: #5

Federal student assistance programs are built on the premise that funding a student's education is primarily the responsibility of the family. To fairly and uniformly assess a family's need, Congress authorizes the Federal Methodology (FM), which through FAFSA conducts a "needs analysis." Which formula most closely represents how to calculate the federal demonstrated financial need?

1. Financial need = What the family wants to pay + Expected Family Contribution.
2. Financial need = The college's own financial aid formula + what the family is willing to borrow
3. Financial need = COA (Cost of Attendance) - Expected Family Contribution
4. The formula for calculating federal financial need is a secret, so we can't tell how the numbers work.

Correct Answer: #3 (Need = COA - EFC)

After graduating from high school, Carolyn went to live with friends for a year, worked part-time and traveled to celebrate her 19th birthday. Is her status "dependent" or "independent?"

1. Dependent
2. Independent

Correct Answer: #1

What are some of the errors people can make when filing the FAFSA?

1. They enter the wrong asset information (e.g., reporting retirement assets on the line for cash, when retirement assets are never counted on FAFSA).
2. Guessing because they are not prepared with all the documents they need to have nearby.
3. Not reading carefully.
4. Entering the wrong Social Security Number.
5. The student completing the parents' section.
6. Not using the IRS Data Retrieval Tool if the DRT is available to them.
7. Not printing the last page of their FAFSA which contains their EFC/SAI
8. Not reviewing their SAR (Student Aid Report) to make sure they entered the correct figures.
9. All of the above.

Correct Answer: #9

What are the annual amounts of federal loans that dependent undergraduate students can borrow for each undergraduate year?

1. A dependent first-year undergraduate student can borrow $5,500. Even if a student has a large financial need, no more than $3,500 of this amount may be subsidized.
2. A dependent second-year undergraduate student can borrow $6,500. No more than $4,500 of this amount may be in subsidized loans.
3. A dependent third-year or fourth-year undergraduate student can borrow up to $7,500. No more than $5,500 of this amount may be in subsidized loans.
4. All of the above.

Correct Answer: #4

True or False? What are the aggregate federal subsidized and unsubsidized loan limits for undergraduate students over the course of the undergraduate years in college?

The total amount of unsubsidized and subsidized loans that dependent students can borrow in their undergraduate years is $31,000. No more than $23,000 of this amount may be in subsidized loans.

Correct Answer: True

The aggregate loan limit is the cumulative amount that students can borrow through a loan program. Federal Direct Loans have established aggregate loan limits. What are the typical Aggregate loan limits for dependent students, independent students, and graduate and professional school students?

1. Typically, a dependent student can borrow up to $31,000 of which students with financial need can borrow no more than $23,000 in subsidized loans.
2. Dependent students whose parent was denied Parent PLUS Loans and independent students can borrow up to $57,500 for undergraduate study of which no more than $23,000 may be subsidized.
3. Graduate and professional students can borrow up to $138,500 in unsubsidized loans. Graduate students are not eligible for subsidized loans.
4. Parent PLUS Loans have no aggregate limits. Parents can borrow up to the full Cost of Attendance minus any other aid awarded to the student.
5. All of the above.

Correct Answer: #5

A senior in high school had to leave home due to an abusive environment. Now he's sleeping at friends' houses and supporting himself by working after school at a local gas station. What might be ways to help this student?

1. Once the student has proven that he's in fact homeless or at risk of being homeless, he will be able to submit a FAFSA as an independent student. This means that his parents income tax returns will not be required.
2. Help the student gather documentation (e.g., police reports, letters from teachers or neighbors, homeless shelters, priests, rabbis, and guidance counselors) that collaborate his story (about his parents being abusive).
3. Inform this student that Independent Educational Consultants (IECs) are committed to helping Pell-eligible and homeless students on a pro-bono basis.
4. IECs can get this student in touch with TRIO/Upward Bound/Talent Development programs available at many public and some private colleges. These programs support students at risk of dropping out of college and may have extra funds in addition to social support.
5. All of the above.

Correct Answer: #5

Under the Federal Methodology (FM), which asset is NOT considered on the FAFSA?

1. Retirement savings.
2. Net worth of farm if it's a principal place of residence.
3. The net worth of the family business if it employs fewer than 100 employees.
4. The family's home.
5. All of the above.

Correct Answer: #5

How is Ability to Benefit (ATB) different from Satisfactory Academic Progress (SAP)?

1. Ability to benefit means that the student is qualified to obtain a college education.
2. Ability to Benefit is demonstrated by the student having a high school diploma or recognized equivalent. A recognized equivalent would be a GED or completing a high school education in a homeschool setting consistent with state requirements, passing an approved ability-to-benefit test, or completing six credit hours toward a degree or certificate.
3. Ability to benefit generally concerns the student's qualifications before enrolling in college.
4. Satisfactory Academic Progress (SAP) refers to the student's academic performance while in college and receiving financial aid.
5. All of the above.

Correct Answer: #5

What is a Subsidized Direct Loan?

This is a Direct loan for undergraduate students only. It's for students who demonstrate need, either because their Expected Family Contribution is low, or the COA (Cost of Attendance) is high and results in a financial need.

1. The government pays the interest on the subsidized Stafford loan while the borrower is in school.
2. The subsidized Stafford loan is given to undergraduate students who demonstrate a financial need.
3. The higher the costs of going to college, the more likely families will experience a gap in funding (unless the colleges meet 100% of need).
4. The subsidized Direct loan is the only federal loan for undergraduate students that is currently available for which the government pays interest while the student is in school.
5. All of the above.

Correct Answer: #5

When undergraduate students have no demonstrated federal financial need, for which Direct student loan do they qualify?

1. The subsidized Direct loan.
2. The Direct Federal Work Study and Grants.
3. All programs under Title IV funding.
4. The Direct <u>un</u>subsidized loan.

Correct Answer: #4

List loans that are available under the Federal Direct Loan Program.

1. Subsidized Federal Direct Stafford Loan for Undergraduate Students
2. Unsubsidized Federal Direct Stafford Loan for Undergraduate Students
3. Unsubsidized Federal Direct Stafford Loan for Graduate Students
4. Federal Direct Grad PLUS Loan
5. Federal Direct Parent PLUS Loan
6. Federal Direct Consolidation Loan
7. Private student loans
8. Private parent loans
9. Private refinance

Correct Answer: #1, #2, #3, #4, $5 and #6

Who is considered the parent who must file the FAFSA?

1. "Parent" refers to a biological or adoptive parent, or a person listed on the student's birth certificate.
2. Grandparents, foster parents, legal guardians, older siblings, and uncles or aunts are NOT the parent unless they have legally adopted the student.
3. If the student's biological parents never married but live together, student should answer questions about both of them.
4. If the student's divorced or widowed parent has remarried, student must provide information about the stepparent.
5. If parents are separated or divorced, the student must give information about the parent he lived with most in the last 12 months.
6. If the student did not live with one parent more than the other, he must give information about the parent who provided the most financial support during the last 12 months or during the most recent year he received support.
7. In 2023-24 the parent who files FAFSA is the parent who provides more financial support to the student.
8. All of the above

Correct Answer: #8

According to Mark Kantrowitz, some of the major FAFSA changes that will take effect in 2023-24 are:

1. More financial aid for single parent households.
2. Less financial aid for middle- and high-income families.
3. Changes in reportable income and assets.
4. Two Federal Pell Grant formulas.
5. Changes in custodial parent and family size.
6. Changes in financial aid appeals.
7. Dropped questions concerning Selective Service registration.
8. No question about drug convictions.
9. Incarcerated people will be able to obtain the Pell Grant.
10. New question about race and gender.
11. All the above.

Correct Answer: #11

As a result of the Consolidations Appropriation Act, 2021, which types of untaxed income will no longer be reported on the FAFSA starting in 2023-2024, and therefore will no longer affect aid eligibility?

1. Cash support and other money paid on the student's behalf.
2. Veterans' education benefits.
3. Workmen's compensation.
4. Gifts to the student will no longer be reported as untaxed income.
5. Qualified distributions from a grandparent-owned 529 college savings plan.
6. All of the above.

Correct Answer: #6

What "power" do Financial Aid Administrators (FAAs) have when reviewing financial aid appeals?

1. Financial Aid Administrators (FAAs) can exercise "Professional Judgment" as per the law: "Nothing… shall be interpreted as limiting the authority of the financial aid administrator, on the basis of adequate documentation, to make adjustments on a case-by-case basis to the COA or the values of the data items required to calculate the EFC of the student or parent to allow for treatment of an individual eligible applicant with special circumstances."
2. FAAs can't change anything.
3. FAAs get paid so well that they can afford to give extra help to families out of their own pocket.
4. FAAs can fulfill each and every wish that families bring up to the FAA

Correct Answer: #1

What might be a possible reason why an aid administrator would request a detailed listing of the family's financial assets?

1. Parents may have made mistakes in reporting their assets.
2. The amount of dividends and capital gains reported on the tax return is inconsistent with the assets reported on the FAFSA and/or CSS Profile.
3. The FAFSA was flagged for verification.
4. All of the above.

Correct Answer: #4

Mr. Jones received his severance pay in a lump sum in December of the prior-prior year. This resulted in an over-statement of income and a higher EFC or SAI. What documentation should he provide to show fluctuation of income?

1. Mr. Jones should provide documentation showing that severance pay is a one-time payment, due to termination of employment, which inflates the base year income.
2. Mr. Jones should collect a minimum of prior-year tax returns so the FAA can average key income and deduction fields, as well as taxes paid. Some FAAs require 3 years of tax returns and some require 5 years.
3. Mr. Jones should show stubs from unemployment collected.
4. Mr. Jones should bring any additional documents that will show the prior-prior year income is not a current measure of his family's ability to pay.
5. All of the above.

Correct Answer: #5

Which considerations are central to the institutional needs analysis formula (e.g., the CSS Profile)?

1. Institutions that award aid based on their internal policies consider the family income to reflect a family's cash flow. How a family spends its money is not a consideration, only the amount available for spending. Specific IRS allowances, such as depreciation and some losses and business deductions, are not allowed in this calculation. Once the income is established, certain non-discretionary expenses are deducted, such as federal tax liabilities.
2. Under IM need-analysis, assets include real estate equity including the family home, savings, investments not in retirement accounts, and business/farm equity.
3. A comparison of assets reported versus dividend and interest income received will be made and figures adjusted if necessary.

4. Both sets of parents must complete the CSS Profile when the student's parents are divorced or separated.
5. If remarried, the income and assets of the new spouses are included.
6. Under IM, each student is expected to contribute to their educational expenses from summer earnings and from their assets.
7. If students cannot earn the amount expected, additional loan eligibility may be available for parents.
8. All of the above.

Correct Answer: #8

What might be legitimate reasons to appeal an award?

1. In the prior-prior year, the family's primary wage-earner was employed, but that's not the situation on the day they file the FAFSA.
2. The family's prior-prior year tax information doesn't reflect their current financial situation.
3. There may be a change in marital status.
4. The award letter shows a large gap between EFC and the family's out-of-pocket net costs which would place an unreasonable burden upon the family.
5. The net cost differential between two similar colleges is significant for the family.
6. The family simply cannot pay the amount the college wants.
7. All of the above.

Correct Answer: #7

Not all colleges meet 100% of demonstrated financial need. Most of them meet much less than 100%. This "unmet need" is referred to as a "gap." What are some ways to describe unmet need in a financial aid award package?

1. Colleges are not obligated to meet 100% of demonstrated financial need, and students are not obligated to attend colleges that are too expensive for them.
2. Gapping is a packaging practice by colleges unable to meet full demonstrated need. If colleges could meet full financial need, there would be no gap in funding and families would need to pay only their EFC/SAI.
3. Financial aid leveraging occurs when colleges gap lower-performing students.
4. It colleges really want a student, they may fill a greater part of the financial need through scholarships and grants.
5. Appeals can result in more financial aid.
6. Some colleges fill the gap (unmet need) with Parent PLUS Loans.
7. All of the above.

Correct Answer: #7

Undergraduate students can work while in school and their income is not considered by the federal financial aid formula, up to what amount?

1. In 2021-22, students can work and have an AAI (Adjusted Available Income) of $6,970, and none of it will be considered in the expected family contribution.
2. The student contribution from income after $6,970 Adjusted Available Income is assessed at 50%.
3. The student contribution from assets is 20%.
4. All of the above.

Correct Answer: #4

On December 27, 2020, the Consolidated Appropriations Act, 2021, was signed into law. This legislation included a $150 increase to the maximum Pell Grant. What is the maximum Pell Grant award for the 2021-2022 award year?

1. In 2021-2022, the maximum Pell Grant is $6,495.
2. The maximum expected family contribution corresponding to Pell Grant eligibility is $5,846.
3. The minimum amount of Pell Grant in the 2021-2022 award year will be $650.
4. A student may be eligible to receive Pell Grant funds for up to 150 percent of the student's Pell Grant scheduled award for an award year, if the student is in an accelerated degree program.
5. The student enrollment status – whether enrolled part or full-time – affects the amount of the Pell Grant award.
6. All of the above.

Correct Answer: #6

Assume you graduated from college, and you are in repayment of your Direct Student Loans. If you get into difficulties, you can use a deferment or forbearance to avoid default. What are deferments and forbearances and what is the difference between a deferment and a forbearance?

1. A deferment or forbearance allows you to temporarily stop making your federal student loan payments.
2. You'll need to work with your loan servicer to apply for deferment or forbearance and be sure to keep making payments on your loan until the deferment or forbearance is approved. Your loan servicer will notify you if further information is needed or if you do not qualify.
3. The main difference is that with a deferment, you will not have to pay the interest that accrues on subsidized loans. You will still have to pay the

interest on unsubsidized loans during a deferment. You will have to pay the interest on both subsidized and unsubsidized loans during a forbearance.

4. A good website for additional information is https://studentaid.ed.gov/sa/repay-loans/deferment-forbearance#differences
5. All of the above.

Correct Answer: #5

What is the American Opportunity Tax Credit (AOTC)?

1. AOTC is an education tax credit that helps with the cost of higher education by reducing the amount of tax owed on your federal income tax return.
2. The AOTC can provide up to $2,500 as a credit on your taxes. It is partially refundable (up to $1,000).
3. The AOTC can be received for tuition and textbook higher education expenses for up to 4 years, yielding a total credit of up to $10,000.
4. All of the above.

Correct Answer: #4

There's one type of debt that colleges, whether they use FAFSA or CSS Profile, do not consider. Which is it?

1. Medical bills.
2. Mortgage.
3. Credit card debt.
4. Interest paid on student loans.

Correct Answer: #3

When IECs work with families that have different EFCs, (e.g. high, medium, low) what considerations might we think about?

1. If a family has a high demonstrated financial need at their "fit" colleges, I'll let them know that going to a college that meets a high percentage of need will be more valuable than going to colleges that award merit aid.
2. If a family has an EFC higher than the COA let them know that merit aid will be the only source of discount
3. If a family has a middle-of-the road EFC and will need both merit and need-based aid. This placement will likely be the more difficult one because more variables will be at play when examining the colleges' aid policies.
4. All of the above.

Correct Answer: #4

Sometimes, the FAFSA will need to be corrected because:

1. Parents reported the value of their retirement account instead of their brokerage account as an asset.
2. The EFC is overstated due to a pension or IRA rollover being counted as untaxed income. It is difficult to see whether this occurred because information transferred from the IRS using the IRS Data Retrieval Tool is redacted on the FAFSA.
3. The wrong parent filled out the FAFSA.
4. Parents didn't report the correct number of people living in the household.
5. Parents reported the net worth of the family home as an asset. Only the CSS Profile requires information about the value of the family home.
6. All of the above.

Correct Answer: #6

What is an award letter?

1. An award letter from a college states the type and amount of financial aid the college is willing to provide.
2. When a student signs on the line next to the financial aid, the award become final.
3. To continue to receive aid they must file FAFSA each year and meet the eligibility requirements of the aid programs.
4. All of the above

Correct Answer: #4

What is interest capitalization?

1. Interest capitalization is the addition of unpaid interest to the principal balance of a loan.
2. With the subsidized Direct loan, the government pays the interest while the student is in school.
3. Interest accrues on an unsubsidized loan while the student is enrolled.
4. Interest may also be charged to the borrower during periods of forbearance and deferment.
5. When interest is not paid as it accrues, it is capitalized at the end of the grace, deferment, or forbearance period. This increases the outstanding principal amount due on the loan.
6. After interest capitalization, interest is charged on the higher principal balance, increasing the cost of the loan.
7. All of the above

Correct Answer: #7

The Consolidated Appropriations Act, 2021, made which of these changes to the way financial aid administrators handle appeals?

1. College financial aid administrators may no longer have a policy of denying all financial aid appeals.
2. It added new examples of special circumstances, such as unusual business, investment and real estate losses, and severe disability of the student, parent or spouse.
3. Dependency overrides will be assumed to continue for the duration of the student's entire college enrollment.
4. Income earned from work may be set to zero due to unemployment during a qualifying emergency.
5. Eligibility for unsubsidized Federal Direct Stafford Loans no longer requires parents to cut off financial support
6. All of the above.

Correct Answer: #6

Starting in the academic year 2023-24, the number of children in college at the same time will no longer increase eligibility for need-based financial aid, although the Income Protection Allowance will increase. What could be the results?

1. The parent contribution will no longer be divided by number of children in college at the same time. This decreases aid eligibility significantly, especially for middle- and high-income families who have multiple children in college at the same time.
2. The income protection allowance will increase, thereby reducing the EFC/SAI. This will increase aid eligibility by roughly a few thousand dollars per child in college.
3. These changes will have a small impact on low-income families with multiple children in college.
4. These changes will have a big impact on middle- and high-income families with two or more children enrolled in college at the same time.
5. Families can appeal for more financial aid based on having multiple family members in college at the same time.
6. All of the above.

Correct Answer: #6

As a result of the Consolidated Appropriations Act, 2021, which parent must complete the FAFSA starting in the 2023-24 academic year? Which old rules will change?

1. When a dependent student's parents are divorced, separated, or never married and do not live together, only one parent files the FAFSA.
2. This parent is the one with whom the student lives with the most. However, starting with the 2023-24 FAFSA, it's the parent who provides more financial support to the student.
3. If this parent has remarried as of the date the FAFSA is filed, the stepparent's info must be reported on the FAFSA.
4. If unmarried parents live together, they are counted as though they were married.
5. All of the above.

Correct Answer: #5

How can IECs help families understand the process of paying for college?

1. Use the Net Price Calculator (NPC) to determine the likely cost of each college of interest.
2. Invite families to use the budget sheet at the beginning of this book.
3. Help the families determine whether their financial resources are enough to cover the net cost they figured using the Net Price Calculator.
4. If families can afford to pay the full cost of attendance, they may still want the student to borrow the limited amounts of federal loans for undergraduate students.
5. If families can't pay and will need a lot of need-based aid, choose colleges with financial aid policies that primarily fill financial need.
6. Cast a wide net to make sure the college list contains a mix of public, in-state institutions, community college, and those less-selective, private colleges known to offer generous merit and need-based aid.
7. If families need a combination of need and merit-based aid, choose colleges known to give generous merit awards where the student can be competitive in the applicant pool.
8. All of the above.

Correct Answer: #8

What are the basic principles of IM (expressed in the CSS Profile form)?

1. A family's capacity to pay is a function of income and assets.
2. The first step in calculating the family contribution is to define income in a reasonable way.
3. After subtracting appropriate allowances from income, a portion of the remainder is available to pay college costs.
4. The same process takes place for assets.
5. All of the above

Correct Answer: #5

Dr. Sandy Baum and Dr. Kathleen Little say the Institutional Methodology (IM) is a formula developed by financial aid professionals, in consultation with economists, to measure a family's ability to pay for college. Which of the following points do they make?

1. The EFC produced by the IM is not the same as the figure calculated by the federal government to determine eligibility for federal student aid dollars.
2. The family contribution is not something most families can realistically take out of one year's income.
3. Most families finance their share of college costs through a combination of saving, paying out of current income and borrowing.
4. All of the above.

Correct Answer: #4

How does the IM define income?

1. IM uses adjusted gross income (AGI) from the federal income tax return to determine family income and then adds in certain types of untaxed income (e.g., Social Security and child support).
2. Like in FM, both parent and student income are taken into account.
3. If parents are divorced or separated, information from the custodial parent, the parent with whom the student lives is required.
4. Information from the non-custodial parent is also required.
5. If the divorced parents have remarried, information from the stepparents are included in the EFC calculation.
6. The IM philosophy is that "You can divorce a spouse but not a child." Regardless of their current marital status, parents have the primary responsibility for paying for their child's college education.
7. Parents are expected to provide reasonable financial support before college resources are used.
8. All of the above.

Correct Answer: #8

Is the Expected Family Contribution the same if more than one child is enrolled?

1. If two children are enrolled, the IM considers 60 percent of the parent contribution for each child.
2. If three children are enrolled, the IM considers 45 percent of the parent contribution for each child.
3. Since the Federal Methodology no longer will allow the discount starting in 2023-24, it remains to be seen if private colleges continue to reduce the EFC when multiple children are enrolled in college at the same time.
4. All of the above.

Correct Answer: #4

When comparing IM treatment of assets and expenses vs. FM, which of these statements are true?

1. Under IM, the parents' full retirement amount of an IRAs or Keogh, or 401(k) is reviewed at least qualitatively. On the other hand, FM does not consider the full amount that may be in an IRA or other retirement plans. FM considers only the contributions to a retirement plan in the base year, not the asset value.
2. IM considers the equity a family may have built in their principal residence as a possible source of funding. The Federal Methodology (FM) does not count the family's equity in their home.
3. Business equity is considered in the IM whereas in FM the net worth of a family business is not considered if they employ fewer than 100 employees.
4. IM takes into consideration exceptionally high medical and dental expenses and deducts an Annual Education Savings Allowance (AESA)
5. IM considers the costs of private K-12 school tuition for the student's siblings. FM does not consider the cost of private school.
6. All of the above.

Correct Answer: #6

Suzy's mother remarried last year and Suzy lives with her mom and new step-dad. Shortly thereafter, Suzy's biological dad remarried as well. Suzy was accepted to Boston College, which uses IM and the CSS Profile form Which forms will BC require?

1. BC will require both the FAFSA and CSS Profile forms filled out by Suzy's mom.
2. BC will also require Suzy's biological father to complete the CSS Profile.
3. The income and assets of the step-dad will be counted.

4. Since Suzy's biological father is also re-married, his new wife's financial information needs to be included.
5. All of the above.

Correct Answer: #5

After subtracting mandatory taxes and other allowances from total income, a portion is counted into the IM EFC. This approach is applied to both parents and students. List the percentage of income families are expected to contribute under IM.

1. The IM assessment rate structure applies a 22 percent contribution to the first dollars of available income and progressively higher rates to additional dollars of discretionary income up to 46%. (The FAFSA assesses income up to 47%.)
2. Students must contribute from $2,000 to $4,000, depending on the college. (For example, Princeton University requires a minimum student contribution of $4,000.)
3. The student's additional available income is assessed at 50 percent, which is a higher rate than parent's graduated income assessment. The reasoning here is that paying for college should be the student's first priority, while parents have other bills to pay.
4. All of the above.

Correct Answer: #4

Recently, there has been a change in the traditional definition of who is considered a parent. In these modern times, who is NOT a parent?

1. Same gender couples who are married.
2. Parents who have legally adopted the student.
3. Divorced spouse with primary custody of the student.
4. Grandmother who takes care of student while her daughter, the student's mom, who was never married, works in another city.

Correct Answer: #4. The grandmother is not a parent unless she has legally adopted the student. Her daughter, the student's mother, must complete the FAFSA.

Describe the purpose of iDoc in the PROFILE form.

1. iDoc is a service offered by the College Board to collect tax documents and other financial information from parents.
2. Not all colleges that use the CSS Profile participate in the iDoc service.
3. This data can be sent to up to five colleges.
4. Colleges require this data to confirm the information reported on the CSS Profile.
5. Students will receive an email notification from the College Board instructing them how to go through the iDoc service.

6. iDoc service has been compared to the FAFSA's Data Retrieval Tool, which downloads tax records directly from the IRS into the FAFSA.
7. CSS Profile colleges collect more than the first two pages of federal income tax returns.
8. All of the above.

Correct Answer: #8

The 'four-legged stool' that makes up the EFC refers to:

1) parent income 2) parent assets

3) student income 4) student assets

Correct Answer: All of the above.

What are the contributions from income and assets under IM and FM?

1. FM Parent contribution from income under FM is a progressive rate from 22% to 47%. Parent assets are considered at the rate of 5.64%.
2. IM Parent contribution from income is a progressive rate from 22% to 46%. Parent assets are considered at a progressive rate of 3%, 4% or 5%.
3. FM Student Contribution from income is 50% after a personal income protection allowance ($6,970 in 2021-22).
4. FM Student Contribution from Assets is 20%.
5. IM Student Contribution from Income is 50% and an obligatory contribution.
6. IM Student Contribution from Assets is 25%.
7. All of the above.

Correct Answer: #7

What is enrollment management?

1. Enrollment management consists of various tools and strategies that colleges can use to attract the type of students they want.
2. Through data analysis, data mining and regression analysis, colleges can predict the probability of specific students enrolling.
3. Enrollment management can include financial aid leveraging as a tool to attract students with paying parents.
4. All of the above.

Correct Answer: #4

Which of these companies provide Strategic Enrollment Management (SEM)?

1. Noel-Levitz and Ruffalo-Cody
2. Maguire and Associates
3. Intelliworks
4. Perceptivesoftware.com; Strategic Enrollment Man.com
5. All of the above.

Correct Answer: #5

What is the "discount rate" for colleges?

1. The discount rate is the average rate by which a college lowers their tuition, typically at least 25%.
2. The average discount rate is 65%.
3. The college's discount rate is a discount calculated by taking the average institutional aid given to students and dividing it by the total gross tuition and fees collected.
4. The discount rate cannot be computed.

Correct Answer: #3

What does Claire Gaudiani, former president of Conn College, say about enrollment management?

1. Merit aid creates real problems from the point of equity.
2. The problem grows if colleges use merit aid not just to recruit better students but also to bolster their bottom line.
3. It's more lucrative for a college to parcel out $30,000 over six students whose parents can pay the rest than to give the entire amount to one student.
4. All of the above.

Correct Answer: #4

What is preferential packaging?

1. Preferential packaging can mean that some students will receive a better financial aid package.
2. A preferential financial aid package includes a greater percentage of grant aid than self-help aid (i.e., loans and work).
3. Students who are admitted but rank in the bottom half of the admitted student group will probably receive a package that contains more self-help aid.
4. All of the above.

Correct Answer: #4

What information would you give to families whose EFC is greater than the COA?

1. Your student has no demonstrated financial need.
2. Federal aid is based on demonstrated financial need.
3. If you don't demonstrate a federal need, you can still borrow federal loans if you file the FAFSA.
4. Most elite colleges and the Ivies award aid based only on demonstrated need.
5. To lower costs this student must seek out colleges that offer merit aid.
6. All of the above.

Correct Answer: #6

What is front-loading of grants?

1. It's when a college's gifting policy is to award larger merit scholarships in the first year of college, in order to attract students and entice them to enroll.
2. It's when the terms for keeping the scholarship are so high that it's unlikely the student can maintain the GPA all 4 years.
3. About half of all colleges practice front-loading of grants, which gives the student a better mix of grants during the freshman year than during the sophomore, junior or senior years.
4. It's when a scholarship is contingent upon the student living in campus-sponsored residence halls all four years.
5. All of the above.

Correct Answer: #5

What are some of the differences between merit aid and need-based aid?

1. Merit scholarships tend to remain static. They usually remain the same over the course of the 4 years unless students can qualify for more merit aid.
2. Need-based aid can change if the family's situation changes. The need-based aid may increase or decrease. This is an unknown for families because colleges award financial aid for one year only.
3. Sometimes a scholarship is simply a tuition discount that entices students to enroll.
4. All of the above.

Correct Answer: #4

Why would parents let their kids take out federal Direct loans in their undergraduate years?

1. Direct loans for undergraduate students typically carry a lower interest rate and more favorable terms than Parent PLUS loans.
2. Studies show that parents take out smaller loans in years 3 and 4 if their kids take out their own loans.
3. If part of the federal Direct loan is subsidized, it means the interest is paid by the government while the student is in school. This is a much better deal than a Parent PLUS loan.
4. Studies show that undergraduate students who graduate typically are able to repay their $30,000 of loans.
5. Having the child borrow a few student loans is a good way for them to have skin in the game without burdening them with excessive student loan debt.
6. All of the above.

Correct Answer: #6

Parents understand that it's their obligation to pay for their children's college education. However, some families' EFCs are much higher than what they can afford. Why is the AFC (Affordable Family Contribution) important?

1. The AFC is an amount based on a family's budget.
2. Families on fixed or low incomes need to carefully evaluate what they can afford to pay from current income, savings and borrowing.
3. By knowing their AFC, students can avoid going to colleges that will place too heavy a debt burden on their families.
4. By knowing their AFC, and working with IECs who know colleges, students will avoid making mistakes, such as ignoring more affordable colleges that would minimize borrowing.
5. All of the above

Correct Answer: #5

Parker is a junior in high school and will graduate in June of 2022. Which FAFSA will he need to complete? Which tax year or income will it use?

1. 2020-21 FAFSA will use the 2018 income.
2. 2021-22 FAFSA will use the 2019 income.
3. 2022-23 FAFSA will use the 2020 income.
4. 2023-24 FAFSA will use the 2021 income.

Correct Answer: #3

Changes to the FAFSA form with its new formulas will go into effect July 1, 2023. Which change is not part of the Consolidated Appropriations Act, 2021?

1. More financial aid for low-income families and single parent households.
2. Less financial aid for middle- and high-income families.
3. Changes in the evaluation of multiple siblings in college at the same time.
4. Twenty-five Federal Pell Grant formulas.
5. Changes in custodial parent and family size.
6. Changes in financial aid appeals.
7. Dropped questions concerning Selective Service and drug convictions.
8. All of the above.

Correct Answer: #4

Index